First World War
and Army of Occupation
War Diary
France, Belgium and Germany

39 DIVISION
Headquarters, Branches and Services
Commander Royal Engineers
5 March 1916 - 31 December 1918

WO95/2573/1

The Naval & Military Press Ltd
www.nmarchive.com
Published in association with The National Archives

Published by

The Naval & Military Press Ltd

Unit 10 Ridgewood Industrial Park,

Uckfield, East Sussex,

TN22 5QE England

Tel: +44 (0) 1825 749494

www.naval-military-press.com

www.nmarchive.com

This diary has been reprinted in facsimile from the original. Any imperfections are inevitably reproduced and the quality may fall short of modern type and cartographic standards.

Contents

Document type	Place/Title	Date From	Date To
Heading	WO95/2573/1		
Heading	39th Division Divl Engineers C.R.E. Mar 1916-Dec 1918		
Heading	War Diary of Headquarters 39th Divisional R.E. From 5th March 1916 to 31st March 1916 (Volume 1).		
War Diary	Milford Camp	05/03/1916	05/03/1916
War Diary	Le Havre	07/03/1916	07/03/1916
War Diary	Blaringhem	08/03/1916	26/03/1916
War Diary	Lestem.	27/03/1916	31/03/1916
Heading	War Diary of C.R.E. 39th Division From 1st April 1916 to 30th April 1916 (Volume 1)		
War Diary	Lestrem	01/04/1916	16/04/1916
War Diary	Locon	17/04/1916	30/04/1916
Heading	War Diary of C.R.E. 39th Division From May 1st to May 31.1916. Vol 3		
War Diary	Locon	01/05/1916	31/05/1916
Heading	War Diary of C.R.E. 39th Division. From June 1st 1916 to June 31st 1916. Vol 4		
War Diary	Locon	01/06/1916	30/06/1916
Heading	War Diary of Headquarters 39th Divl. R.E. From 1st July 1916. to 31st July 1916. Vol 5		
War Diary	Locon	01/07/1916	11/07/1916
War Diary	Bethune	12/07/1916	15/07/1916
War Diary	Locon	16/07/1916	31/07/1916
Heading	War Diary of 39th Divisional R.E. From August 1st 1916. to August 31st 1916. Vol 6		
Heading	War Diary of H.Q. 39th Divl. R.E. From August 1st 1916. to August 31st 1916		
War Diary	Locon	08/08/1916	10/08/1916
War Diary	Rollecourt	11/08/1916	12/08/1916
War Diary	Boirin	12/08/1916	23/08/1916
War Diary	Bus Les Artois	24/08/1916	26/08/1916
War Diary	Acheux	27/08/1916	31/08/1916
Miscellaneous	39th Divisional R.E. Training Programme. 225th Field Company R.E. Appendix A.	13/08/1916	13/08/1916
Miscellaneous	39th Divisional R.E. Training Programme. 227th Field Coy. R.E.	13/08/1916	13/08/1916
Miscellaneous	39th Divisional R.E. Training Programme. 234th Field Coy. R.E.	13/08/1916	13/08/1916
Miscellaneous	Wire Entanglements. Materials Required For 50 Yard Line of Various Types At Found By Actual Test.	16/08/1916	16/08/1916
Miscellaneous	225" Co.	20/08/1916	20/08/1916
Miscellaneous	227th CRE	22/08/1916	22/08/1916
Miscellaneous	H.Q. 39th Divn. G.S.	25/08/1916	25/08/1916
Miscellaneous	OC 227th Fd. Co.	26/08/1916	26/08/1916
Miscellaneous	OC 234th Fd. Coy.	26/08/1916	26/08/1916
Miscellaneous	227th Fd. Co. RE.		
Miscellaneous	39 Div H.Q.	29/08/1916	29/08/1916
Miscellaneous	O.C. 13 Gloster R.	28/08/1916	28/08/1916
Miscellaneous	O.C. 13 Gloster Regt.	29/08/1916	29/08/1916

Miscellaneous	O.C. 227th Field Coy. R.E.	27/08/1916	27/08/1916
Miscellaneous	O.C. 13th Gloster Regt.	29/08/1916	29/08/1916
Miscellaneous	O.C. 225th Field Coy. R.E. Working Parties.	30/08/1916	30/08/1916
Miscellaneous	Work Report	01/09/1916	01/09/1916
Operation(al) Order(s)	Special Orders To O.C., Section, 227 Company R.E., To Accompany 117th Infantry Brigade Order No. 50. Appendix O.	30/08/1916	30/08/1916
Heading	39th. Division H.Q., C.R.E. 39th Division, Royal Engineers September, 1916		
War Diary	Acheux	01/09/1916	30/09/1916
Miscellaneous	To CRE 30th Div Stores Forwarded To King Brigade. A	31/08/1916	31/08/1916
Miscellaneous	To CRE 39th Div.	01/09/1916	01/09/1916
Miscellaneous	Report on Active Operations Sept. 3. 1916	03/09/1916	03/09/1916
Miscellaneous	L.P.833	03/09/1916	03/09/1916
Miscellaneous	Brief Report on Active Operation Moving of 3rd Sept 1916. Party of 13th Glosters Attached 116th Inf. Bde.	03/09/1916	03/09/1916
Miscellaneous	To C.R.E. 39th Div. From O/C. 227th Co Rg	07/09/1916	07/09/1916
Miscellaneous	Report Upon Operation of R.E. Section in Attack on 3/9/16	03/09/1916	03/09/1916
Miscellaneous	R.E. Section in Attack on 3/9/16	03/09/1916	03/09/1916
Miscellaneous	Report on R.E. Operation 3/9/16	03/09/1916	03/09/1916
Miscellaneous	To C.R.E. 39th Div.	03/09/1916	03/09/1916
Miscellaneous	Employment of R.E. on at attack by 116th & 117th Brigades on the German position immediately North of R. Ancre.	09/09/1916	09/09/1916
Operation(al) Order(s)	Extracts from 116th Infantry Brigade Order No. 43		
Miscellaneous	Attack on Thiepval.	26/09/1916	26/09/1916
Miscellaneous	Attack on Schwaben Redoubt.	28/09/1916	28/09/1916
Miscellaneous	Casualties.		
Miscellaneous	Consolidation Of Trenches.	16/09/1916	16/09/1916
Miscellaneous	Consolidation Of Captured Positions.	27/09/1916	27/09/1916
Map	Plan Of Hasty Fire Trench.		
Heading	War Diary Of Headquarters 39th Divl. R.E. From 1st October To 31st October 1916		
War Diary	Acheux	01/10/1916	01/10/1916
War Diary	Hedauville	02/10/1916	05/10/1916
War Diary	Bouzincourt	06/10/1916	31/10/1916
Miscellaneous	243/a. Headquarters, 39th Division	11/10/1916	11/10/1916
Operation(al) Order(s)	Headquarters 39th Div R.E. Operation Order No. 1	11/10/1916	11/10/1916
Miscellaneous	O.C. 234th Field Coy. R.E. 247/a.	12/10/1916	12/10/1916
Miscellaneous	248/A	12/10/1916	12/10/1916
Miscellaneous	Report on R.E. Action in Connection with Operations of Oct 14th at The Schwaben Redoubt.	17/10/1916	17/10/1916
Miscellaneous	Headquarters, 39th Division.	06/10/1916	06/10/1916
Miscellaneous	Recommendations as a Result of Experience Gained.	17/10/1916	17/10/1916
Miscellaneous	II Corps. G. 3029. 39th Division.	18/10/1916	18/10/1916
Diagram etc	Q.24.a		
Miscellaneous	Report on Brigades Over Ancre in Q.24.a	20/10/1916	20/10/1916
Heading	War Diaries For 39th Divisional R.E. From November 1st to November 30th 1916. Vol 9		
Heading	War Diary For Headquarters 39th Divisional R.E. From November 1st 1916 to November 30th 1916		
War Diary	Bouzincourt	01/11/1916	15/11/1916
War Diary	Doullens	16/11/1916	17/11/1916
War Diary	Esquelbecq.	18/11/1916	30/11/1916

Miscellaneous	225th Field Coy. R.E.	04/11/1916	04/11/1916
Operation(al) Order(s)	H.Q. 39th Division R.E. Operation Order No. 6	12/11/1916	12/11/1916
Operation(al) Order(s)	H.Q. 39th Division R.E. Operation Order No. 5	29/10/1916	29/10/1916
Miscellaneous	Report on R.E. Cooperation in Connection with The Operation of 39th Division of Nov. 10th-14th.	10/11/1916	10/11/1916
Miscellaneous	Operation Of November 13th.	17/11/1916	17/11/1916
Operation(al) Order(s)	HQ. 39th Div. R.E. Operation Order No. 7	23/11/1916	23/11/1916
Miscellaneous	O.C. 225th Field Coy R.E.	30/11/1916	30/11/1916
Operation(al) Order(s)	H.Q. 39th Division R.E. Operation Order No. 5	29/10/1916	29/10/1916
Map	Operation Trench Map 3 Pierre Divion		
Operation(al) Order(s)	H.Q. 39th Division R.E. Operation Order No. 6	12/11/1916	12/11/1916
Heading	War Diary For 39th Divisional R.E. From 1st December To 31st December 1916. Vol 10		
Heading	War Diary For Headquarters 39th Divisional R.E. From 1st December 1916 to 31st December 1916		
War Diary	Esquelbecq	01/12/1916	11/12/1916
War Diary	St. Sixte Belgium.	12/12/1916	31/12/1916
Operation(al) Order(s)	Headquarters 39th Div. R.E. Operation Order No. 8	09/12/1916	09/12/1916
Heading	War Diary for 39th Division R.E. from January 1st 1917 to January 31st 1917. Vol XI.		
Heading	War Diary for Headquarters 39th Division R.E. from January 1st 1917 to January 31st 1917		
War Diary	St Sixte Belgium	03/01/1917	15/01/1917
War Diary	Hamhoek Belgium	15/01/1917	29/01/1917
War Diary	Hamhoek	30/01/1917	31/01/1917
Miscellaneous	Distribution of Work in Right Division Area.	13/01/1917	13/01/1917
Miscellaneous	O.C. 225th Field Coy R.E.	15/01/1917	15/01/1917
Miscellaneous	225th Field Coy. R.E.	17/01/1917	17/01/1917
Miscellaneous	Divisional Programme of Work. Instructions for No. 4 Party. Extension Cambridge Trench North from Piccadilly.	19/01/1917	19/01/1917
Miscellaneous	A Table of Work on Following Line Will be Prepared by Infantry Officer in Charge.		
Miscellaneous	Instructions For Deepening Muddy Lane.		
Miscellaneous	Instruction in Consolidation.	28/01/1917	28/01/1917
Miscellaneous	Pumps For Dug-Out.	01/02/1917	01/02/1917
Miscellaneous	Head Quarters "G" 39th Division.	31/01/1917	31/01/1917
Miscellaneous	Pumps And Pumping Deep Dug-Outs.		
Heading	War Diary of C.R.E., 39th Division. From February 1st 1917. to February 28th 1917. Vol 12		
War Diary	Hamhoek	01/02/1917	17/02/1917
War Diary	Esquelbecq	18/02/1917	26/02/1917
War Diary	Reninghelst	27/02/1917	28/02/1917
Miscellaneous	Headquarters "G". C.R.E. 55th Division.	11/02/1917	11/02/1917
Miscellaneous	A Form. Messages And Signals.		
Operation(al) Order(s)	H.Q. 39th Division R.E. Operation Order No. 10	14/02/1917	14/02/1917
Operation(al) Order(s)	Headquarters 39th Divl. R.E. Operation Order No. 11	19/02/1917	19/02/1917
Operation(al) Order(s)	Headquarters 39th Divl. R.E. Operation Order No. 12	20/02/1917	20/02/1917
Operation(al) Order(s)	Headquarters 39th Divl. R.E. Operation Order No. 13	21/02/1917	21/02/1917
Operation(al) Order(s)	Amendments To H.Q. 39th Div. R.E. Operation Order No. 11	24/02/1917	24/02/1917
Operation(al) Order(s)	Headquarters, 39th Divisional R.E., Operation Order No. 15	22/02/1917	22/02/1917
Heading	War Diary of 39th Divisional R.E. From March 1st 1917. to March 31st 1917. Vol 13		

Heading	War Diary of Headquarters, 39th Divisional R.E. from March 1st 1917 to March 31st 1917		
War Diary	Reninghelst	01/03/1917	01/04/1917
Heading	War Diary of Headquarters 39th Divisional R.E. From April 1st, 1917 to April 30th, 1917. Vol 14		
War Diary	Reninghelst	01/04/1917	29/04/1917
War Diary	D Camp.	30/04/1917	30/04/1917
Operation(al) Order(s)	Headquarters, 39th Divl. R.E. Operation Order No. 16	04/04/1917	04/04/1917
Operation(al) Order(s)	Amendment To 39th Div. R.E. Order No. 16	04/04/1917	04/04/1917
Operation(al) Order(s)	Headquarters, 39th Divl. R.E. Operation Order No. 17	05/04/1917	05/04/1917
Operation(al) Order(s)	Headquarters, 39th Divl. R.E. Operation Order No. 18	07/04/1917	07/04/1917
Operation(al) Order(s)	Headquarters, 39th Divisional R.E. Operation Order No. 19	12/04/1917	12/04/1917
Operation(al) Order(s)	Headquarters, 39th Divl. R.E. Operation Order No. 20	13/04/1917	13/04/1917
Operation(al) Order(s)	Headquarters, 39th Divl. R.E. Operation Order No. 22	15/04/1917	15/04/1917
Heading	War Diary. of Headquarters, 39th. Divisional. R.E. From May 1st 1917. to May 31st 1917. Vol 15		
War Diary	D Camp A.30.b.27	01/05/1917	31/05/1917
Heading	War Diary Of The Headquarters, 39th. Divisional Royal Engineers. From June 1st. 1917 To June 30th. 1917. Vol 16		
War Diary	Border Camp	01/06/1917	30/06/1917
Heading	War Diary. Headquarters, 39th. Divisional Royal Engineers. From 1st July 1917. To 31st July 1917. Vol 17		
War Diary	Border Camp	01/07/1917	02/07/1917
War Diary	C. Camp	03/07/1917	15/07/1917
War Diary	C. Camp A.30.d.0.0. Sh. 28 N.W.	18/07/1917	31/07/1917
Operation(al) Order(s)	Headquarters 39th Divisional R.E. Order No. 32	10/07/1917	10/07/1917
Operation(al) Order(s)	Headquarters, 39th Divisional R.E. Order No. 33	10/07/1917	10/07/1917
Operation(al) Order(s)	Headquarters, 39th. Divisional R.E. Order No. 34	14/07/1917	14/07/1917
Operation(al) Order(s)	Headquarters, 39th. Divisional R.E. Order No. 35	22/07/1917	22/07/1917
Operation(al) Order(s)	Headquarters, 39th. Divisional R.E. Order No. 36	30/07/1917	30/07/1917
Miscellaneous	Appendix "A"		
Miscellaneous	Instruction No. 12		
Heading	War Diary For Headquarters 39th Divl. R.E. From 1st August To 31st August 1917. Vol 18		
War Diary	C Camp A.30.d.0.0. Sh 28	01/08/1917	05/08/1917
War Diary	A.23.G.H. Sh 28	06/08/1917	06/08/1917
War Diary	Meteren	08/08/1917	09/08/1917
War Diary	Meteren France	11/08/1917	13/08/1917
War Diary	Westoutre Belgium	15/08/1917	31/08/1917
Miscellaneous	Instruction No. 12. Appendix A.		
Operation(al) Order(s)	Instruction No. 12. (Issued in Connection with 39th Division Order No. 125.)		
Miscellaneous	Work of Field Companies And Pioneer Battalion on July 31st. 1917. App A.2	10/08/1917	10/08/1917
Miscellaneous	Work of Field Companies And Pioneer Battalion on July 31st. 1917	10/08/1917	10/08/1917
Operation(al) Order(s)	Headquarters, 39th. Divisional. R.E. Order No. 38	07/08/1917	07/08/1917
Operation(al) Order(s)	Headquarters, 39th. Divisional. R.E. Order No. 38. Appendix B.		
Operation(al) Order(s)	Headquarters, 39th Divisional. R.E. Order No. 38	07/08/1917	07/08/1917
Operation(al) Order(s)	Headquarters, 39th Divisional. R.E. Order No. 39. Appendix C.	12/08/1917	12/08/1917
Operation(al) Order(s)	Headquarters, 39th Divisional. R.E. Order No. 39	28/08/1917	28/08/1917

Miscellaneous	G.772. Appendix D.	28/08/1917	28/08/1917
Miscellaneous	G.772	28/08/1917	28/08/1917
Miscellaneous	C.E. Xth Corps 975 Xth Corps G.S.	17/11/1917	17/11/1917
Heading	War Diaries of 39th Divl R.E. from 1st 30th September 1917, Vol 19		
Heading	War Diary Of Headquarters 39th Divl. R.E. From 1st September To 30th September 1917		
War Diary	Westoutre	01/09/1917	11/09/1917
War Diary	De Zon Camp.	12/09/1917	14/09/1917
War Diary	De Zon Camp Belgium.	15/09/1917	21/09/1917
War Diary	Zevecoten Belgium	22/09/1917	26/09/1917
War Diary	St Jans Cappel France	28/09/1917	30/09/1917
Miscellaneous	G.969. Appendix A.	17/09/1917	17/09/1917
Miscellaneous	Instructions For R.E. And Pioneers. Appendix B.	24/09/1917	24/09/1917
Heading	War Diary For Headquarters, 39th Divl. R.E. From October 1st To October 31st 1917. Vol 20		
War Diary	St Jans Cappel	01/10/1917	15/10/1917
War Diary	De Zon Camp	16/10/1917	31/10/1917
Heading	War Diary of Headquarters 39th Divl. R.E. From 1st to 30th November 1917. Vol 21		
War Diary	De Zon Camp	01/11/1917	16/11/1917
War Diary	Westoutre	17/11/1917	23/11/1917
War Diary	Goldfish Chateau	24/11/1917	30/11/1917
Operation(al) Order(s)	C.R.E. 39th Division Operation Order No. 48	23/11/1917	23/11/1917
Miscellaneous			
Miscellaneous	H.465. H.Q. 39th Division. C.E. Xth Corps.	09/11/1917	09/11/1917
Miscellaneous	Four Separate Sectors of the Ypres Salient have been Prepared for Offensive Operations by this Division.	09/11/1917	09/11/1917
Miscellaneous		18/11/1917	18/11/1917
Heading	War Diary of H.Q., 39th Divl. R.E. From 1st December to 31st December 1917. Vol 22		
War Diary	Goldfish Chateau	01/12/1917	01/12/1917
War Diary	H.11 Central Sheet 28	02/12/1917	07/12/1917
War Diary	Eecke	08/12/1917	09/12/1917
War Diary	Colembert Sheet 13 1/100000	10/12/1917	23/12/1917
War Diary	Canal Bank Ypres	24/12/1917	31/12/1917
Operation(al) Order(s)	C.R.E., 39th Division Operation Order No. 49	07/12/1917	07/12/1917
Miscellaneous			
Operation(al) Order(s)	C.R.E., 39th Division Order No. 50	27/12/1917	27/12/1917
Miscellaneous	Table Showing Movements of 234th Field Coy.		
Heading	War Diary For Headquarters 39th Divl. R.E. From 1st January To 31st January 1918. Vol 23		
War Diary	Canal Bank Ypres	01/01/1918	22/01/1918
War Diary	Tunnelling Camp	23/01/1918	24/01/1918
War Diary	Mericourt Sur Somme	25/01/1918	31/01/1918
Heading	War Diary of Headquarters 39th Divl RE. From 1st to 28th Feb. 1918. Vol 24		
War Diary	Mericourt	01/02/1918	01/02/1918
War Diary	Nurlu	02/02/1918	28/02/1918
Heading	War Diary Headquarters, Royal Engineers, 39th Division. March 1918. Attached:- Narrative of Operations 21st to 31st March.		
Heading	War Diary Of Headquarters 39th Divl. R.E. From 1st March 1918 To 31st March 1918. Vol 25		
War Diary	Nurlu	01/03/1918	11/03/1918
War Diary	Haut Allaines	12/03/1918	21/03/1918

Miscellaneous	Detailed Narrative March 21st-31st H.Q., 39th Divl. Engineers.		
Heading	39th Divisional Engineers. C.R.E. 39th Division. April 1918		
Heading	War Diary of H.Q. 39th Divl. R.E. From 1-4-18 to 30-4-18. Vol 26		
War Diary	Guignemicourt (Amiens Sheet)	01/04/1918	02/04/1918
War Diary	Belloy-St Leonard (Dieppe Sheet)	03/04/1918	03/04/1918
War Diary	Oisemont	04/04/1918	08/04/1918
War Diary	Wolphus	09/04/1918	11/04/1918
War Diary	Eperlecques	12/04/1918	30/05/1918
War Diary	Eperlecques	01/05/1918	31/05/1918
War Diary	Eperlecques	26/05/1918	31/05/1918
Heading	War Diary of H.Q. 39th Divl. R.E. From 1st to 30th June. Vol 28		
War Diary	Eperlecques (Map 1/100000 Hazebrouck 5.A)	01/06/1918	07/06/1918
War Diary	La Recousse	08/06/1918	30/06/1918
Heading	War Diary For H.Q., 39th Divl. R.E. From 1st July to 31st July, 1918. Vol 29		
War Diary	La Recousse		
Heading	War Diary of H.Q. 39th Divl RE From 1st-31st Aug 1918. Vol 30		
War Diary	La Recousse	01/08/1918	31/08/1918
Heading	War Diary For H.Q., 39th Divisional R.E. From 1st to 30th Sept. 1918. Vol 31		
War Diary	Sheet 27 N.30.d.7.0	01/09/1918	29/09/1918
War Diary	Phincboom Sheet 27 X.8	30/09/1918	30/09/1918
Heading	39th Div. R.E. War Diary For H.Q., 39th Div. RE (1-10-18-31-10-18) Vol 32		
War Diary	Phincboom Sheet 27 X.8 Central	01/10/1918	28/10/1918
War Diary	Arques	29/10/1918	31/10/1918
Miscellaneous	D.A.G., G.H.Q., 3rd Echelon.	01/12/1918	01/12/1918
Heading	War Diary. Headquarters, 39th Divisional Royal Engineers November, 1918. Volume XXXIII		
War Diary	Arques	01/11/1918	11/11/1918
War Diary	Vichte	12/11/1918	12/11/1918
War Diary	Escanaffles	13/11/1918	30/11/1918
Heading	War Diary. Headquarters, 39th Divisional Royal Engineers, December 1918. Volume XXXIV.		
War Diary	Escanaffles	01/12/1918	02/12/1918
War Diary	Menin	03/12/1918	17/12/1918
War Diary	Hazebrouck	18/12/1918	31/12/1918
Miscellaneous	D.A.A.G., G.H.Q., 3rd Echelon.	29/10/1918	29/10/1918
Miscellaneous	D.A.G. 3rd Echelon., G.H.Q.	10/10/1918	10/10/1918
Miscellaneous	C.R.E. VIIth Corps Troops.	24/10/1918	24/10/1918
Miscellaneous	C.E. VIIth Corps.	02/09/1918	02/09/1918

39TH DIVISION
DIVL ENGINEERS

C. R. E.

MAR 1916-DEC 1918

CRE 39th Div Vol 1

Confidential

War Diary

of

Headquarters, 39th Divisional R.E.,

from 5th March 1916 to 31st March 1916.

(Volume 1.)

Dec 1918

Instructions regarding War Diaries and Intelligence Summaries are contained in F. S. Regs., Part II. and the Staff Manual respectively. Title Pages will be prepared in manuscript.

WAR DIARY

~~or~~

~~INTELLIGENCE SUMMARY~~

(Erase heading not required.)

Army Form C. 2118

I.

Place	Date	Hour	Summary of Events and Information	Remarks and references to Appendices
Milford Camp	5/3/16		Left Camp 4.a.m, entrained departed 7.15a.m. arrived Southampton, embarked on Courtfield & left at 7.45 pm for Le HAVRE, where HQ disembarked about 11. a.m. next day. Marched to No 1 Rest Camp.	C.P.
Le Havre	7/3/16		Marched to Pt 6 & entrained, left 1 pm.	C.P.
Blaringhem	8/3/16		Arrived Thiennes at 10 a m, wrongly directed to billets so arrived to find nothing, telephoned DHQ, resumed march & arrived at BLARINGHEM at 3 p.m. Found that after drawing extra blankets & rugs not enough accomodation in baggage wagon. Great difficulties over entraining & detraining as no. of personnel hardly sufficient to look after horses. Companies over 5 miles away. This is likely to occur frequently & Divisional Head Quarters state that they are seldom likely to have a car for the CRE. It seems that a car is absolutely essential.	C.P.
ditto	9/3/16.		225th Field Company moved to front area for instruction. Major Harrison O.C. of the unit sent to hospital with pleurisy. O.C. 227th ordered, on instructions from CE III Corps, to detail an officer (Lt HMS Meares) to take over the dump at STEENEBEQUE & to sort out & erect a TARRANT HUT & report on it. No plans available.	C.P. C.P.
do.	10/3/16		CRE reported to CE 1st Army afterwards visited RE dump at STEENEBEGUE & met 234th Company on arrival from England.	C.P.
do	11/3/16		227th Fd Coy moved to front area for Instruction	
"	12/3/16		Church Service in Morning. Heavy firing all the morning.	
"	13/3/16		234 Fd Coy moved to front area for Instn. Adj 39th Div RE. " " " "	
	14.3.16		C.R.E. visited all camps in Divisional Area with [illegible]	

1875 Wt. W593/826 1,000,000 4/15 J.B.C. & A. A.D.S.S./Forms/C. 2118.

Instructions regarding War Diaries and Intelligence Summaries are contained in F. S. Regs., Part II. and the Staff Manual respectively. Title Pages will be prepared in manuscript.

WAR DIARY
or
~~INTELLIGENCE SUMMARY~~
(Erase heading not required.)

Army Form C. 2118

2

Place	Date	Hour	Summary of Events and Information	Remarks and references to Appendices
Blaringhem	15.3.16		Eng Clerk Browning to front area for instruction	
"	16.3.16		~~Visit~~ C.R.E. visited C.E. 3rd Corps. afterwards inspected R.E. Dump at Steenbecque.	
	17.3.16		Nothing of importance occurred.	
	18.3.16		Nothing of any importance. Arranged for car for 21st to visit front area	
	19.3.16		Visited Hut for Canteen & then to La Motte with A.D.M.S. In afternoon inspected huts near R.E. Dump & decided to take down & re erect 3 Armstrong huts for use as Disinfector for Blankets. New site selected at the Hospital at Morbecque.	
	20.3.16		Work on E.F.C. & Huts at Morbecque approaching completion	
	21.3.16		C.R.E. 39th to C.R.E. 8th Div for a few days instruction.	Cb
			Adjutant returned to Blaringhem.	
	22.3		C.R.E. visited Home Counties Field Company section of the line with Major Bryant on the assumption that 39th Division would take over this section as part of their front.	Cb
	23.3	—	227th Field Company moved from Bac St Maur to Estaires	Cb
			234th from 34th Division area to Neuf Berquin.	Cb
	23.3		C.R.E. returned Blaringhem	
	24.3	—	227th moved to Les Lauriers area K 11 d 7.8	Cb
			234th " " " " K 11 b 0 4.	
	24.3.		39th Division joined XI Corps from 10 am.	(X 5a.) Cb
	25.3		225th Company attached XIX division, left Nouveau Monde 4. pm marched to LA COUTOURE	Cb
			Adjutant visited all Field Companies on a motor bicycle borrowed from the Signal Company.	
	26.3		Adjutant took orders for moves to Field Companies as under then visited LESTREM to arrange Billets for HQ. 227th to move to L'ECLÈME leave pontoons spare horses etc parked there & move on to BETHUNE area to be attached to 33rd DIV. 234th Div Field Company. 1 section attached 123rd Company LETOURET 2 sections to 124th & 151st Field Coys at GORRE 1 section attached 29th Siege Bde R 9A at LES LOBES	Cb
			Moves to be carried out on 27th	

1875 Wt. W593/826 1,000,000 4/15 J.B.C. & A. A.D.S.S./Forms/C. 2118.

Instructions regarding War Diaries and Intelligence Summaries are contained in F. S. Regs., Part II. and the Staff Manual respectively. Title Pages will be prepared in manuscript.

WAR DIARY

~~or~~

~~INTELLIGENCE SUMMARY~~

(Erase heading not required.)

Army Form C. 2118

Place	Date	Hour	Summary of Events and Information	Remarks and references to Appendices
	27/3/16		Moves carried out by units.	CJ
LESTEM.	28/3/16.		Divisional Headquarters moved to LESTREM. Divisional workshop arranged at ST VENANT. present staff 1 officer, 4 carpenters, 1 fitter, 3 labourers, all supplied by pioneer battalion 13th Gloucesters. It is intended to make this a permanency replacing pioneers by tradesmen from infantry units.	CJ
"	29/3/16		Flammenwerfer exhibition near LES LAURIERS. Flame played on occupied trench at 20 feet range, sandbags burned + 2 men's coats badly singed. Flames appeared to strike down, according to some reports, but this is thought to be due to the setting alight of the parados sandbags.	CJ
"	30/3/16		CRE visited all Field Companies + also CRE 33rd DIV.	CJ
"	31/3/16		Major Harrison returned from hospital + took over command of 225th Field Company from Capt. Hammonds.	CJ.

C. J. Turner Jones
Capt RE
Ag CRE 39th DIV.

31/3/16

1875 Wt. W593/826 1,000,000 4/15 J.B.C. & A. A.D.S.S./Forms/C. 2118.

Confidential

War Diary
of
C. R. E., 39th Division

From 1st April 1916 to 30th April 1916.

(Volume I)

Instructions regarding War Diaries and Intelligence Summaries are contained in F. S. Regs., Part II. and the Staff Manual respectively. Title Pages will be prepared in manuscript.

WAR DIARY
or
~~INTELLIGENCE SUMMARY~~
(Erase heading not required.)

Army Form C. 2118

Place	Date	Hour	Summary of Events and Information	Remarks and references to Appendices
LESTREM	1/4/16		Nothing of Importance	CL
	2/4/16		do.	CL
	3/4/16	10 15pm	L/C Parkinson J W 131442 ~~of~~ of 234th Field Coy RE wounded slightly Sapper Pearson C H 101229 of 225th " " " " in thigh at Boars Head S16a25 36	CL
	4/4/16	9 30am	CE called for CRE + took him round a section of the 2nd line S of ESTAIRES	
		3pm	CRE left for corps HQ at HINGES to take over the duties of CE	CL.
	5/4/16		Adj went to BETHUNE on local purchase	CL
	6/4/16		nothing of importance	CL
	7/4/16		visited Haazbrook on local purchase, no success	CL.
	8/4/16		No 104144 Sapr W. Foley. 227th Field Coy RE killed Conference at Div Hd Qrs in connection with XI corps policy of warfare.	CL
	9/4/16		CE picked up adjutant at 2.30 pm; visited reserve line VIELLE CHAPELLE. LES 8 MAISONS, RIEZ BAILLEUL, CARTERS.POST.	CL.
	10/4/16		Order marked A (attached) received.	
	11/4/16		visited LOCON, CRE 38th Division + discussed preliminaries arranged for each field company to send officers to learn 38th Division area	

Army Form C. 2118

Instructions regarding War Diaries and Intelligence Summaries are contained in F. S. Regs., Part II. and the Staff Manual respectively. Title Pages will be prepared in manuscript.

WAR DIARY
or
INTELLIGENCE SUMMARY
(Erase heading not required.)

Place	Date	Hour	Summary of Events and Information	Remarks and references to Appendices
LESTREM	11.4.16	(Cont)	Arranged for 225th Field Coy to relieve 123rd near LE TOURET at X 15 d 8 2 Sheet 36A for work in FESTUBERT section.	
			227th to relieve 157th at GORRE F 3 c 5 4 sheet 36(b) for work on right of GIVENCHY section	
			234th to relieve 124th at GORRE F 3 d 1 4 sheet 36(b) for work on left of GIVENCHY section.	
			Preliminary Div order received & attached (B). also 39th D O no 6 (C).	
	12.4.		Visited LOCON & CRE dump at LE TOURET.	
	13.4		Visited 124th Coy area* with the O.C. a tremendous lot of work to be done in this portion especially in mine area *(Left half of Right Bde GIVENCHY section)	
			Lt H M S MEARES reported for duty with HQ RE during the absence of the CRE.	
	14.4		Visited right half of right bde in GIVENCHY section 157th Coy area.	
			Selected position for Divisional Bomb Store in consultation with G.	
			227th Coy took over from 157th at 9 a.m. & Handing over report attached (D.)	
			Capt D H Hammonds 225th Field Coy RE admitted into 131 Field ambulance & evacuated to No 2 London CCS. MERVILLE suffering from German measles.	
	15		Attached (E) Divisional instruction drawn up & submitted for approval. A very temporary measure to bridge over till further knowledge of the line is gained. (Adapted from CRE 8th Division's instructions.	

1875 Wt. W593/826 1,000,000 4/15 J.B.C. & A. A.D.S.S./Forms/C. 2118.

Instructions regarding War Diaries and Intelligence Summaries are contained in F. S. Regs., Part II. and the Staff Manual respectively. Title Pages will be prepared in manuscript.

WAR DIARY
or
INTELLIGENCE SUMMARY
(Erase heading not required.)

Army Form C. 2118

Place	Date	Hour	Summary of Events and Information	Remarks and references to Appendices
Lestrem	16 4/16		C.R.E assumed duty from Hd. qrs. Visited 225th Coy a.m. Le Touret with C.E.	CGB
Locon	17 4/16		Hd Qrs. 39th Divn moved in from Lestrem. O.	CGB
			Order of urgency of work in left section received from Hd Qrs. Copies of O.C. 225th Coy	Marked F
"	18 4/16		O.C. 13 Gloucesters (Pioneers) together with suggestions as to method of carrying on work. Visited C.R.E.s dump at Le Touret. O.C.'s 225 Coy & 227th & 234th Coy at Gorre. Studying records handed over by 38th Div. Conference at Corps Hd Qrs	CGB
"	19th		Studying records. Visited G.O.C. 118 Bde to arrange details of work. Conference at Divn Hd Qrs afterwards discussed with Brigadier the organization of Infantry working parties.	CGB
	20th		Met Sargent 225th Coy who explained progress of work in left section	CGB
	21st		Visited FESTUBERT – FESTUBERT E – & CAILLOUX POSTS	CGB
	22		with G.S.O 1 & 3.	
	23rd		Started with Major Harrison to visit Fife Road got hung up near Tuning Fork by heavy shelling. Went thoroughly into condition of posts etc in left sector with plans in this office	CGB
	24th		Visited Wolfe Road, Coventry Street, Front line Trenches etc with O.C 227th Field Coy afterwards conferred with G.O.C. B section re urgency of work to be carried out therein.	CGB
	25th		Visited Le Tourret, Le Touret E, Wine food but parapets etc require attention. Some good concrete dugouts in latter	CGB

1375 Wt. W593/826 1,000,000 4/15 J.B.C. & A. A.D.S.S./Forms/C. 2118.

Instructions regarding War Diaries and Intelligence Summaries are contained in F. S. Regs., Part II. and the Staff Manual respectively. Title Pages will be prepared in manuscript.

WAR DIARY
or
INTELLIGENCE SUMMARY
(Erase heading not required.)

Army Form C. 2118

Place	Date	Hour	Summary of Events and Information	Remarks and references to Appendices
26.4.16			Visited Givenchy with C.E.'s 1st Army & XI Corps. Heaps of fallen brick in village require clearing to ~~put~~ improve Field of fire from Keep H.Q.'s. Caledonian Road should be stopped so as to be used as fire trench it has an excellent field of fire to N.W.	Cy/B
			Conference with O.C. 7th Cov. O.C. 13 Gloucesters & Drainage Officers.	Cy/B Cy/B
27.4.16			G.O.C. Divisional Conference at Hd. Qrs.	
28.4.16			Visited Dump near Estaminet, La Plantin N. Cheshire Rd. O.B.L. Fife Rd. Barnton Rd.	
29.4.16			Visited Dump at Spinnette, Village W. & Brigade advanced Report centre. Pioneer Rd. Brigade advanced Report centre should be completed to O.B.L. as early as possible. Cheshire Road & Barnton road should be brought forward. This would enable Rd. material to be brought forward in the day time & so facilitate the Reclaiming of Fife & Barnton Roads to the Islands & Pioneer Rd. to Richmond Terrace at night owing to the saving in carrying stores by night. Instructions have been given for the improvement of advanced Brigade Report centre. Pioneer Road from O.B.L. to Village Line wants improving, the existing portion is only waist high & hardly bullet proof. Several places in the O.B.L. require the parapet heightened a little as one can see over when standing upright behind.	Cy/B
30.4.16			Visited Army workshops Bethune. Butts at Essars.	Cy/B

1875 Wt. W593/826 1,000,000 4/15 J.B.C. & A. A.D.S.S./Forms/C. 2118.

CONFIDENTIAL

War Diary

of

C.R.E 39th Division

from May 1st to May 31.1916

Instructions regarding War Diaries and Intelligence Summaries are contained in F. S. Regs., Part II. and the Staff Manual respectively. Title Pages will be prepared in manuscript.

WAR DIARY
or
~~INTELLIGENCE SUMMARY~~

(Erase heading not required.)

Army Form C. 2118

Place	Date	Hour	Summary of Events and Information	Remarks and references to Appendices
Hohn[?]	1 5/16		work in office. Went to Hinges to look for & destroy reported aeroplane Bomb. not found	
			fallen here from A.A. gun dug up about x7d13 below.	
"	2 5/16		Visited B.G. 116 Bde (Right sector). Visited Pont Fixe proposed O.P. explained they are Walk	
			Sidbury Defences O.P. Artillery Road. Strathcona Walk & front line Trenches	
			from Canal to Gap North of Thames Road. Givenchy Section	
	3 5/16		Nothing of importance. Visited B.G. 116 Bde to discuss some of his work in front line	
	4 5/16		Visited 231st Fd Coy RE. went with O.C. round some of new advanced Batt. Hd Qrs. M.G. Emp.	
			Grenadier Rd, Hitchin Road & new advanced Batt. Hd Qrs. M.G. Emp. in afternoon.	
			at Windy corner. Conference of O.C. Fd Coy. in afternoon. inspected proposed new site	
	5 5/16		Visited Le Touret with A.D.M.S. re Baths inspected proposed new site. Enquiries from Corps if R. La Loisne	
			question of Water supply to be considered. Saw St Thomas	
			dries in Summer or if there is always water in it.	
			re posts back of Village line. question of advanced aid Posts in Village Line	
	6 5/16		Discussed with A.D.M.S. question of advanced aid Posts in Village Line	
			& further forward.	
	7th		Visited Posts at Essars. Croix de Fer. Lawe Bridge & Long Cornet.	
	8th		Visited Orchard Rd & Orchard Redoubt. Road not good but being	
			recovered. Redoubt in bad condition existing M.G. Empmt poor	
			found a very good site just topping the crest of Ridge & commanding	
			all the ground E & N of it to Marie Redoubt. Also found some	
			apparently R.E. abandoned dug out shelters of Orchard Trench a little	
			W of the Farm. Possibly a good site for advanced Batt. H.Q.	
			Sidbury a difficult proposition. Old mined dug outs must be	
			pumped out to see what accommodation there	
			is. If extra are required they must be mined as it will	

1875 Wt. W593/826 1,000,000 4/15 J.B.C. & A. A.D.S.S./Forms/C. 2118.

Instructions regarding War Diaries and Intelligence Summaries are contained in F. S. Regs., Part II. and the Staff Manual respectively. Title Pages will be prepared in manuscript.

WAR DIARY
or
INTELLIGENCE SUMMARY
(Erase heading not required.)

Army Form C. 2118

Place	Date	Hour	Summary of Events and Information	Remarks and references to Appendices
Locon			be almost impossible to dig deep owing to looseness of soil. The defences are in poor condition.	
	9th		Work in office & visited 225th Fd Coy at the Tourret.	
	10th		Visited all Rd Dumps with C.E. XI Corps. Visited B[illegible] with G.S.O.1 & G.O.C. B Sectn to settle order of urgency of work. Cambridge Terrace, Oxford Terrace, Bayswater & Rat Road to be immediately reclaimed & made capable of firing. 2 M.G. Empts S.E. corner Orchard redoubt to be improved & good dug outs provided. Sidbury finally decided on as site for Rt Battn Hd Qrs. Steel shelters suggested. Possibly Brick & Concrete dug outs may be better. Bomb store near Castle & [illegible] requires to be made for safety of Bomb site.	
	11th		Explained policy arrived at on 10th to O.C. 227th & 234th Fd Coys & to G.O.C. & instructed them to put in hand at once, leaving work temporarily of less immediate importance & to see on certain work G.O.C. B Section re details.	
	12th		Conference at Hd Quarters.	
	13th		Visited 225 Coy at Le Touret. Visited Festubert, Barnton Rd to O.B.L., Fife Rd to the Loop, Le Plantin N. & O.P. Called at 227th Coy on way home & discussed certain work in hand	
	14th		Work in office.	
	15th		Visited 227th Fd Coy. Inspected Pont Fixe Defences.	
	16th		Visited proposed new training ground re material required	

Instructions regarding War Diaries and Intelligence Summaries are contained in F. S. Regs., Part II. and the Staff Manual respectively. Title Pages will be prepared in manuscript.

WAR DIARY
or
INTELLIGENCE SUMMARY
(Erase heading not required.)

Army Form C. 2118

Place	Date	Hour	Summary of Events and Information	Remarks and references to Appendices
Locon	17th		Visited 225 Fd Coy. Visited Loisne N & Loisne E. Tuning Fork W & the Breastwork line from latter to Le Touret Rd. Loisne N very good except that dug outs & Empts fill with water. Loisne E wants a lot of work on it to put in good state. Breastwork Line in fair state in places but revetment wants a lot of work on it. There are a number of M.G. Empts in various stages of completion some only want the roofs completing, others have only had the entrance [illegible].	
	18th		Visited 234th Fd Coy. Visited work in progress at New Cut Wave(?) Road Caledonian Road. Pumping St. Ry Aid Post & Hut Redoubt & Windy Corner Defences. Office lecture by B.G.G.S. 1 Corps on	
	19.		Defended Localities. Compiling Report on Defended Localities	
	20th		Visited our Battn Billets of Bns in Reserve with A.D.M.S. re water supply and drainage. Also Bomb school.	
	21st			
	22nd		Visited 227th Coy. Wolf Road. Coventry St. Gunner Siding. M.G. Empt. Orchard Road & Sidbury in advanced Battn. H.Q. Met B.G. R.A. Corps who spoke to me about O.Ps	
	23		work in Office	

1375 Wt. W593/826 1,000,000 4/15 J.B.C. & A. A.D.S.S./Forms/C. 2118.

Instructions regarding War Diaries and Intelligence Summaries are contained in F. S. Regs., Part II. and the Staff Manual respectively. Title Pages will be prepared in manuscript.

WAR DIARY
or
INTELLIGENCE SUMMARY
(Erase heading not required.)

Army Form C. 2118

Place	Date	Hour	Summary of Events and Information	Remarks and references to Appendices
Locon	24th		Visited 234th Coy with Lt Col Mowat CRE 6th Dn. Hitchin Rd to Scottish Trench T.M. Position Caledonian Road. Adv. Batt HQrs given by Pringles Pt. Adv. Aid Post. Herts Redoubt & Pringles Pride.	
	25th		Visited 227th & 234th & Battn Billets at Gorre with A.A.Q.M.G. visited O.C. Mining Coy with reference to mine work & instn of 72 Coy with push pipe method of making Commn Trenches. Conference with O.C. 225 Visited works at Le Hamel & Le Hamel N.W. Conference with C.E. 1st Army & XI Corps Divisional Conference	
	26th		Round Le Touret. Loone N & S. Gorre Wood & Le Hamel with	
	27th		arrangements for visiting back billets with A.A & Q.M.G cancelled owing to certain moves.	
	28th		To Gorre to reconnoitre site for bridge over canal. Gave O.C. 227th orders to collect stores. 9pm ordered him to carry on. Bridge completed 4am 30th.	
	29th		Conference of CRE's at Hinges at C.E. XI Corps office re stores chiefly. Divisional Conference 6.30pm.	
	30th		Inspected bridge at Gorre. In afternoon visited CRE 33rd Dn re section one of our Brigades is holding. Conference 6.30. Dn HQ. afterwards ordered O.C. 227 to reconnoitre approaches from Bridges on Bethune Canal to those on Bourry Canal & onwards. also site for shelters for advanced Dn HQrs to be reconnoitred	
	31st		Visited B Section HdQrs & RA Bde HdQuarters re dugouts for staff afterwards visited 227th Coy on same matter & gave instructions.	

C G Burnaby
Lt Col RE
CRE 39th Dn

1875 Wt. W593/826 1,000,000 4/15 J.B.C. & A. A.D.S.S./Forms/C. 2118.

CONFIDENTIAL.

W A R   D I A R Y

O F

C.R.E. 39TH DIVISION.

FROM JUNE 1st 1916   TO   JUNE 31st 1916.

Instructions regarding War Diaries and Intelligence Summaries are contained in F. S. Regs., Part II. and the Staff Manual respectively. Title Pages will be prepared in manuscript.

WAR DIARY
or
INTELLIGENCE SUMMARY
(Erase heading not required.)

Army Form C. 2118

Place	Date	Hour	Summary of Events and Information	Remarks and references to Appendices
	June			
Locon	1st		Work on experimental periscope. Conference of Fd Coy Comdrs in afternoon. Practice forming bridge over Bethune Canal at night.	
			Conference at Corps Head Quarters. 9 Div Hd Qrs later.	
	2nd		Conference at Corps Head Quarters. 9 Div Hd Qrs later.	
	3rd		Visited [illegible] 33rd Div'n Bethune & afterwards with 11th Fd Coy.	
	4th		Conference at Canal House. Handing over to Lt Col Smith.	
	5th		Visited 227th Field Coy. and arranged work.	
	6th		Visited 1st Army Workshops, BETHUNE, re experimental large periscope.	
	7th		Visited R.E. yard re experimental trolly for carrying 3 stretchers.	
	8th		Inspected dug outs for Advanced Div! Hqrs at CANAL HOUSE, and at "B" group R.F.A. Hqrs. Went round lines with O.C. 234th Fd Coy., inspecting Left Battalion Hqrs., GIVENCHY Pumping Station, KILBY'S WALK, AVENUE, PICCADILLY, BOND ST., NEW CUT.	
	9th		Attended Conference at XI Corps Hqrs. No Divisional Conference held.	
	10th		Visited Distillery O.P., PONT FIXE, and site for Right Battalion Hqrs. SIDBURY, with Chief Engineer XI Corps.	
			2/2nd South Midland Fd Coy. R.E.(T.) 61st Division was attached for instructional work to this Division on 30th May, and was withdrawn on this date.	
	11th.		Nothing of importance	
	12th.		Visited 1st Army Workshops, BETHUNE, and inspected progress on experimental periscope.	

Instructions regarding War Diaries and Intelligence Summaries are contained in F. S. Regs., Part II. and the Staff Manual respectively. Title Pages will be prepared in manuscript.

WAR DIARY
or
INTELLIGENCE SUMMARY
(Erase heading not required.)

Army Form C. 2118

Place	Date	Hour	Summary of Events and Information	Remarks and references to Appendices
LOCON	13-6-16		Received Divisional Defence Scheme on readjustment of front, taking over part of line from 35th Divn and giving up part to 33rd Divn	
			Visited LESTREM and conferred with CRE. 35th Divn	
	14-6-16		Conference at LESTREM with CRE. 35th Divn and O.Cs. 227th + 234th Fd. Coys. who met the OCs. 203rd 204th + 205th Fd Coys. and arranged about handing over.	
			CRE. 33rd Div. visited GIVENCHY area, to be taken over by him.	
	15-6-16		Conference with CRE 33rd Div Handing over Documents etc.	
			" " CRE 35th " Taking over Documents etc.	
	16-6-16		Conference with G.O.C., G.S.O. & Q. Visited CE XI Corps & CRE 35th Div.	
			Working out details with Companies moving to new Billets.	
	17-6-16		Arranging working parties etc. & arranging [illegible] Visited 227th & 234th Fd Coys.	
			Drawing stores. Compiling report with Q.	
	18th-6-16		Work in office. Return of Defended Posts. Compiling arrangements [illegible]	
	19-6-16		Return of Defended posts completed. Report on certain arrangements [illegible] completed report. [illegible]	
	20-6		Conference with O.C. Pioneers & [illegible] 227th Coy	
	21-6		Visited G.O.C. 118 Bde. Conference with O.C. [illegible]	
	22-6		Visited 225th Coy. [illegible] Conference of CRE's at O.E. Office	
	23-6		Conference with O.C. 13 Gloucesters. Talking [illegible] Visited model near ZELOBES. Saw G.O.C.	
	24-6		Conference with O.C. 234th Coy. Conference with O.C. Gloucesters [illegible]	
	25-6		Preparing & sorting papers in office [illegible] with O.C. 227 & 234 afterwards.	
	26th		Visited Ferme du Bois section. Conference [illegible]	
	27th		Visited model etc. at Zelobes with O.C. 234 Coy [illegible] & discussing proposed schemes	

1875 Wt. W593/826 1,000,000 4/15 J.B.C. & A. A.D.S.S./Forms/C. 2118.

Instructions regarding War Diaries and Intelligence Summaries are contained in F. S. Regs., Part II. and the Staff Manual respectively. Title Pages will be prepared in manuscript.

WAR DIARY
or
INTELLIGENCE SUMMARY
(Erase heading not required.)

Army Form C. 2118

Place	Date	Hour	Summary of Events and Information	Remarks and references to Appendices
28th	—	—	Work in office	
29th	—	—	Heavy preliminary Bombardment of enemy trenches. attack on enemy trenches night of 29th–30th. 234th Co took part. (10 W 5 M.)	
	—	—		
30th	—	—	Getting reports of operations. 10 W. 5 M. Visited CE XI Corps re Pin in Marriage	C.J. [illegible] Lt Col (RE) CRE 39th Div

1875 Wt. W593/826 1,000,000 4/15 J.B.C. & A. A.D.S.S./Forms/C. 2118.

39/CRE
Vol 5

CONFIDENTIAL.

W A R D I A R Y.

OF

Headquarters 39th Divl. R.E.

FROM 1st JULY 1916. TO 31ST JULy 1916.

39/C.R.E.
Vol 5

CONFIDENTIAL.

W A R D I A R Y.

OF

Headquarters 39th Divl. R.E.

FROM 1st JULY 1916. TO 31ST JULy 1916.

Instructions regarding War Diaries and Intelligence Summaries are contained in F. S. Regs., Part II. and the Staff Manual respectively. Title pages will be prepared in manuscript.

WAR DIARY
or
~~INTELLIGENCE SUMMARY.~~
(*Erase heading not required.*)

Army Form C. 2118.

HQ 39th Div[l] RE

Place	Date	Hour	Summary of Events and Information	Remarks and references to Appendices
Locon				
"	1.7.16		Work in office	
"	2.7.16		Visited St Vaast Dressing Station also that at R. George's Road with [illegible] afterwards visited 234 Fd Coy at Le Hamel [illegible] with OC [illegible]	
	3.7.16		Visited Festubert left section & whole front of Ferme du Bois section [illegible] back via Lansdowne C.T. & Rue des Berceaux.	
	4th		Writing up report on work visited on 3rd	
	5th		Visited proposed extension of Grenade [illegible] with OC 234 Fd Coy & left of front line Ferme du Bois. Later visited CRE 61st Div with reference to connection of our proposal with works in Neuve Chapelle Section	
	6th		Received warning to move. Visited CRE 33 & arranged for officers to visit sections	
	7.		Taking over plans etc from CRE 33rd & handing over to CRE 61st. Companies moved to new billets starting 9.45 pm & 10.15 pm resp	
	8th		Moved to Bethune. Ordered Bridge over Canal to be made ready	
	9th		Conference with OC units arranged programme of work	
	10		Work in Office. Visited [illegible]	
	11th		Visited part of Cuinchy Section with OC 227 Coy	

T2134. Wt. W708-776. 500000. 4/15. Sir J. C. & S.

Instructions regarding War Diaries and Intelligence Summaries are contained in F. S. Regs., Part II. and the Staff Manual respectively. Title pages will be prepared in manuscript.

WAR DIARY

~~or~~

~~INTELLIGENCE SUMMARY.~~

(*Erase heading not required.*)

Army Form C. 2118.

HQ 39th Divl RE.

Place	Date	Hour	Summary of Events and Information	Remarks and references to Appendices
Bethune	12th		Work in Office Conference with Q re preparations for advance	
"	13th		Work in office Visited La Gorgue re stores. Inspected model at Locon	
"	14th		Orders to move received 7.30 am. Handing over to CRE 8th Div T	
	15th		Taking over plans from CRE 61st Div. Moved from Bethune to Locon.	
LOCON	16th		Arranging programme of work & distribution of units	
	17		Standing by. Conference of O.C.'s. CE 1st Army called in Office.	
	18		Work in office.	
	19		Bombardment of Enemy Lines	
	20		Attack on Enemy lines by Div on left of Corps.	
	21		Getting out scheme for work on Divl front	
	22		& working parties required	
	23		Corps Conference. Visited CE re Drainage.	
	24		Divl Conference. 7th Cy Comdr came [illegible] stores 4 S.O.1	
	25		~~Choosing~~ site for [illegible] Bomb store with Q. x	
	26		x	
	27		Work in Office	
	28		Work in Office	

T2134. Wt. W708–776. 500000. 4/15. Sir J. C. & S.

Instructions regarding War Diaries and Intelligence Summaries are contained in F. S. Regs., Part II. and the Staff Manual respectively. Title pages will be prepared in manuscript.

WAR DIARY
~~or~~
~~INTELLIGENCE~~ SUMMARY.

(*Erase heading not required.*)

Army Form C. 2118.

HQ 39th Div RE

Place	Date	Hour	Summary of Events and Information	Remarks and references to Appendices
LOCON	31-7-16		Lt Col BURNABY left for MERVILLE.	
			Major & Hon Lt Col S. SMITH took over duties as acting CRE.	
			No events of importance	
			S. Smith Major & Hon Lt Col RE a/CRE 39th Div	

T2134. Wt. W708–776. 500000. 4/15. Sir J. C. & S.

CRE Vol 6

CONFIDENTIAL.

W A R   D I A R Y

OF

39th Divisional R.E.

FROM AUGUST 1st 1916.   TO AUGUST 31st 1916.

....

CONFIDENTIAL.

W A R D I A R Y

OF

H.Q. 39th DIVL. R.E.

FROM August 1st 1916 TO AUGUST 31st 1916.

Instructions regarding War Diaries and Intelligence Summaries are contained in F. S. Regs., Part II. and the Staff Manual respectively. Title pages will be prepared in manuscript.

WAR DIARY
or
~~INTELLIGENCE SUMMARY.~~
(Erase heading not required.)

Army Form C. 2118.

HQ 39 Div RE

Place	Date	Hour	Summary of Events and Information	Remarks and references to Appendices
LOCON	8-8-16		Preparing Handing-over Reports &c	
	9-8-16		Do. do do. Meeting CREs. 30th & 31st Divs and discussing work to be carried on, on taking over.	
			39th Div. Secret Order No 36 received, detailing moves of Division 10th to 12th Augt Field Coys. to move on 10th to CAUCHY À LA TOUR, on 11th to MARQUAY & BAILLEUL-AUX-CORNAILLES, on 12th to respective Brigade areas. Orders issued in accordance	
	10-8-16		Completed handing over to CRE 30th Div.	
			Field Coys. moved to CAUCHY À LA TOUR. Lt Col LE Hopkins RE took over duties of CRE	
ROLLECOURT	11.8.16		RE Head Qrs moved to ROLECOURT & Field Cos to MARQUAY & BAILLEUL	
	12.8.16		Div! Head Qrs moved to ROLLECOURT. 225th Co to ROCOURT & 234th Co to BETHENCOURT	
BOIRIN			RE Head Qrs moved to BOIRIN.	
	13.8.16		visited training area with GSO II & fixed site & gave orders for rifle range to be constructed – submitted training programme to DHQ. visited CE 17 Corps.	
	14.8.16		visited 227th Co at Training. &	A
	15.8.16		completed Riflerange. One section 227th Co & 2 Cos Pioneers employed on it.	
	"		arranged for material for incinerators for camps – [illegible]	B

Aug 1916. LE Hopkins Lt Col RE

T2134. Wt. W708–776. 500000. 4/15. Sir J. C. & S.

Instructions regarding War Diaries and Intelligence Summaries are contained in F. S. Regs., Part II. and the Staff Manual respectively. Title pages will be prepared in manuscript.

WAR DIARY
or
~~INTELLIGENCE SUMMARY~~
(Erase heading not required.)

Army Form C. 2118.

HQ. 39th Div ~~RE~~.

Place	Date	Hour	Summary of Events and Information	Remarks and references to Appendices
BOIRIN ~~[illegible]~~	16.8		Issued instructions re wiring + strong points. Put in hand construction of latrines + washplaces at St MICHEL + Baths at BETHENCOURT + THIEULOYE + repairs to bath at MAGNICOURT.	
	17.8		Conference at 5th Corps HdQrs + MARIEUX. with 6th Divn. whose line is to be taken over. + advanced	
	18.8		CRE. went to ACHEUX + visited dumps + Company billets with CRE 6th Divn.	
	19.8		CRE went round trenches with CRE 6th Divn	
	20.8		CRE went round trenches with CRE 6th Divn + OC 12th Co. + returned to BOIRIN in evening.	
	21.8		advanced parties of 227th + 234th + Head Qrs went to 6th Divn area by bus. orders for march to new area issued to Companies	C
	23.8		225 Co marched with 116th Brigade - 227th with 117 Brigade - 234th with 118th Brigade	
			CRE attended trench attack practice by Infantry	
BUS LES ARTOIS	24.8		H.Q moved with DAQ to BUS LES ARTOIS.	

[illegible] Lt Col RE
CRE 39th Divn

T2134. Wt. W708-776. 500000. 4/15. Sir J. C. & S.

Instructions regarding War Diaries and Intelligence Summaries are contained in F. S. Regs., Part II. and the Staff Manual respectively. Title pages will be prepared in manuscript.

WAR DIARY
or
~~INTELLIGENCE SUMMARY.~~
(Erase heading not required.)

Army Form C. 2118.

39th Div RE. HQrs

Place	Date	Hour	Summary of Events and Information	Remarks and references to Appendices
BUSLES ARTOIS.	25.8		CRE went round trenches in front of AUCHONVILLERS with CRE 6th Divn saw 3rd Avenue Hunter Trench WHITE CITY etc.	
	26.8		Companies & Pioneers took over trenches & billets as in attached orders.	D E F G
ACHEUX	27.8		HQ took over from CRE 6th Div at 10am. CRE went round trenches with OC 13 Glosters. Spoke to GOC 118 Brigade about clearing mine bags & debris from Roberts & Gordon trenches & arranged for maintenance of CTs. Instructions	H
	28.8		orders re forward dumps issued. orders received from DHQ 10am for attack for attack issued to Cos.	J. K.
	29.8		orders received re date of attack and instructions issued to Pioneers re their role. Instruction for working parties	L. M.
	30.8		Heavy rain & great demand for trench boards. Work report attached.	N
	31.8		CRE visited Charles Avenue & new trench to connect it with Royal Avenue. Brigade orders to 227th Co for attack.	O

Sept 2 1916

[signature]
Lt Col RE
CRE 39 Divn

T2134. Wt. W708–776. 500000. 4/15. Sir J. C. & S.

1916 War Diary CRE 39th Div
Appendix A July

39th Divisional R.E. TRAINING PROGRAMME.

225th Field Company R.E.

Date.	Nature of Training. Morning 6 - 7 a.m. and 8 - 11 a.m.	Afternoon 2 - 5 p.m.	Position of Training Ground or Route of March.	Remarks.
August 14th.	Physical Exercises. Rifle Exercises.	Squad Drill & Kit Inspection.	H.Q. ROCOURT.	
" 15th.	Route March 8 - 12.	Feet Inspection.	LA COMTE - CURTON - DIEVAL - LA THIEULOYE - ROCOURT (12 miles).	
" 16th.	Physical Exercises & Demolitions. instruction & practice in use of bombs.	Recreation.	H.Q. ROCOURT & BRIGADE AREA.	Lecture by C.R.E. to O.C. Companies at 10 a.m. at BOIRIN.
" 17th.	Fire Discipline and recognition of targets & range finding.	Knotting & Lashing.	H.Q. ROCOURT.	GENERAL. A proportion of Officers & N.C.Os are to be employed on reporting on roads, bridges & water supply & reconnoitring trench positions & strong points.
" 18th.	Physical Exercises & Section Drill.	Demolitions & Map Reading.	H.Q. ROCOURT & Map Reading in Divisional Area.	
" 19th.	Route March 8 - 12.	Feet Inspection.	MONCHY-BRETON - CHELERS - FREVILLERS - FOUVELIN - ROCOURT (12 miles).	
" 20th.	Physical Exercises, Practice in use of Weldon trestles.	Knotting & Lashing & bomb throwing.	H.Q. ROCOURT.	
" 22nd.	Physical Exercises & Rifle Exercises.	Pay & Recreation.	H.Q. ROCOURT.	
" 21st	Drill & Demolitions, instruction & practice in use of bombs.	Tactical scheme in Bde. Area.	H.Q. ROCOURT & BRIGADE AREA (morning) (afternoon).	

August 13th 1916.

[signature]
ADJT. 39TH DIV. R.E.
for LT. COL. R.E.
C.R.E. 39TH DIVISION.

39th Divisional R.E. TRAINING PROGRAMME.

227th Field Coy. R.E.

Date.	Nature of Training. Morning 8 - 12.	Afternoon 2 - 5 p.m.	Position of Training Ground or Route of March.	Remarks.
August 14th.	Section & Company Drill	Instruction on Demolitions Testing Exploders & Leads.	Field at Company H.Q.	1 Section on construction of Rifle Range.
" 15th.	Weldon Trestle & Pontoon Drill.	Musketry & Fire discipline	-do- -do-	
" 16th	Route March.	Lecture on preparations for the attack.	BAILLEUL-AUX-CORNAILLES - CHELERS - HERLIN-LE-VERT - U.6.d.8.8. - MAGNICOURT - ROCOURT - HOME.	Lecture by C.R.E. to O.C.Companies at 10 a.m. at BOIRIN.
" 17th.	Rifle & bayonet exercise	Recreation.	Field at Company H.Q.	GENERAL. A proportion of Officers & N.C.Os are to be employed on reporting on roads, bridges & water supply & reconnoitring trench positions & strong points.
" 18th	Officers & some N.C.Os Scheme x Remainder Section Drill & Bayonet exercise, under C.S.M.	all day.	x Field at Company H.Q.	
" 19th.	Route March.	Lecture on Bridging, if time available.	BAILLEUL-AUX-CORNAILLES - ORLENCOURT - LA THIEULOYE - ROCOURT - HOME.	
" 20th.	N.C.Os Map Reading &c. Remainder, Musketry.	Recreation.	Field at Company H.Q.	
" 21st.	Officers & some N.C.Os Scheme x Remainder Section Drill rifle & bayonet exercise.	All day. Company drill.	Field at Company H.Q.	
" 22nd.	Section & Company Drill	Weldon Trestle Drill.	Field at Company H.Q?	

x Details will be given later.

Specialists - Cyclists - Training in Map reading &c (in connection with schemes & Route Marches).
Signallers - Practice 2 hours daily.

August 13th 1916.

[signature]
ADJT. 39TH DIV. R.E.
for LT. COL. R.E.
C.R.E. 39TH DIVISION.

39th Divisional R.E. TRAINING PROGRAMME.

234th Field Ccy. R.E.

Date.	Nature of Training. Morning 8 - 12.	Afternoon 2 - 5 p.m	Position of Training Ground or Route of March.	Remarks.
August 14th.	Physical Exercises & Squad Drill.	Bayonet fighting.	H.Q. BETHENCOURT.	
" 15th	Rifle Exercise Ditto. & KIT INSPECTION.	Demolitions, instruction and ditto. practice in use of bombs.	H.Q. BETHENCOURT.& BRIGADE AREA (morning). (afternoon).	
" 16th.	Route March & Feet inspection.	Recreation.	BETHENCOURT - VILLERS-BRULIN - FREVILLERS - HOUVELIN-ROCOURT - MONCHY-BRETON - ORLENCOURT - MARQUAY - BAILLEL-AUX-CORNAILLES. - TINQUES. - BETHENCOURT.	Lecture by C.R.E. to O.C. Companies at 10 a.m at BOIRIN.
" 17th.	Squad & Company Drill.	Rapid wiring.	H.Q? BETHONCOURT.	GENERAL.
" 18th.	ditto. Signalling	Tactical Schemes.	H.Q. BETHONCOURT.& BRIGADE AREA (morning). (afternoon).	A proportion of Officers & N.C.OS are to be employed on reporting on roads, bridges & water supply & reconnoitring trench positions & strong points
" 19th.	Instruction in demolitions.	Knotting & Lashing.		
" 20th.	Route March & Feet Inspection.	Recreation. ~~Knotting & Lashing.~~	TINQUES - CHELERS - MAGNICOURT-EN-COMTE - HOUVELIN - LA COMTE - BEUGIN - HOUDIN - FREVILLERS - VILLERS-BRULIN.	
" 21st.	Practice in use of Weldon trestles.	Fire discipline & recognition of targets	H.Q. BETHONCOURT.	
" 22nd.	Map Reading.	Pay & Recreation.	H.Q. BETHONCOURT.	

August 13th 1916.

ADJT. 39TH DIV. R.E.
for LT. COL. R.E.
C.R.E. 39TH DIVISION.

CRE 39 Divn
1916 War Diary July
Appendix B.

WIRE ENTANGLEMENTS.

MATERIALS REQUIRED for 50 YARDS LINE of VARIOUS TYPES AS FOUND BY ACTUAL TEST.

FRENCH WIRE ENTANGLEMENT.

DESCRIPTION	FRENCH WIRE SMALL COILS	SCREW STAKES LONG β	SCREW STAKES SHORT	STAPLES γ	BARBED WIRE COILS α
One double row, staked down to short stakes, front & rear, to form aprons, 5 strands to each apron	10	25	25	50	25
	Each coil extends 10x	5 yds apart		2 yds apart	
Add for wastage in the dark	1	4	4	10	3
Total	11	29	29	60	28
Two double rows, with aprons as before	20	50	50	100	50
Add for wastage in the dark	2	8	8	20	6
Total	22	58	58	120	56

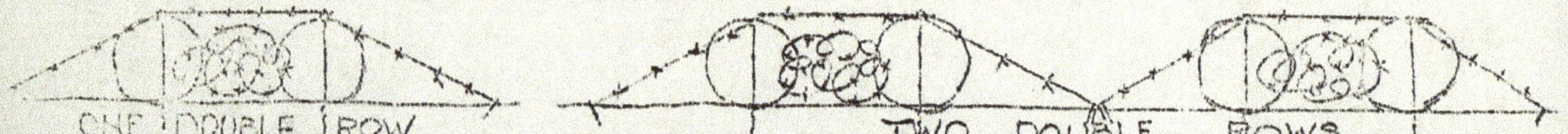

BARBED WIRE ENTANGLEMENT

DESCRIPTION	BARBED WIRE COILS α	GREEN PICKETS LONG	GREEN PICKETS SHORT
Trip wire [illegible] 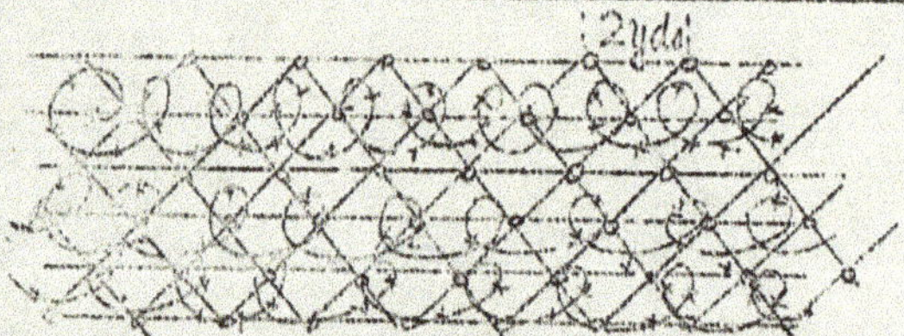	25		150
High wire entanglement similar to above but alternate long and short pickets. Each picket wired top & bottom to each neighbouring picket	42½	68	80
Entanglement for Rear Lines. Green pickets 3 yds apart, apron both sides, diagonals on aprons 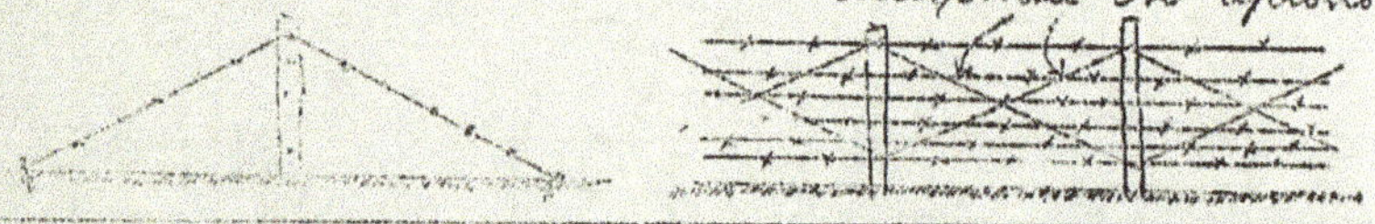	17½	18	35

PARTIES ETC. required for WIRING

	FRENCH WIRE SMALL COILS	GREEN PICKETS LONG	GREEN PICKETS SHORT	SCREW STAKES LONG β	SCREW STAKES SHORT	STAPLES (γ) (IN SANDBAGS)	BARBED WIRE COILS α
ONE MAN CAN CARRY	1	3	5	4	8	60 (1/5 Box)	1

WIRING PARTY One double row French wire with aprons 12 men
" " Two " rows " " " " 23 "

CARRYING " for each 50 One " row " " " " 51 "
" " yds length Two " rows " " " " 102 "

NOTES: α BARBED wire coils are averaged as containing 70 yds. The new pattern with long barbs contains about 70 yds. The short barb pattern 114 yds.
β LONG screw stakes should be tied together in bundles of [illegible] for carrying.
γ A BOX of staples contains 300 and should be split up into 5 sandbags.
SPECIAL Barbed wire concertinas are made up in 5 yds lengths. They are carried by 2 men and set out in 2 minutes!

16-8-16 [illegible]

225th Co.
227th Co.
234th Co.

SECRET

CRE 59 Div War Diary Aug 16 Appendix C.

Reference to CRE [illegible] of 17th advanced party of 225th Co will not be sent.

Party of 2 officers & 6 NCOs & men of 227th Co take over from London Field Co & the Party of 2 officers & 6 NCOs & men of 234th Co will take over from 12th Field Co.

Both parties should visit as much as possible of the whole of the trenches to be taken over by the Div from Mary Redan to the Lancashire post & CTs in rear.

The 225th Co will be in reserve & will receive further orders as to billets.

The 227th Co will take over the dressing station at Mesnil if not completed from the West Riding Fd Co. also the advanced Divl Report Centre at P22b 72

12th Co is at Q32a 43
London Fd Co is at P24 c 52

[illegible]
for CRE
CRE 39th Divn

Aug 20th

227th
234th
CRE 6th Divn

Aug 22nd

Arrangements Brigades for march on morning of 26th Aug in time to complete relief by 9/30 am in case of 234th C & 2pm in case of 227th C.

2) On completion of relief inform 6 HQ by wire

3) As soon as possible after relief send me lists of trench & other stores & material received and lists of maps & plans

4) Maps & plans of British trenches & MG positions should be numbered & registered and copy sent to CRE

5) 1/2 Co of Pioneers are placed at disposal of each company for their works.

[illegible]
Lt Col RE
CRE 39 Divn

CRE 39 Divn
War Diary July 16
appendix D

H.Q. 39th Div G.S. copy CRE 6th Div

Head Qrs R.E. 39 Div relieve 6th Div RE at Acheux at 10 am 27th (unless otherwise ordered)

234th Field Co relieve 12th Co at Martinsart Q32 a1.5 at 2pm on 26th

227th Field Co relieve London 1st Co at P24 C52 at 2pm on 26th

225th Field Co take over billets of West Riding Field Co at Englebelmer at 11 am on 27th

13th Gloster R take over harness of 11 Leicester R at Englebelmer and move there on 27th under own arrangement

A Field Co of 48th Div take over billets of ~~West Riding~~ 1st London Field Co at Mailly Maillet and take over the RE dump at same place from CRE 6th Div on 27th

CRE 39 Div War Diary, July 16

Appendix E

Aug 15

[illegible signature]

[illegible]

OC
227th F.C.

SECRET

Your Co will work in the area between GABION AV. CONSTITUTION HILL – LONGMERE GORDON. LOVEROY – CHARLES AV. Exclusive of last named two C.Ts which are in 232nd area.

The 118th Brigade will carry on maintenance & deepening of old trenches in front of [illegible] Street.

You will continue deepening & maintaining in front & start a sap at once from the front line about Q17 a 8 2 to meet the German sap opposite to it at Q17 b 0 3. This should tunnel under the parapet & afterwards be an open sap 6 ft deep. The earth removed in sand bags. Arrange to carry on the work continuously day & night.

[illegible]
[illegible]
CRE 39 Divn

Aug 26th

7.

OC
23rd Fd Co.

You will work in the area LOUVERCY ST - CHALES AVENUE inclusive down to the river ANCRE.

The 18th Brigade will maintain & deepen trenches & CTs in front of the front line. Louvercy & PEAKE ST especially want deepening & Gordon & Roberts trench.
The deepening is required to prevent these trenches being overlooked from across the river.

Continue deep dugouts left unfinished by 6th Divn & start a sap from the east end of GORDON TRENCH towards pt 36 on the German front line.

[illegible signature]
Lt Col RE
CRE 32 Divn

Aug 26th

G.

227th Fd Coy RE URGENT. Aug 28
234th " " 2 pm.

Please examine the Brigade and Forward dumps & let me know what they contain.

The materials should be made up into one man loads. i.e. stakes & pickets tied in bundles. Sandbags in bundles of 100 staples in bags.

The dumps are as follows.

Right sector.	Q24a26	Forward
	O17d45.	"
&	Q23d45	Brigade dump.
Left sector	Q17c37	
	Q17c44	
	Q16c91	Brigade dump.

Each forward dump should contain as follows & Brigade dumps twice the amount :—
Picks 500 shovels 500 300 coils barbed wire
100 French wire. 500 screw stakes 500 staples
2 coils plain wire 500 5ft screw pickets 5000 sandbags
50 Prs wirecutters 20 pairs hedging gloves

20 notice boards. 20 direction arrows.
10 sets mine casing at Brigade Dumps.
10 axes. 10 saws 10 mauls.
black paint 1 tin + 2 brushes.

Please consider if anything else should be added to this list or amounts increased.

Arrange with brigades that nothing is removed from these dumps until required in action.

2. acknowledge

A Hopkins
Lt Col CRE
39 Divn CRE

CRE 39 Divn
War Diary I
Appendix

39 Div. HQ 68.

Reference to Div. order No 41 para 7b. & 8b. May carrying parties of 200 men to move material forward from Brigade dumps be earmarked for use if required. i.e 100 men at each Brigade dump.

20 G.S. wagons may also be required to move stores from Englebelmer to Knightsbridge + Hamel

[signature]

N.C. Collins

Aug 29th.

K.

OC. 13 Gloster R.
copy 118 Brigade

Aug 28th.

You will maintain in order & improve the CTs as follows.

Jacobs ladder
Royal avenue
Charles avenue
} Up to Battn HQrs.

Gabion avenue & Constitution Hill
Up to Buckingham Palace Road

The last 100 yds in Royal Avenue to Cottage requires trench boarding & some repairs & Trenchboards are wanted in Jacobs ladder. Please have this done

The new portion of Charles Av connecting to Royal avenue must be completed at the earliest possible moment

[signature]
Lt Col CRE

Appendix to
War diary July 16 CRE 39 Div
L.

OC 13 Gloster Regt.
copy 39 Divn HQ
" 117 & 116 Brigades

SECRET
urgent

67.
Aug 29th.

Reference to Div order No 41 para 8(a) the half company attached to 117 Brigade will extend the two Galleries across No mans land by open trenches to the German front trench. You will arrange details of assembly & time with 117 Brigade Report completion to 117 Brigade

2. The half company with 116 Brigade will extend No 4 gallery by an open trench to meet the German trenches at the nearest point. They will also dig a trench from the east end of Gordon Trench to the nearest point in the German trenches at about Q 18 c 2½ 7½. 116 Brigade has arranged to assist with half a company of infantry ~~the party working on the trench~~

3. all parties will get across to the German trenches ~~as soon as they are~~ immediately behind the first wave of infantry & start working backwards towards ~~the ...~~ Gordon Trench.

CRE 39 Divn
War Diary July 16
Appendix L

[signature]
CRE 39th

SECRET H.

O.C. 227th Field Coy. R.E. No 61.
O.C. 234th -do-

An attack will be made shortly on the German trenches by the 116th and 117th Brigades. The 116th on right and 117th on left. The O.C. 227th Coy. will attach one section to 117th Brigade and O.C. 234th one section to 116th Brigade to assist in consolidation of captured trenches. A platoon of infantry will be attached for carrying materials. The R.E. will go over with the 3rd wave of infantry so as to avoid hostile barrage.

The role of the R.E. in consolidation will be.-

1. Making it impossible to approach the position from German C.T. and other trenches. For this, trenches must either be filled in for 40 yards from the fire trench or they must be covered by our fire. Obstacles and blocks not under fire are of no use.
Traverses can be moved by means of 15 lb charges of guncotton dug into the corners about 2 ft. The trenches to be dealt with should be settled before hand and parties told off.

2. Clearing entrances to damaged deep dugouts and blocking any underground galleries by which the Germans may get into the trenches. Dugouts should not be destroyed with charges of guncotton as they will be wanted to shelter our men.

3. The clearing out of trenches blown in by shell fire - the making of Lewis gun positions near deep dugouts, - the making of a few fire trenches and wiring them - as described in my note on strong points will best be done by the infantry and the details of this can be largely settled beforehand.

4. Please report to your Brigade Commanders at once and take instructions from him. 116th is at Q.19.b.4.5.

5. Plan of dumps attached. 118th Brigade has been asked to give you lists of what has been put at these dumps by 6th Division.

6. The Pioneers are undertaking the trenches across NO MANS LAND.

7. Acknowledge.

8. Your Headquarters will be with Brigade Hd. Qrs, remainder stand to at Coy. Headquarters.

sd. L.E.Hopkins, Lt-Col R.E.
C.R.E., 39th Division.

27th August 1916.

39 Divn CRE War diary July 16
appendix H.

SECRET No. 61.

O.C. 227th Field Coy. R.E.
O.C. 234th "

An attack will be made shortly on the German trenches by the 116th and 117th Brigades. The 116th on right and 117th on left. The O.C. 227th Coy. will attach one section to 117th Brigade and O.C. 234th one section to 116th Brigade to assist in consolidation of captured trenches. A platoon of infantry will be attached for carrying materials. The R.E. will go over with the 3rd wave of infantry so as to avoid hostile barrage.

The role of the R.E. in consolidation will be,

1. Making it impossible to approach the position from German C.T. and other trenches. For this, trenches must either be filled in for 40 yards from the fire trench or they must be covered by our fire. Obstacles and blocks not under fire are of no use. Traverses can be removed by means of 15 lb charges of gun cotton dug into the corners about 2 ft. The trenches to be dealt with should be settled beforehand and parties told off.

2. Clearing entrances to damaged deep dugouts and blocking any underground galleries by which the Germans may get into the trenches. Dugouts should not be destroyed with charges of guncotton as they will be wanted to shelter our men.

3. The clearing out of trenches blown in by shell fire - the making of Lewis gun positions near deep dugouts - the making of a few fire trenches and wiring them - as described in my note on strong points will best be done by the infantry and the details of this can be largely settled beforehand.

4. Please report to your Brigade Commanders at once and take instructions from him. 116th is at Q.19.b.4.5.

5. Plan of dumps attached. 118th Brigade has been asked to give you lists of what has been put at these dumps by 6th Div.

6. The Pioneers are undertaking the trenches across NO MAN'S LAND.

7. Acknowledge.

8. Your Headquarters will be with Brigade Headquarters remainder of Company stand to at Coy. Headquarters.

sd. L.E.Hopkins, Lt-Col R.E.
C.R.E., 39th Div.

August 27th 1916.

SECRET

O.C. 13th Gloster Regt.
Copy to 39th Div. H.Q.
" 117th & 116th Bdes.

Reference to Division Order No. 41 para 8(a), the half company attached to 117th Brigade will extend the two galleries across NO MAN'S LAND by open trenches to the German front trench. You will arrange details of assembly and time with 117th Brigade. Report completion to 117th Brigade.

2. The half company with 116th Brigade will extend No. 4 gallery by an open trench to meet the German trenches at the nearest point. They will also dig a trench from the East end of GORDON TRENCH to the nearest point in the German trench at about Q.18.c.2½.7½. 116th Brigade has arranged to assist with half a company of infantry.

3. All parties will get across to the German trenches immediately behind the last wave of infantry and start working backwards towards GORDON TRENCH.

sd. L.E.Hopkins, Lt-Col R.E.
C.R.E. 39th Division.

August 29th 1916.

O.C. 225th Field Coy. R.E.
O.C. 227th do.
O.C. 234th do.
Copies to 116th Inf. Bade.
117th do.
118th do.
O.C. 13th Gloucester Regt.

WORKING PARTIES.

1. Field Company C.Os. should see the G.O.C. of the Brigade in whose area they are working daily and should as a rule bring in their demands for working parties personally.

2 Working parties should be demanded on the attached form. When the Revised Brigade working party list is received, it shoulfl be posted in a position where all concerned can quickly refer to it. If a Field Company is getting working parties from several different units they should all be shewn on the list.

3. The officer in charge of a working party should have with him a slip shewing time and place of rendezvous, strength of party, and to whom it is to report and work to be done, and tools required.

4. R.E. working parties may be diverted to other work if required by the officer in charge and can only be dismissed by the R.E. officer or N.C.O. in charge .

5. Brigade working party lists should shew all parties including those reporting to Field Companies, or Infantry Battalions or C.R.E. or A.P.M.

sd. L.E.Hopkins, Lt-Col R.E.
C.R.E., 39th Div.

August 30th 1916.

CRE 39th Div War Diary July 16.
Appendix M.

39th Div

Work Report. Sept. 1. 1916.

Saps at top of Paris St. 20 yds.

Dugouts.
R. Brigade Hd Qrs. strutted inside with pit props
Signal Hd Qrs do.
tunnel on DEVIAL 1 yd. excavated. trench revetted
225 Co Hd Qrs. dugouts deepened.

Collecting station hut. Englebelmer finished
Med Aid Post do 4%.
Mesnil dressing station excavated. 60%.
Advanced Dressing Stn Hamel 7 cub yds excavated
cellar cleared.

Well at Englebelmer 34 ft. deep.
70 yds of Charles Avenue west of Rly duckboarded

Road Mesnil Martinsart drained + shellholes filled.
Royal Avenue Ry trench Comm's laid.

16 Wagon loads stores material to Knightsbridge.

Appendix IV
[illegible] [illegible] CRE 39th Div
Warden, CRE 39th

SECRET.

Copy No. 2

Special orders to O.C., Section, 227 Company R.E., to accompany 117th Infantry Brigade Order No. 50.

30.8.1916.

1. Your section will be divided into 2 parties to work with the 2 assaulting Battalions.
1 section (less 1 N.C.O. and 10 men) will be attached to 17th Notts and Derby.
1 N.C.O. and 10 men to the 16th Rifle Brigade.
They will accompany the rear assaulting wave of each Battalion across NO MAN'S LAND.

2. On arrival in the German trenches they will at once begin the construction of Strong Points at Points 04, 33 and 36 working in three parties in conjunction with available Infantry at those spots.

3. The O.C. Section should as far as the situation allows of it give help and advice to the Infantry in the construction of the other strong points laid down in Infantry Brigade Order No.50, para.4(c).

4. The section will march from ENGLEBELMER in Rear of 16th Rifle Brigade. O.C. Section should report to O.C., 16th Rifle Brigade not later than 5 hours before Zero in VITERMONT Q.19.b.

5. 1 Platoon, 16th Notts and Derby, will join your section at ENGLEBELMER at 5 p.m.

6. Acknowledge.

for [signature] Captain,
Brigade Major, 117th Brigade.

Issued at 12.30 p.m.
No.1. H.Q., 39th Division.
No.2. C.R.E.
No.3. 17th Notts & Derby Regt.
No.4. 16th Rifle Brigade.
No.5. 227 Company, R.E.
No.6. G.O.C.
No.7. B.M.
No.8. S.C.
No.9. War Diary.
No.10. War Diary.
No.11. Order file.

Appendix O
C.R.E. War Diary

H.Q., C. R. E.

39th. DIVISION, ROYAL ENGINEERS

SEPTEMBER, 1916.

Instructions regarding War Diaries and Intelligence Summaries are contained in F. S. Regs., Part II. and the Staff Manual respectively. Title pages will be prepared in manuscript.

WAR DIARY
or
~~INTELLIGENCE SUMMARY.~~
(Erase heading not required.)

Army Form C. 2118.

CRE 39th Divn

Place	Date	Hour	Summary of Events and Information	Remarks and references to Appendices
ACHEUX	1.9.16		Pushing up RE materials to Dumps at Hamel + Knightsbridge + forward dumps which had been left ~~[illegible]~~ with very little in them. The left sector had practically no wiring material only picks + shovels. Lot of materials sent to Knightsbridge. Personally instructed Lt Ellen about his duties in attack.	A
	2.9.16		Saw 2nd Lt Panton + spoke to him about his role when he reaches German trenches + what he might expect to have to do. Sap from Pondtt towards German trenches carried 32yds by the 227th Co. Sap from E end of Gordon Trench nothing done by 234th Co + Pioneer party owing to hostile fire. 13 Glouc R. (Pioneers) report completion of new CT 400yds connecting Charles Av with Pottage. 6ft deep + Charles av. Trench boarded + usable from Prowse Fort to Royal Avenue. Martinsart Mesnil road repaired with over 100 tons of stone besides material collected at site. Work done by Pioneers (13 Glouc R)	
	3.9.		Division attacked German position at 4/30 am. Lt Ellen 227th Co wounded 2nd Lt PANTON wounded + missing. Special report attached	B
	4.9.		All RE + Pioneers clearing damage to trenches. CRE inspected front line [illegible]	

Sept 3rd

[illegible]
Lt Col CRE

T2134. Wt. W708-776. 500000. 4/15. Sir J. C. & S.

Instructions regarding War Diaries and Intelligence Summaries are contained in F. S. Regs., Part II. and the Staff Manual respectively. Title pages will be prepared in manuscript.

WAR DIARY
or
~~INTELLIGENCE SUMMARY.~~
(Erase heading not required.)

Army Form C. 2118.

CRE 39th Division

Place	Date	Hour	Summary of Events and Information	Remarks and references to Appendices
ACHEUX.	4/9/16		and CT^s. Work hindered by gas shells	
	5/9/16		Visited 145 Brigade + 3rd Field Co. + arranged for taking over	
	6/9.6		225 Fd Co. took over from 3rd Midland Field Co. ordered them to repair tramways	
	7.9.6		Visited Pioneers 225. 234 + 227 Field Cos + 118 Brigade – arranged for Construction of 3 new Trench Mortar Emplacements	
	8.9.		Visited 234th + 118th Brigade also Corps Head Qrs. re supply of trench boards	
	9.9.16		Visited Centre Brigade trenches from Auchonvillers to Mary Redan [illegible] OC 225th Co. New trench for Corps Commander along railway in Ancre valley reconnoitred + reported on by Col Boulton + Capt Wood. Attended meeting of AQMG's + CRE's at Corps Headquarters in connexion with [illegible] etc.	
			Report on operation of Sept 3.	C
	11.9		Visited 225 + 227th + Pioneers + arranged for Pioneers to dig new CT up railway in Ancre valley. 234th Co relieved 3 Midland Field Co in the Broadway Watling Street sector on the left which was taken over from 48th Division.	

Sept 30th

[signature] Lt Col RE

T2134. Wt. W708–776. 500000. 4/15. Sir J. C. & S.

Instructions regarding War Diaries and Intelligence Summaries are contained in F. S. Regs., Part II. and the Staff Manual respectively. Title pages will be prepared in manuscript.

WAR DIARY
or
~~INTELLIGENCE SUMMARY.~~
(Erase heading not required.)

Army Form C. 2118.

39 Divn RE Hd Qrs.

Place	Date	Hour	Summary of Events and Information	Remarks and references to Appendices
ACHEUX.	11/9		Inspected 234th Co lines at Mailly Maillet.	
	12/9		Inspected flint quarry at Warnimont Wood + Expt Horse standing Authie with Road Engineer	
	13/9		Inspected sites for Horselines for Artillery - Train - DAC at Louvencourt with OC Train	
	14/9		Examined left ~~Brigade~~ front trenches with OC 234th Co. and told him to concentrate on one trench only	
	15.9		Inspected Horselines at Bus + to meet CE V Corps at Acheux in afternoon re. consolidation of trenches about which wrote following note D	D
	16.9		Inspected work at Louvencourt in morning + right + centre brigade trenches in afternoon, new trench in railway bank progressing well and new ATME in Hongarre	
	17.9		Heavy rain.	
	18.9		Heavy rain went to Marieux to see CE 5th Corps in afternoon	
	19.9		Heavy rain. Went Couin in afternoon to arrange about transfer with the 2nd Divn went to Sucrerie water supply + tramways with OC 234th Co.	
	20.9		Went round Redan section in morning with GSO I very wet + muddy. to 116 Brigade in evening. re work	

M. Chapman (?) Lt Col RE

T2134. Wt. W708-776. 500000. 4/15. Sir J. C. & S.

Instructions regarding War Diaries and Intelligence Summaries are contained in F. S. Regs., Part II. and the Staff Manual respectively. Title pages will be prepared in manuscript.

WAR DIARY
or
~~INTELLIGENCE SUMMARY.~~
(Erase heading not required.)

Army Form C. 2118.

39 Divn HQ RE.

Place	Date	Hour	Summary of Events and Information	Remarks and references to Appendices
			Visited 234th Co in morning + inspected stabling work at Louvencourt.	
ACHEUX.	21.9			
	22.9.		CRE went up Gabion Av + down Charles St + visited 118 Brigade HQs. Submitted attached note to CE 5.	E
	~~22.9~~		Went to Bus with ADMS inspected Fd Ambulance buildings there and at Acheux. 13 Corps Cyclists ordered to Mailly for work under CRE. 234th Co ordered to take over from 226th Co in the Redan Section in addition to Auchonvillers but order cancelled.	
	23.9.		Office work.	
	24.9.		Visited Pioneers + discussed work. OCs Field Cos came in to HQrs for conference. Ordered commencement of classes of instruction.	
	25.9		Visited stabling + ambulance huts at Bus + Bertrancourt. and Dump at Beaussart. Spoke to CE about lack of small timber + want of circular saws which make progress of work impossible.	
	26.9.		Visited stables with B.G. G staff + 39 Divn AQMG. at Louvencourt Bus + Bertrancourt. Visited 5 Corps Dump at Varennes about supply of material + getting it sawn by 2nd Corps	
	27.9		Classes of instruction commenced. Pioneers put on to fill up advanced dumps.	
	28.9		Visited 227 + 234 Fd Cos. rain in evening. Started digging new reserve line trench between 5th + 6th Avenues.	

[illegible]
Lt Col
CRE 39 Divn

T2131. Wt. W708-776. 500000. 4/15. Sir J. C. & S.

Instructions regarding War Diaries and Intelligence Summaries are contained in F. S. Regs., Part II. and the Staff Manual respectively. Title pages will be prepared in manuscript.

WAR DIARY
or
~~INTELLIGENCE SUMMARY.~~
(*Erase heading not required.*)

Army Form C. 2118.

H.Q. 39. Divn

Place	Date	Hour	Summary of Events and Information	Remarks and references to Appendices
ACHEUX	29.9		Inspected 5th Avenue New Trench 86th + Broadway & visited 234th Co Foggy day + some rain	
"	30.9		Inspected Stabling at Bus + Louvencourt. Adjt. went to Amiens to purchase materials. Fine + dry weather. Got one small circular saw going at Beaussart dump, which will help a little in supplying small timber for Stables + Hutting + trench boards.	

[illegible]
Lt Col RE.
CRE 39 Divn

To C.R.E. 39th Div
From O/C. 227th Coy R.E.

A

Stores forwarded to Knightsbridge

Date	29/8/16	30/8/16	31/8/16
Sandbags	10,000		4250
Barbed Wire, coils		50	195
French " "			52
Plain " "			5
Long Screw Pickets			
Short Iron Pickets (Bundles)		50	
Short Green "			290
Trench Boards	60		55
" Bridges		10	
" Ladders		10	
Plain Notice Boards			50
Direction Arrows			
Mauls			10
Staples for French wire, boxes			6

These are being pushed forward by 118th Bgde.
Can we have some G.S. wagons tomorrow.
Roads terribly cut with shell holes & transport difficult

W. Mackesy
Capt R.E. 31/8/16

To CRE 39th Div.
From O/C. 227th Field Coy. RE

Date	Description	Quantity
1-9-16	Sandbags	6000
"	Barbed Wire Coils	50
"	French "	60
"	Plain "	5
"	Long Screw Pickets	350
"	Short Green Pickets bundles	200
"	Trench Bridges	20
"	Mauls	6
"	Staples for French Wire boxes.	4

Total Wagon Loads 11.

1/9/16

Mackesy
Capt RE

L.P. 838.

B

Report on active operations
Sept. 3. 1916
Half Coy. of 13th Glosters attached to 117th Inf. Bde.

This half coy was employed in Nos. 1 & 2 saps and duly assembled there in time. Major Howman was in charge and as he could not discover when the third wave went over and believed the enemy line was still occupied by Germans, he sent a message to the Bde. Commander asking for information. He received a reply ordering him to begin work at once.
The men were got out of the sap & set out on the trench & proceeded to dig it. After they had been at work for a short time, the Germans commenced bombing them from their front line. After some men had been knocked out, Major Howman withdrew the men nearest the German line & continued the work at our end of the C.T.
The party then came under M.G. fire directed on the sap head. They were withdrawn into the sap. Major Howman went out with his orderly to try & get

some information, & found our infantry coming back
Shortly after this he received a message from the Bde Commander to take his men away, and he left the Saps about 5.30 P.M. 3rd
Saps were blocked before leaving.

L. Brodie Capt & Adj
for

4 9/16

LP 833

To/
C.R.E
39th Div.

Ref. your note on my T.754. Under 118th Inf. Bde. Order No. 37 we are to move into trenches Q 33 a. c & d and Q 27 c.
Only half our company has returned from the operation of this morning. Very briefly they report as per attached.
I am leaving instructions that when the O.C. Coy. returns (Major HOWMAN) he reports direct to you to save time.
Col. Boulton has gone to see G.O.C 118th Inf. Bde. with a view to our remaining in present quarters, as he considers work on trench repairs etc. would probably be better conducted from here, where we can get our men fed and so on, than in reserve trenches wh. are apparently rather imaginary ones.

H Procter Capt & Adj
for
LT. COL.
O.C. 13th (FOREST OF DEAN) BATT.
THE GLOUCESTERSHIRE REGIMENT.

3/9/16

L.P. 834

Brief Report on Active Operations, morning of 3rd Sept 1916.

Party of 13th Glosters attached 116th Inf Bde.

The two C.Ts laid out for this party were not dug, owing to failure of Infantry to make good.
The right flank party was ordered out to withdraw by O.C 13th Royal Sussex at 2 P.M on 3rd
Left Party, owing to attack failing sent message to Bn. H.Q. Pottage Trench asking what they shd do & stating that C.T had not been dug. Meantime orders were given to this party by O.C. 14th Hants to go over parapet with his men as Infantry. This was complied with, but before all men were out, the wave on left went over, and at the same time an order came from a Hants. officer confirmed by Tunnelling Officer R.E for all Glosters to return to sap. All were stopped except 1 off and 4 O.R. who are reported missing. A few minutes after orders were received from Bde. H.Q to withdraw & report at HAMEL, where the party was ordered back to P 18 central

5 9/16.

[illegible] Capt & Adj
13th Glosters

To C.R.E. 39th Div
FROM O/C. 227th Co R.E.

In handing you the attached report on this Coys operations on 3/9/16 I have to call your attention to the excellent work done by the Section officers & men in sapping out in preparation. This was a dangerous operation done with such skill that it was not noticed by the enemy & no casualties were suffered. It was carried on with energy in spite of frequent want of working parties, terribly difficult communications & bad weather. Lt D Huffam R.E. was the life & soul of this work as he was of the equally difficult & dangerous front line & Duck's Bill work at Givenchy.

W Mackesy
Capt R.E.

4/9/16

FROM O/C 227th Co RE.
TO CRE. 39th Div

Report upon Operation of R.E. Section in attack on 3/9/16

Section No 3 of the 227th Co RE. under Lt. C. W. Ellen RE. took part in the attack. It was ordered to go over with the third line of Infantry who were to occupy the 3rd line of Enemy trench. The objective of the Section was to consolidate 3 definite points in the captured trenches.
The assembly was conducted according to 117th Inf Bgde orders.
The Section of RE. was organised into 3 parties of 10 O.R. each.
Two assembled on left with 17th Sherwoods under Lt Ellen, Sergt Hudson & 2/Cpl Harland. The third party assembled on the right with the 16th R.B. The Section was attached to the Inf. Bgde & the parties were allotted to the respective Battalions.
Just prior to time of assault Lt Ellen RE. was unfortunately wounded in throat. He handed over to Lt Brown of the 16th Sherwoods & to Sergt Hudson

After doing this he started his men over the open, following as best he could. When the section returned to our lines he went to the Dressing Station. After having his wound dressed the traffic control insisted on his going down according to the orders issued them.

To return to the two left parties. They advanced over the open after the 3rd wave & on reaching near the German wire they found our infantry checked. They lay down in shell holes. Here ~~&~~ during the check Sapper J Young crawled about attending to wounded infantry. The infantry retired & Sergt Hudson withdrew his men to our trenches. As our front line became congested with retiring Infantry Sergt Hudson withdrew his men to Long Sap. He made frequent visits to the front line to see whether the situation was improving. As things did not brighten up he withdrew to a dug out in POND ST where he remained until ordered to withdraw. Sergt Hudson & 2nd Cpl Harland (who was in charge of one party on the left) both were perfectly cool throughout the whole operation & paid no attention to personal risk in trying to carry out their orders nor in looking after their men

The right party consisted of 10 o.r. under Cpl Blumer. It was attached directly to the 16th R.B. ~~Before~~ the start of the attack Cpl Blumer was wounded & the command devolved upon Sapper W. Garland who carried on in a cool & collected manner & seems to have done the right thing at the right time.

The party went over with the 3rd wave. Before reaching the German line the infantry recoiled to our own trenches. Sapper Garland took his men back with them. They waited in GORDON TRENCH, frequently going to Sergt Stuart of D. Coy. R.B. who seemed to be taking command as his Captain was knocked out. At last Sergt Stuart told Sapper Garland that they had given it up & he had better withdraw his party. This he did. The whole party seems to have behaved very well & in particular Sapper H Bellwood showed great pluck.

- 4 -

He was waiting in a firebay with some infantry. The Infantry Officer gave the order for the 2nd man to get up & give the word when the previous wave had gone over. Sapper Bellwood jumped up, leaned over the parapet & gave the word for the next wave to go.

The figures as to casualties are

Went out	1 OFFICER	30 O.R.
Returned wounded	1	8
" unwounded		22

In general the Section set out to do a specific work. It went with the attack; suffered a loss of 30% of its strength; and never had a chance of doing a single stroke of R.E. work. Not only did it suffer this loss but in addition for several days to come, until the men have had a rest, the Company will have lost 25% of its working strength

4/9/16

W Mackesy
Capt R.E.

To C.R.E. 39th Div

FROM O/C. 227th Co R.E.

R.E. Section in attack on 3/9/16

No 134425 Sapper W Garland distinguished himself by taking over from Cpl T S Blumer the command of the right party & carrying through in a cool & efficient manner. He has been made L/Cpl but this would have happened in any case. I would strongly recommend him for some decoration.

The remainder all did their duty in an excellent manner but there is nothing to distinguish any one man above another sufficiently to call for reward.

15/9/16

W Mackay
Capt R.E.

To C.R.E. 39th Div
From O/C 227th Co R.E.

B

Report on R.E. Operations 3/9/16

The last party of No 3 Section has not yet returned – with it is Sergt Hudson; & until he returns a complete report cannot be rendered.

	OFF	O.R.
Section went out	1	30
Wounded Returned	1	8
Unwounded Returned		21
Not Yet returned		1

Lt C.W. Ellen R.E. went in charge of No 3 Section: the assembly was conducted according to orders: just before the attack Lt Ellen R.E. was wounded in the throat. He handed over to Sergt Hudson & Lt Brown who commanded the infantry carrying part. After doing this he started his men for the rush over the open & followed them as quickly as he could.

Our parties got mixed up among the attacking & retiring infantry. They suffered a considerable number of casualties: and at no time was it possible for them to do any R.E. work at all.
A full report will be sent tomorrow

W Macleay
Capt R.E.

3/9/16

P.S. Sergt Hudson just returned – hence above figures of casualties &c

W.M.
Capt R.E.

To C.R.E. 39th Div

FROM O/C. 227th Field Co R.E.

Lt Ellen R.E. has returned wounded & dazed. Some of the men of Section have taken refuge in our trenches. I expect some are carrying on

W Macleay
Capt R.E.

3/9/16

10.55 am.

About 6 ~~this~~ of his men have returned wounded to this dressing station – I know nothing about any seriously wounded cases or fatal ones

W.M.

HEADQUARTERS
148/A.
9 SEP 1916
39th DIVISION R.E.

Headquarters,
39th Division.

Employment of R.E. on attack by 116th & 117th Brigades on the German position immediately North of R.ANCRE.

Two sections of R.E. were allotted to assist the attacking infantry in consolidating their position. Lieut. Ellen with a section of 227th Company with 117th Brigade and 2/Lt. Panton of the 234th Company with 116th Brigade.

They each had a platoon of infantry as carriers and took with them sandbags, tools and some explosives.

The sections followed the 3rd wave of infantry in the attack and were to make strong points at 3 points on the left and 2 points on the right.

The section with the 117th Brigade, less Lt. Ellen and 8 men wounded before leaving the trenches, reached the German front line but soon returned as the infantry had not made good their objective and were never in possession of the points to be consolidated.

2nd Lt. Panton and party reached their objective and appear to have done very well, but as all those present were wounded and evacuated to base, or are missing, no direct evidence is available. A sergeant and 10 men of the section who were detailed to assemble at a different point, never actually left our trenches.

2nd Lt. Panton was wounded and missing.

It is probable that his party were valuable on the consolidation of this portion, which appears to have been held for some time.

The Pioneers detailed to extend the saps on the left (No. 1 and 2), report that they were unable to work as the Germans were never quite cleared out of the trench in front of them.

The parties to extend No 4 sap and trench across from south end of GORDON TRENCH also did no appreciable work and report that the Infantry attack did not clear their front.

It appears doubtful if Pioneers and R.E. can effect any useful work until a position has been thoroughly made good. At the same time, by keeping them back till later, they will probably be too late.

The parties sent should not exceed in number those detailed for the attack and I think that ~~this~~ the attempt to dig the trenches across NO MAN'S LAND from No 4 sap and from the South end of GORDON TRENCH might in any future operations, be postponed till night. No trench of any value could be made here in less than 8 hours, in the hard chalk.

[signature]

Lieut-Colonel R.E.
C.R.E., 39th Division.

Sept. 9th 1916.

SECRET

EXTRACTS FROM 116TH INFANTRY BRIGADE ORDER No.43

5. OBJECTIVES & TASKS.

(a). 11th Batn. R.Sussex R. will be right assaulting Battalion.

Ultimate objective. German reserve line from Q.18.b.½.2. to Q.18.a.6½.2.

(b). 14th Batn. Hampshire R. will be the left assaulting Battalion and the following will be its objectives.

Ultimate objective. German reserve line from Q.18.a.6½.2. to Q.18.a.0.4.

(i). No 3 section 234th Field Coy. R.E. will assist the assaulting Battalions with the construction of strong points at

(i) Q.18.c.5½.9½. (½ section R.E.)
(ii) Q.18.a.3½.¼. (½ section R.E.)

These two half sections will cross NO MAN'S LAND immediately behind the 3rd Coys. of the assaulting Battalions.

O.C. 12th Bn. R.Sussex R. will detail ½ platoon to be attached to each half section 234th Field Coy. R.E. for the purpose of carrying stores etc. etc.

EXTRACT FROM REVISED WORKING PARTY TABLE OF 12th Batt. Sussex R. (116th Infantry Brigade amended order 43).

Ref. no. of Party.	No. of men.	To work for.	Task.	To work under orders of
5	15	½ Sect R.E.	To assist in consolidating strong points to carry materials for same.	O.C. No 3 Sect. 234th Fld.Coy. R.E.
6	15	do.	do.	do.

Parties No. 5 & 6 to be attached to 234th Field Coy. R.E. from 4 p.m. on Z. day.

ATTACK ON THIEPVAL.

26/9/16.

1. The trenches for the attack were taken over from the C.R.E. 49th Division on the 21st Sept. 1916.

Work was immediately started preparing for the attack on THIEPVAL. The front line trenches taken over were in very bad order, therewas only one communication trench - PRINCE STREET - existing, this also, was in very bad order.

2. The following troops were employed on preparing sundry trenches and communication trenches, as shewn in red on the accompanying map:

Royal Engineers	-	79th Fd Co.
		80th Fd Co.
		92nd Fd Co (from 1/10/16).
Pioneers.	-	8th Royal Sussex.
Infantry	-	8th East Surrey (nights 23/24/25th).
	-	7th Queens (nights 24/25th).

The C.R.E., 49th Division with his Field Cos and the Pioneer Battalion of the 49th Division gave all the assistance in their power before their Division was withdrawn.

3. The following work was carried out:-

Assembly trenches.

Two were prepared for the Right Brigade Front and three for the Left Brigade front, total length about 2,500 yards, existing trenches being used as far as possible.

Communication Trenches.

Right Brigade.

A good line of communication was arranged for from WOOD POST to the assembly trenches and grids laid from our old front line forward. This trench is now known as PIP STREET.

Left Brigade.

CAMPBELL AVENUE was selected as a line of approach to FIFTH AV. which was improved and then up PRINCE STREET which was deepened and gridded. The enemy's old front line was also dug out and made into a communication trench

A second line of approach was made from THIEPVAL AVENUE and a trench dug across NO MAN'S LAND to Point 42.

4. Dumps.

Right Brigade Dump at WOOD POST.

Left Brigade Dump at AUTHUILLE and PAISLEY RAVINE.

Forward Dumps.

Right Brigade	-	3 along PIP STREET.
Left Brigade	-	Enemy's front line at MAISON GRIS and at PAISLEY AVENUE near our old front line.

5. Consolidation.

The work of consolidation for R.E. was very difficult owing to the uncertainty of the amount of ground actually held and the difficulty of working in the front line owing to the number of troops holding thetrenches

The 79th Fd Co. (Right Bde) apparently were only able to consolidate the point marked 36 on the map, on the night of the 26th.

As regards the 80th Fd Co (Left Bde), owing to the N.W. corner of THIEPVAL being still in the hands of the enemy, the Coy was unable to consolidate the point marked 43 on the attached map until the day of the 27th September.

The above represents the work done by the R.E. and Pioneers in connection with the capture of THIEPVAL and is shewn in red on the accompanying map.

ATTACK ON SCHWABEN REDOUBT.
28/9/16.

All work done or proposed is shewn on the accompanying map in green.

There was no time for making forming up trenches but immediate Steps were taken to improve the communications to THIEPVAL.

The following work has been put in hand and steadily proceeded with:-

ROADS. The old metalled road from AUTHUILLE to THIEPVAL has been cleared and a brushwood screen has been erected along the whole length, approximately about 1000 yards. This road is now in use and has turned out invaluable as so far it has not been shelled to any extent.

This communication is of such importance at the present juncture that I would urge most strongly that no wagons be allowed to use it by day for fear that the enemy may shell it and thus render traffic most difficult.

TRAMLINES.

A tramline has been laid across SOUTH CAUSEWAY to connect the AVELUY - HAMEL Roadwith PAISLEY RAVINE Tramline.

COMMUNICATION TRENCHES.

PIP STREET has been extended into THIEPVAL: grids are in process of being laid.

DUGOUTS.

A Company of Pioneers and 2 Sections of the 179th (T) Co RE have been employed on clearing and repairing tunnelled dugouts in and around THIEPVAL. I am unable to state the exact number of dugouts available in THIEPVAL, but in addition to those immediately made use of by Infantry approximately 15 others have been put in order, sufficient to accommodate about 300 men.

A systematic survey of THIEPVAL should be taken in hand as soon as possible to ascertain the dug-out accommodation available and also to make an inventory of captured war material; a great deal of which is still lying about.

WELLS.

4 wells have been found in THIEPVAL, 2 of which are now in use. These are marked"1" and "2" on the map - the water is good.

CONSOLIDATION.

In all 7 points have been consolidated by the Field Cos.

These are shown on the accompanying map. The work has been carried out under great difficulty, as continuous fighting has been proceeding in this area, the work being done without covering parties and under shell fire.

WORK NOT YET COMPLETED.

It has been impossible to clear MARTIN'S TRENCH and BULGAR TRENCH owing to the constant shelling of these trenches.

As both trenches are well known to the enemy, it is suggested that a new trench should be dug between these two as shown by the dotted line on the map, and it is also suggested that the old BOSCHE line due East through the line of trees to the Collecting Station, see dotted line on Map.

I consider this communication if made, very necessary, and if dug on the line suggested would be practically clear of the daily shelling that THIEPVAL is subjected to.

In conclusion, as regards the employment of R.E. and Pioneers, the following points appear to me more than ever important :-

(i). Before a Division undertakes an operation the necessity of sending these units up as many days beforehand as possible.

(ii). Too much time cannot be devoted to the study of the ground and communications. In these last operations the R.E. were used to an appreciable extent as guides.

(iii). The great difficulty of consolidating unless the attacking troops push beyond the line that it is proposed to consolidate. R.E. and Pioneers were used on several occasions for

carrying

ammunition and bombs. I consider this justified as consolidation was impossible at the time.

(iv). Before an advance, the consolidating parties should be put under cover as far forward as possible, so as to be available for consolidation at the crucial period which may be very short. If consolidation is impossible they are available for use as in (iii) in case of an emergency.

Colonel,

5th Oct 1916. Commanding Royal Engineers, 18th Division.

CASUALTIES.

R.E.	Employed.	Killed.	Wounded.	Missing.
227th Field Coy.				
Officers.	1	-	1	-
O.R.	30	-	8	-
234th Field Coy.				
Officers.	1	-	1 & missing.	
O.R.	29		12	4
13th Gloucester R.				
Officers.	7			1
O.R.	164	3	9	3

C.E. V Corps.

Consolidation of Trenches.

The principlew which C.R.E. 18th Division demonstrated yesterday at ARQUEVES seem open to many objections and do not agree with the principles followed in this Division and others in which I have served.

The first idea shown us was the rapid construction of deep dugouts as being the best way to obtain protection quckly. The Infantry were to carry up mine casing on their backs in the first assault, I think, and proceed at once to dig deep dugouts.

A mine gallery cannot be dug in chalk (which is practically the only subsoil in this country) by ordinary untrained men, i.e. not professional miners, at a greater rate than 6 feet a day, with reliefs every 6 hours, and working without any molestation. Assuming that in attack, this progress is made, even in 12 hours the protection arrived at is practicaaly of little use, and in six hours the same men could get much better protection digging a slit trench.

The infantry are already overloaded and cannot bring up mine casing, and, if they do, very little mine casing is likely to arrive at any particular point where it is wanted. In fact nothing more complicated than carrying up pick and shovel and working with these, is either necessary or advisable.

It is also necessary to have a trench from which to start the deep dugout and find a place where there is a good working face to start from. The starting of a deep dugout is always the slowest part of the construction, as the face crumbles away and requires sand bagging, or revetting. The German trenches get all the shelling by our guns before the attack, and by the enemy guns afterwards, and it is better to look for existing deep dugouts and repair them, rather than start new ones before that can be done deliberately, after the fighting has quietened down a bit.

The immediate consolidation to be done is,

1. To get out 20 or 30 yards in front of the captured trenches, and dig slits off the C.Ts or between shell holes.

2. Get the approaches up C.Ts and other trenches under fire or filled up.

3. Look for fire position for Lewis guns and men in the old trenches near deep dugouts.

4. Repair entrances to deep dugouts.

5. Wire.

The second idea presented, was the training of infantry in schools to what is described as "intensive digging". I do not think it possible to give instruction of much value in a school, unless the men are already good diggers, and have learnt by experience how to get to work at once on a trench which has been knocked to pieces, and dig alternative trenches.

In this division the principle is to get the Infantry thoroughly accustomed, not merely to digging, but to tackling a job at once without waste of time. This is done by placing all the front line work in the trenches in charge of the Infantry holding the trenches. In this way, every man becomes a trench expert and will automatically know what to do when captured trenches have to be consolidated.

A further note on consolidation in general will follow.

L.E.Hopkins, Lieut-Col R.E.
C.R.E., 39th Division.

Sept 16th 1916.

161/A.

Headquarters,
39th Division.

Copy of above forwarded for your information.

sd. L.E.Hopkins, Lt-Col R.E.
C.R.E. 39th Div.

Sept 16th 1916.

VE

Consolidation of Captured Positions

It has hitherto always been the duty of the R.E. to lead the attack of fortified positions, clear away obstacles and make good the captured work. Under the conditions developed during the present war, where almost every action has been the attack of a fortified position, it has been no longer possible for R.E. to carry out these duties - there are not enough of them. Small parties of R.E. are still sent with the attack but it is doubtful whether their presence in such small numbers can ever seriously affect the course of events. When used in the early stages of attack, R.E. should be given one work and never split up into parties smaller thanone section of a Field Company.

2. As it is no longer possible to provide R.E. for every attack, the duty of consolidation devolves on the Infantry and their training in trench work of all kinds becomes as important as their training in musketry. This training should begin in England at the same time as musketry and every man should be taught that the practice of digging is a necessary accomplishment to every soldier and is not a "fatigue". The mere power to dig being acquired, the experience to apply the knowledge can only be obtained by practical work in the trenches. For this reason, Infantry should always make and repair their own support and front line trenches and so acquire a knowledge of the tactical application of digging as well as gain experience in all the difficulties of getting men and materials to the place where they are to work ; such difficulties, under war conditions are created by shells, gas, mud, darkness, Machine Gun fire, and traffice congestion of the trenches.

3. With Infantry trained on these lines, there only remains the question how to ensure them the most favourable conditions for the work of consolidation and what exactly in detail is the work they should do. In two successful attacks of which I have had practical knowledge, the attacking troops took their objective and rushed 500 to 800 yards beyond it without a check. In the attack at YPRES in June made by the Germans on the Canadians' position, the attacking troops were immediately followed by x large working parties who set to work to make new trenches on the main position under cover of the advenced troops. The latter tried to consolidate their position but were soon removed by the Canadian counter-attack, but not before those in rear had made a strong line on the main position.

These are the lines on which all attacks run. There are always the advanced troops consolidating themselves in close touch with the enemy, and, if the attack is successful, there are troops under the protection of those in advance consolidating the main position more or less unmolested.

There are also attacks made with the enemy's front trenches only as objective, which it is intended to join up with our line and provide with C.Ts. Such attacks have seldom been successful unless quickly followed by a further advance and the attempts to join up captured trenches with our own have usually failed unless carried out on an extended front.

It is possible that too much stress is laid on trenches as an objective, rather than positions. Schemes of attack should consider the consolidation of a main position under cover of advanced troops : the objective of either need not necessarily be a trench.

4. The action of both the most advanced troops and of those of the main position will be guided by the same principles which are to (1) to avoid offering a target to the enemy's artillery, (2) to get cover from the enemy's artillery, (3) to provide fire bays from which to repulse attack of infantry, and (4) to prevent approach of enemy bombers or attacking infantry.

To avoid offering a target, the advanced troops will make use of banks, ditches, shell-holes, and, if possible, occupy ground rising gently towards the enemy for a short distance rather than ground falling towards them. Those occupying the main position, which may have been already entrenched by the enemy, will usually avoid the enemy's trenches as a fire trench. Such trenches will usually be full of dead and all the debris of revetments and, if not entirely obliterated, certainly will be difficult to repair quickly ; they will be conspicuous and a well-known mark to the enemy ; they will often be wrongly sited for fire in a contrary direction ; in short, it will often be better to dig new trenches either in front of the captured trenches or in rear, about 40 yards distant, where the old trenches and wire will form a formidable obstacle.

To get cover and at the same time provide fire bays, the quickest form of trench is a slit 6 to 7 ft deep. For the advanced line it will be zig-zag in plan, and with portions dug 3 ft deep only to act, at first, as fire trenches, and to be afterwards filled up for traverses.. This is very simple, gives very efficient cover and lends itself to
See drawing. improvement into a complete fire trench with traverses. The zig-zag plan gives fire over a wide arc enabling all the ground to be covered without the necessity for a continuous trench. The fire bays may be made for fire in either direction. The men available for digging will usually be few in number in the advanced line, and they will concentrate in digging short trenches or 'strong points' about 40 yards in length for 15 or 20 men and at about 40 yards interval. In consolidating the main position with working parties from the rear, trenches will be dug deep and narrow with traverses ; Wooden forms will be brought up for use as fire steps.

Wiring for the advanced troops will often be impossible except with the wire they may find on the spot and they can only deal with old trenches which form dangerous approaches by filling them up. The main position wiring can be most quickly done by means of barbed concertina wire, ready made, and carried up in 5 yards lengths, by two men each. Old trenches must be straightened out and brought under enfilade rifle fire, or must be filled in.

Old deep dugouts left by the enemy may be repaired and the trenches to them opened out for use as communication or traffic trenches. Positions for Machine Guns for flanking fire should be chosen near these dugouts.

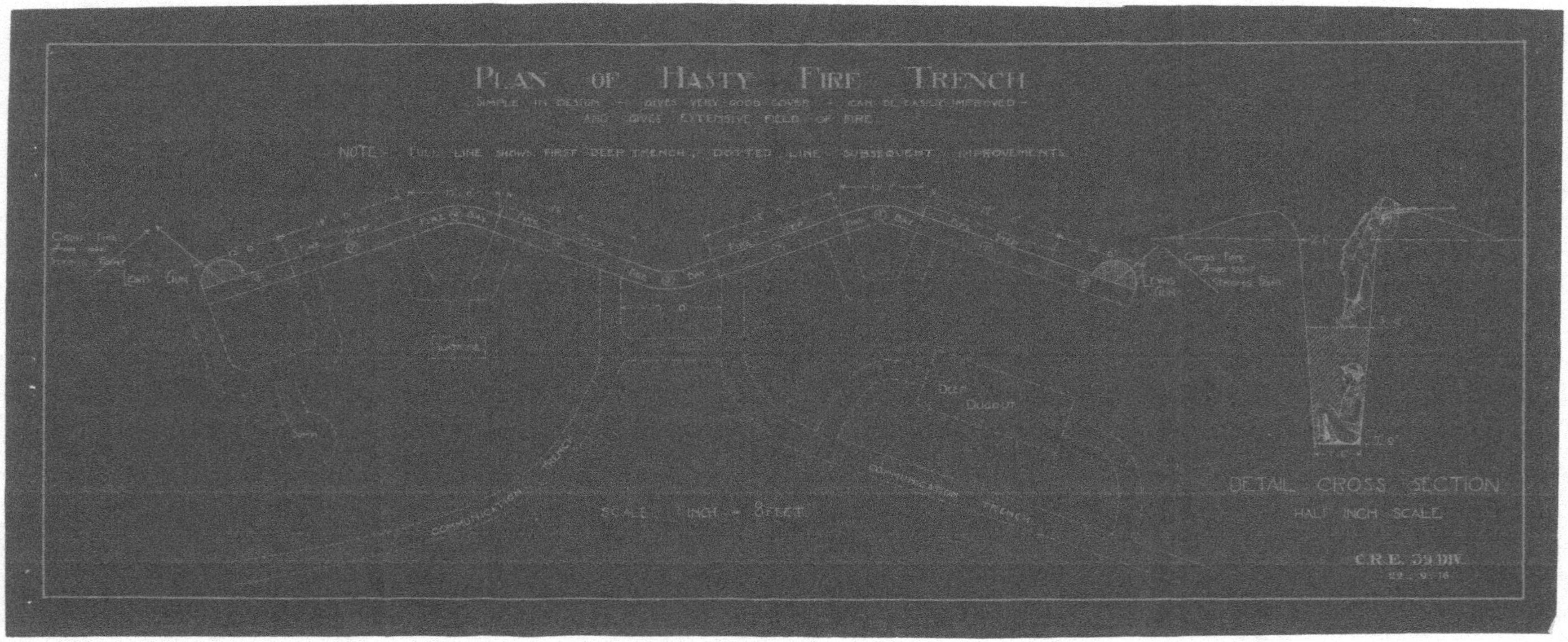
PLAN OF HASTY FIRE TRENCH
SIMPLE IN DESIGN – GIVES VERY GOOD COVER – CAN BE EASILY IMPROVED –
AND GIVES EXTENSIVE FIELD OF FIRE.
NOTE:– FULL LINE SHOWS FIRST DEEP TRENCH, DOTTED LINE SUBSEQUENT IMPROVEMENTS.
LEWIS GUN
DEEP DUGOUT
COMMUNICATION TRENCH
COMMUNICATION TRENCH
SCALE 1 INCH = 8 FEET
DETAIL CROSS SECTION
HALF INCH SCALE
C.R.E. 39 DIV.

Vol 8

CONFIDENTIAL.

W A R D I A R Y

O F

Headquarters 39th Divl R.E.

FROM 1ST OCTOBER TO 31ST OCTOBER 1916.

Instructions regarding War Diaries and Intelligence Summaries are contained in F. S. Regs., Part II. and the Staff Manual respectively. Title pages will be prepared in manuscript.

WAR DIARY
or
~~INTELLIGENCE SUMMARY.~~
(Erase heading not required.)

Army Form C. 2118.

H.Q. 39th Divn RE.

Place	Date	Hour	Summary of Events and Information	Remarks and references to Appendices
ACHEUX	Oct 1	1916	Arranged for 8 huts and dugout to accomodate Div HQrs on Englebelmer Martinsart Road.	
HEDAUVILLE	Oct 2		HQrs moved to camp in Hedauville	
	Oct 3		Fixed site + prepared plans for hutting Divisional HQrs at Englebelmer P36d	
	Oct 4		Went round Thiepval + 18 Divn area with CRE 18 Divn. visited CE at Senlis	
	Oct 5		Took charge of trenches south of R Ancre as far as R20 central. with 234th F Co in Thiepval. 225th in Martinsart + 13 Glouc R. in Quarry Post and Thiepval. 227th remain North of Ancre with area extending to Watling Street	
	Oct 6		Put up huts at Bouzincourt for Divisional Head Qrs	
BOUZINCOURT.	Oct 7		Div Head Qrs moved to Bouzincourt. Went round trenches with OC 13 Glouc R + arranged details of work to be done	
	Oct 8th		visited CE. at Senlis + to Varennes siding about materials	
	Oct 9th		visited Field Cos + Pioneers.	
	Oct 10th		Went round trenches + Thiepval with GSO 2	
	Oct 11th		Note on defence of Thiepval area with plan copy attached visited field Cos. Operation order for attack issued	A B.

[signature]
[signature] CRE 39th Divn

T2134. Wt. W708-776. 500000. 4/15. Sir J. C. & S.

Instructions regarding War Diaries and Intelligence Summaries are contained in F. S. Regs., Part II. and the Staff Manual respectively. Title pages will be prepared in manuscript.

WAR DIARY
or
INTELLIGENCE SUMMARY.
(Erase heading not required.)

Army Form C. 2118.

Place	Date	Hour	Summary of Events and Information	Remarks and references to Appendices
BOUZINCOURT	Oct 12th		visited works at Mesnil with OC 227th Co. Instructions for Coalwoods' action in attack issued. visited CE II Corps 227 Co 234th Co & 13 Glosc Pioneers. Copy attached.	~~B~~ C
	Oct 13		visited 234th Co & 225th Co. Adjutant went to Amiens for materials. Capt Mackesy went on leave & Lt West officiates in command of 227th Co.	
	Oct 14		3 sections of 234th Co. & 1 Coy Pioneers assisted in consolidation of north side of SCHWABEN REDOUBT. 2nd Lt Reed wounded. & 7 O.R.	
	Oct 15.		225th Co continued consolidation 234th Co one section in Thiepval remainder resting. 2nd Lt Cotton 234th Co wounded. took CRE 63rd Div round Y Ravine section.	
	Oct 16.		Handed over sections north of Ancre to 63rd Div. & took over 500 yds on right from 25th Div. visited Field Cos & Pioneers.	
	Oct 17		Report on operations of Oct 14th attached with recommendations	D
	Oct 18.		CRE visited Thiepval Tank ~~Street~~ Zollern trench Paisley avenue with OC 234 Fd Co	
	Oct 19		Heavy rain & gale from North West. Operations postponed. Billets of 225 & 227 Fd Co shelled all night 1 Killed 7 wounded. 1 Horse killed 3 wounded	

[signature]
Lt Col
CRE 39 Div

T2134. Wt. W708–776. 500000. 4/15. Sir J. C. & S.

Instructions regarding War Diaries and Intelligence Summaries are contained in F. S. Regs., Part II. and the Staff Manual respectively. Title pages will be prepared in manuscript.

WAR DIARY
or
INTELLIGENCE SUMMARY.
(Erase heading not required.)

Army Form C. 2118.

39 Divn RE HQ.

Place	Date	Hour	Summary of Events and Information	Remarks and references to Appendices
BOUZINCOURT			Visited Pioneers + Field Cos. Divl Head Qrs Camp shelled at night	
	20.X.	16	2 killed OR 1 officer 20 OR wounded of artillery Head Qrs. Frosty night	
	21.X.	16.	Attack & capture of Stuff Trench 225 + 227th + 13 Glouc R employed on consolidation. Frost at night.	
	22/X		Handed over to 19th Divn, the right section of Schwaben + Stuff Trenches	
	23.10		Digging assembly + other trenches in Schwaben Redoubt + preparing dumps for tank routes.	
	24.10		Heavy rain work stopped.	
	25.10		Heavy rain. Work continued at night. Examined Speyside road & working of tramways.	
	26.10		Ground & trenches too muddy for work – put all labour onto trench boarding.	
	27.10		Visited Thiepval + Thiepval wood + old German front line to corps conference in evening about tramways & roads.	
	28.10		Took officers of 227 + 234 over new reserve line to be dug on 29th + gave them full instructions about the work to be done	

[illegible signature]
LT. COL. R.E.
C.R.E. 39TH DIVISION.

T2134. Wt. W708–776. 500000. 4/15. Sir J. C. & S.

Instructions regarding War Diaries and Intelligence Summaries are contained in F. S. Regs., Part II. and the Staff Manual respectively. Title pages will be prepared in manuscript.

WAR DIARY
or
~~INTELLIGENCE~~ SUMMARY.
(Erase heading not required.)

Army Form C. 2118.

HQ 39 Divn RE

Place	Date	Hour	Summary of Events and Information	Remarks and references to Appendices
BOUZINCOURT	Oct 29.		Rain interferes with work on reserve line. — Visited Fd Cos.	
	Oct 30.		Visited Passerelle de Magenta with GOC & GSO1. Heavy rain in afternoon which stopped all work.	
	Oct 31.		Fine & cold. Went to Advanced Brigade HeadQrs with GOC. arranged for clearing road through Thiepval & ~~[illegible]~~ routes to front line.	

[illegible signature]
LT. COL. R.E.
C.R.E. 39TH DIVISION.

T2134. Wt. W708–776. 500000. 4/15. Sir J. C. & S.

COPY

A.

243/a.

SECRET

Headquarters,
39th Division.

The attached plan shows proposals for defence of the THIEPVAL area.

FRONT LINE.

Front line being on the crest, is mainly for observation.

SUPPORT LINE.

Support line is full of dugouts and better situated for resistance.

RESERVE LINE.

Reserve line has a fair number of dugouts existing.

STRONG POINTS.

Strong points are chosen to include dugouts as a rule.

C.Ts.

C.Ts are sited after considering following points:-
(1) Access to front line.
(2) Communication to Battalion Headquarters, water supply, ration dumps, yard, tramways and R.E.dumps.
(3) New trenches are sited to avoid heavily shelled areas.
(4) Old trenches sometimes chosen to get into chalk soil.
(5) Across trench TANK STREET provides communication between Brigade and all Battalion Headquarters.

WATER SUPPLY.

Water supply is developed from existing ANCRE supply and from THIEPVAL well.

TRAMWAYS.

PAISLEY AVENUE line may be extended up to FRONT LINE along CENERAL AVENUE and onto R.20.c.

ROADS.

Road through THIEPVAL from AUTHUILLE is being cleared for Ambulance traffic and R.E. stores and rations.

sd. L.E.Hopkins.
Lieut-Colonel R.E.
C.R.E. 39th Division.

11.10.16.

COPY

B.

SECRET. 11.10.16.

HEADQUARTERS 39TH DIV R.E. OPERATION ORDER NO.1.

Reference 1/5,000 Map.

1. The 118th Brigade are to attack and capture the remainder of SCHWABEN REDOUBT on 13th October at 2.5 p.m.
The new general line will be R.20.c.2.7 - R.19.d.9.9. - 69 - 49 - 39 - 19 with observation posts in front of this at R.20.a.15.06 - R.19.b.95.10 - R.19.b.62 - d.19.

2. 3 Sections of 234th Field Company R.E. and 1 Company of Pioneers will leave THIEPVAL as soon as it is dark to consolidate the position. They should start not later than 6 p.m.

3. The operations will be in charge of Capt Wood, O.C. 234th Field Company R.E. Strong points of type design will be placed near deep dugouts, or, if no dugouts, across the C.Ts. at 19 (49-69) 99. One section R.E. and a platoon of 13th Gloucester Regt will be detailed for each of the above three points and one platoon of Pioneers clearing dugouts.

4. Tools and materials will be collected at forward dumps at 45 and 15 tomorrow by the R.E. and Pioneers who will carry out the consolidation.

sdl. L.E.Hopkins.
Lieut-Colonel R.E.
C.R.E. 39th Division.

Copies issued at 8 p.m. to
234th Field Coy R.E.
13th Gloucester Regt.
118th Infantry Brigade.
H.Q. 39th Div "G" (2 copies).

SECRET 11.10.16.

AMENDMENT TO H.Q. 39TH DIV. R.E. OPERATION ORDER NO 1.
d/- 11.10.16.

Reference paragraph 1, Line 2.

Date and time is now cancelled, and will be notified later.

sd. L.E.Hopkins.
Lieut-Col R.E.
C.R.E. 39th Division.

Copies issued at 10.10.p.m.
234th Field Coy R.E.
13th Gloucester Regt.
118th Infantry Brigade.
H.Q. 39th Div "G"

COPY

247/a.

C

O.C. 234th Field Coy R.E.

Cancel my note asking to see your orders before issue. Send one copy orders after issue for my information:-

I make following suggestions:-
Keep R.E. and Pioneers separate.
Tell off R.E. as wiring parties.
Tell off R.E. as dugout parties.
Tell off R.E. as C.T.blocking parties.
Tell off Pioneers as digging parties.
Tell off Pioneers as clearing parties.
Tell off Pioneers as filling in trench parties.

If the C.Ts. are much damaged, they need not be taken into account. They cannot give much better approach to the enemy than do the shell holesm but, if they are in good order, they must be filled in or blocked for 50 yards in front of the strong point.

Strong point trench is shewn on the type plan, it need not be circular. Your progress report speaks of trenches dug "round" the strong points.

sd L.E.Hopkins.
Lieut-Colonel R.E.
C.R.E. 39th Division.

12.10.16.

COPY 248/A.

VERY SECRET

With reference to Headquarters 39th Div R.E.Operation Order No 1 of 11.10.16.

1. Date and ~~hour~~ ZERO hour of Operations is 13th October at 3.17 p.m.

2. Please acknowledge.

sd L.E.Hopkins.

Lieut-Col R.E.
C.R.E. 39th Division.

12.10.16.

Copies to:-
234th Field Coy R.E.
13th Gloucester Regt.
118th Infantry Brigade.

19

COPY

Headquarters,
39th Division.

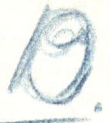

REPORT ON R.E.ACTION IN CONNECTION WITH OPERATIONS OF OCT 14TH AT THE SCHWABEN REDOUBT.

In accordance with 39th Division Order No 57, 3 sections of 234th Field Coy R.E. and "A" Company, 13th Gloucester Regt. (Pioneers) were detailed to proceed at 6 p.m. to consolidate Northern face of SCHWABEN REDOUBT.

Captain Wood, O.C. 234th Field Coy R.E was placed in charge of the operations, and ordered to make strong points at R.19.d.3.9. (49-69) and 99.

The form of strong point was left to the officer on the spot, but the R.E. were advised to construct new deep trenches 40 yards North of the German trench, to clear out old trenches leading from them to existing dugouts, to repair such dugouts and to block communication trenches if they were not destroyed by shell fire.

Lieut Reid took his section and a platoon of pioneers to consolidate point 99, which was not captured till 4 p.m.

Lieut Reid went about 200 yards beyond the German trench and there was some discussion with the infantry about the best line to consolidate, and it was decided to work on the German North face of SCHWABEN REDOUBT. This was done, and the trench was made fit for defence.

Lieut Reid was wounded in the foot about 1 a.m. and returned to Dressing Station.

2/Lieut Gandy took his section and a platoon of pioneers to consolidate point 49 to 69. Deep trenches and fire steps were made between 49 and 69, and a bomb stop near 48. A dugout was included near 49 in the strong point.

2/Lieut Dryland proceeded with his section and a platoon of pioneers, from THIEPVAL up the old GERMAN FRONT LINE where he was stopped by barrage till 10 p.m. He was then able to proceed to point 39 where he found that the CAMBRIDGESHIRES had already cleared the trenches, and required wire. He then returned and brought up wire from R.20.b.4.9. where a dump had been formed.

Lieut Kirby R.E. with the fourth platoon of pioneers, superintended digging of a C.T. from point 65 to 69 across centre of SCHWABEN REDOUBT. About 80 yards of this was dug 5 ft deep. More would have been done but at request of the Infantry, wiring materials were taken up by this party to the North side of the redoubt.

Reports of O.C. 13th Gloucester Regt and O.C. 234th Field Coy R.E. are attached.

Also copies of C.R.E's orders and instructions.

Casualties R.E.	1 officer wounded.
	O.R. 4 wounded.
Engaged:-	3 wounded at duty.
4 officers, 75 O.R.	

Casualties 13th Gloucester R.	
	11 wounded.
	1 shell shock.
Engaged:-	1 missing, believed wounded.
5 officers, 129 O.R.	

List of recommendations for rewards is forwarded separately.

17.10.16.

sd L.E.Hopkins.
Lt-Col R.E.
C.R.E. 39th Division.

225/A.

Headquarters,
39th Division.

I visited some of the new THIEPVAL Area with C.R.E. 18th Division.

The work done by the 18th Division and proposed, is described with C.R.E's note and plan of which I understand you have a copy.

As regards Road to THIEPVAL, the clearing extends up to the old German front line, beyond it is impassable. The road is deep in mud and requires metalling.

PIP STREET is narrow and unrevetted, and sides are falling in. The grids extend to the apple trees South of THIEPVAL.

The clearing of THIEPVAL roads and metalling, clearing of MARTIN'S TRENCH and of dugouts, has been allotted to the 13th Bn Gloucester Regt, consolidation of the front line is being taken up by the 234th Field Company (3 Sections in THIEPVAL).

The 225th Company is working in the THIEPVAL WOOD Area and should put on working parties to clear INNISKILLING AVENUE and extend it across NO MAN'S LAND to the German lines, which will give a good C.T. up to SCHWABEN REDOUBT. The front line along the Sunken road requires clearing out.

Sd. L.E.Hopkins, Lt.Col.R.E.
C.R.E. 39th Division.

Oct 6th 1916.

Copy of C.R.E. 18th Division note and map herewith. Please return.

COPY

Recommendations as a result of experience gained.

As the Infantry commanders are solely responsible for deciding what work shall be done by R.E. and Pioneers, there must be close co-operation between Infantry and R.E., both before and during the operations.

The O.C. R.E. must bring strongly to the notice of the Brigade Commander what his views are before operations begin, and the Brigade Commander must decide and communicate his views to the junior infantry commanders, who will have to decide what should be done on the spot.

In this case, the C.R.E's recommendations were to dig a new trench in front of the captured trench with access to any dugouts found. This is generally advisable unless the existing trench is a good one. The commanders on the spot decided to retain existing German trench. Actually no harm appears to have resulted, as the enemy's artillery fire in the counter attack seems to have been ineffective, but it may yet be found, that the old trench is untenable, owing to artillery fire, and that a new trench will be required in front of it.

2. The sending up of R.E. and Pioneers only after the objective has been well secured, proved quite satisfactory. In the case of point 99 which was not captured till 11 p.m. this course was well justified.

There was delay to the left party owing to barrage, but the remainder all got up without much difficulty.

sd L E.Hopkins.

Lieut-Col R.E.
C.R.E. 39th Division.

17.10.16.

Pressing

SECRET.

II Corps.
G.3029.

18/10/16.

39th Division.

1. Would you kindly arrange for an R.E? Officer to reconnoitre the bridges shown on the attached sketch of the ground to the East of HAMEL.

2. Information is especially required as regards the width of each Bridge, the weight it will carry and its present condition, as also of the type and condition of the road between X and Y.

3. It is thought that the reconnaissance will have to be carried out by night; and it is desirable that the Officer carrying it out should get in touch with the troops holding the line to the North of the R.ANCRE as it is understood that the Mill is occupied at night by a patrol from these troops.

4. . I should be glad if you canarrange for the reconnaissance to be carried out on the night 19th/20th October and let me have a report as early as possible for the information of the Reserve Army.

5. Please return sketch.

Sd. S.H.Wilson,
B.G.G.S.

-2-

G.S.O.3 ✓

39/G/364/9

39th Divisional R.E.

For information and necessary action.
G.S.O.3. will let C.R.E. have a summary of information atpresent available re these Bridges.
The Officer detailed should communicate with 63rd Division before proceeding.

R. Coper.

19/10/16.

Lieut-Colonel,
General Staff,
39th Division.

Q24 a

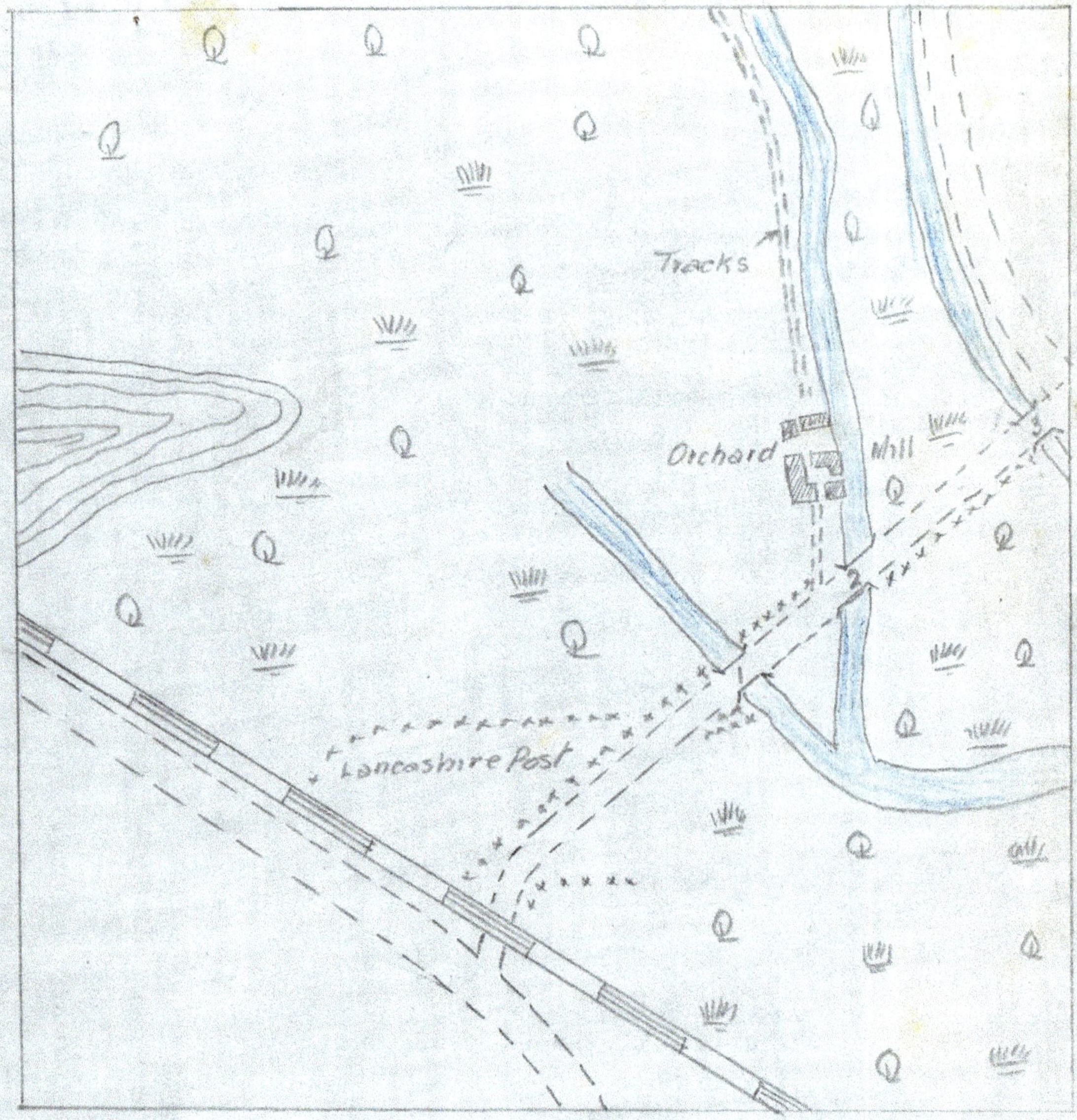

1. Stone Bridge
2. Iron Bridge
3. Stone Bridge

SECRET. 264/A.

Report on Bridges over ANCRE in Q.24.a.

C.R.E. 39th Division.

There is a lot of R.E. material on the road by the embankment and then a trench next the railway embankment on the East (? West) side, another trench and some three trees lying across the road.

The average width is from 15 to 18 feet, but there are shell holes here and there, but not many, the worst being a large one on the S.E. abutment of the centre bridge (No. 2), this should be rebuilt but would, I fancy, be strong enough pro tem if the shell hole were filled in.

No. 1 Bridge.

Consists of a strong arch with low stone parapet walls about 2 feet high and 1 foot wide at each side. As the water was flush with the top of the arch, it was rather hard to estimate the span, which I put at from 10' to 12', the width of the roadway in the clear is 17' 10".

This bridge was capable of taking heavy motor traffic prior to the war and does not appear to have been damaged in any way.

The surface of the roadway is about 2' 6" to 3' above the water level.

No. 2 Bridge.

Is an iron one, width 19' 7" in the clear. The span is about 15 feet to 20 feet; the bridge consists of plate girders about 2 feet deep; there is an iron rail on e ch side more or less damaged, and a large shell hole at the down stream side of the East end of the bridge. This corner of the abutment should be rebuilt to make a permanent job, but I consider that the bridge is strong enough for heavy motor traffic, provided the shell hole is well filled in.

No. 3 Bridge.

This amounts to a brick culvert with ample width. A shell hole has caught the up stream end which is crumbly a little, otherwise it appears quite sound.

There is another obstacle of fallen trees beyond this, and then the end of our trenches.

Obstacles. There is some wire here and there along this road which is on the whole in very good condition (by moonlight).

5 a.m.
20.10.1916.

sd. J.C.I. Wood, Capt. R.E.
O.C. 234th Field Company R.E.

H.Q. 39th Division.

Forwarded. Sketch attached.

The Maire of Martinsart says the road was used for heavy motor traffic before the war.

See also para 5, page 6 Notes on Achiet Le Grand Area.

Oct 20th.

sd. L.E. Hopkins, Lt. Col. R.E.
C.R.E. 39th Division.

8069

CONFIDENTIAL.

W A R D I A R I E S

F O R

39TH DIVISIONAL R.E.

FROM NOVEMBER 1st TO NOVEMBER 30th 1916.

308

CONFIDENTIAL.

W A R   D I A R Y.

FOR

Headquarters 39th Divisional R.E.

FROM NOVEMBER 1st 1916 TO NOVEMBER 30hh1916.

...ding War Diaries and Int... ...e contained in F. S. Regs... ...f Manual respectively... ...pared in manuscript.

...elligence ..., Part II. Title pages

WAR DIARY
or
~~INTELLIGENCE SUMMARY.~~
(Erase heading not required.)

Army Form C. 2118.

HQ. 39th Divn RE.

Place	Date	Hour	Summary of Events and Information	Remarks and references to Appendices
BOUZINCOURT.	Nov 1st.		Visited Reserve line + Thiepval with GSO I WMG.	
	Nov 2nd		Working parties cut down owing to reliefs + large parties for Corps works. WMG.	
	Nov 3rd		No working parties again. visited trenches. Conference of CREs at Corps Head Qrs re winter schemes WMG.	
	Nov 4th		night parties cancelled for above reasons. conference of CREs at Corps Head Qrs re supply of stores + transport. WMG.	
	Nov 5.		Preparation of dugout plan ordered. Thiepval road & winter defence works begun. High wind + some rain. Visited Thiepval + reserve line WMG.	A.
	Nov 6		Offensive action to be resumed. Issued orders to allow for this. WMG.	A
	Nov 7		visited 118 Brigade with OC 234th Co + prepared scheme for constructing a trench system in Thiepval area. WMG.	
	Nov 8.		Heavy rain WMG.	
	Nov 9		visited Schwaben with GSO I trenches all mud except on trench board routes. Lt Gillespie went on 10 days leave. WMG.	
	Nov 10		prepared scheme of work for front line and dugout scheme. Lt Kirby appointed officiating adjutant WMG.	
	Nov 11		Preparing trench scheme + dugout scheme for Thiepval area WMG.	
	Nov 12		Preparations for attack. taping out assembly positions, tank routes + forward dumps WMG.	B

Nov 14th.

WMHopkins
Lt Col RE

T2134. Wt. W708-776. 500000. 4/15. Sir J. C. & S.

Instructions regarding War Diaries and Intelligence Summaries are contained in F. S. Regs., Part II. and the Staff Manual respectively. Title pages will be prepared in manuscript.

WAR DIARY
or
~~INTELLIGENCE SUMMARY.~~
(Erase heading not required.)

Army Form C. 2118.

HQ 39th Divn RE.

Place	Date	Hour	Summary of Events and Information	Remarks and references to Appendices
BOUZINCOURT.	Nov 13		Attack by 118 Brigade. One section of 225th Co under Lt HOLLEY went with attacking infantry & helped consolidate. Two more sections of 225th under Lt DIBDIN went up at night to dig support trench in front of St Pierre Divion. Capt EGERTON OC 227th Co went up & examined St Pierre Divion road & with Pioneers repaired it as far as old German front line. WWG.	C
	Nov 14.		Handed over to 32 Divn CRE. & front ~~line~~ to CRE 19 Divn WWG.	
	Nov 15.		Very cold NE wind. CRE 11th Divn arrived to take over camp. WWG.	
DOULLENS	Nov 16		Moved from BOUZINCOURT today. Camp was not taken over by 11th Div: but had to be left under sentries WWG.	
	Nov 17		A/Adj. visited 225th & 227th Field Co. Weather still cold. WWG.	
ESQUELBECQ	Nov 18		Moved from DOULLENS this morning, detraining at HOPOUTRE at 7 PM. HQ personal came on by road here. Weather warmer. WWG.	
	Nov 19		Got in touch with CE 8th Corps by telephone. Back area work required in erection of NISSEN HUTS at L & K Camps, also finishing off Y & Z Camps. Ordered 225th Field Co to carry out the work. WWG.	

W.W. Gillespie [illegible]
ADJT. 39TH DIV R. E.
for CRE.

Army Form C. 2118.

WAR DIARY
or
~~INTELLIGENCE SUMMARY.~~
(Erase heading not required.)

Instructions regarding War Diaries and Intelligence Summaries are contained in F. S. Regs., Part II. and the Staff Manual respectively. Title pages will be prepared in manuscript.

HQ 39th Divn RE

Place	Date	Hour	Summary of Events and Information	Remarks and references to Appendices
ESQUEL-BECQ.	Nov. 20		Sent lorry into 8th Corps RE Park to draw materials required by Field Cos. A/adj visited 227 & 225 Fld Co. WWG.	
	Nov 21.		Obtained 3 lorries for Corps, and sent them to draw materials required for instructional purposes. WWG.	
	Nov 22.		8th Corps handed over work on K, L, Y, & Z camps to be carried on under direction of C.R.E. A adj went over works with Staff Officer & OC 225th Fld Co. WWG.	
			CRE Prepared and issued notes "Pioneer Work in the Trenches."	
	Nov 23.		C.R.E visited C.E. 8th Corps. Orders issued to 234th Field Co RE for move into line. WWG.	D
	Nov 24th		CRE visited 225th Field Co, and inspected Z Camp. Weather mild. WWG.	
	Nov 25th		C. RE visited site for 39th School at VOLKERINGHOVE suitability of position questioned WWG.	
	26		Lt Gillespie returned from leave. A/adj Lt Kirby returned to unit. CRE issued orders regarding his departure on leave. WWG.	

WW Gillespie Lt RE
ADJT. 39TH DIV. R.E.
for Lt Col

T2134. Wt. W708-776. 500000. 4/15. Sir J. C. & S.

Instructions regarding War Diaries and Intelligence Summaries are contained in F. S. Regs., Part II. and the Staff Manual respectively. Title pages will be prepared in manuscript.

WAR DIARY

~~INTELLIGENCE SUMMARY~~

(Erase heading not required.)

Army Form C. 2118.

H.Q. 39 DIV. R.E.

Place	Date	Hour	Summary of Events and Information	Remarks and references to Appendices
	Nov.			
ESQUELBECQ	27		C.R.E. proceeded to England for 10 days leave. ~~A/C.R.E.~~ Capt. Egerton, appointed officiating C.R.E., became acquainted with R.E. work on hand. Weather – Fine + mild W.M.G.	
	28		A/C.R.E. visited work in progress at Div! Schools at VOLKERINCKHOVE Weather – Fair becoming showery W.M.G.	
	29		A/C.R.E. and Col. Robertson G. Staff. 2nd Army visited site of rifle range at FORET DE TOURNEHEM in 2nd Army training area. Weather – Fair – cold N.E. wind. W.M.G.	
	30		A/C.R.E. visited site of rifle-range. ~~[illegible]~~ Orders issued to 225 Fd. C. R.E to moves into line. Weather – Fine + cold. W.M.G.	E

W.M. Gillespie Lt R.E.
ADJT. 39TH DIV. R.E.
for C.R.E.
3/12/16

T2134. Wt. W708–776. 500000. 4/15. Sir J. C. & S.

SECRET 339/A.

A.

225th Field Coy R.E.	116th Infantry Brigade.
227th " "	117th " "
234th " "	118th " "
13th Gloucester Regt.	Headquarters, 39th Div. For information.

Reference 39/G/37/9 of 30th October 1916 with Trench Map attached.

The following orders will come into force from the morning of Nov 5th 1916.

The 225th and 234th Field Companies R.E. will work in the area in front of the Reserve Line separated by the N & S line through 19.central.

The construction of the Front Line trenches by means of firebays near dugouts connected by trench board routes which develop into trenches as time permits; or by clearing out existing trenches where that is possible, will be carried out by the Infantry Brigade in Front Line, and 225th and 234th Field Companies R.E. will each detail a section to assist.

The Field Companies will get sandbags and wire materials, firesteps and trench boards carried up to dumps near the Front Line by carrying parties obtained through C.R.E.

Field Companies will arrange working parties with the Brigade in line (H.Q. PASSERELLE DE MAGENTA). The Brigade is only in the line for 2 days and working parties will put in not less than 12 hours work during that period.

O.C. 13th Gloucester Regt will detail 1 company to work under the supervision of O.C. 225th Field Coy R.E. on communication trenches across old NO MAN'S LAND. and new deep dugouts in Front Line and 1 company to work under supervision of O.C. 234th Field Coy R.E. on communication trench across SCHWABEN and new deep dugouts in Front Line near 79.

2 sections of each Field Company R.E. will work on clearing and making Support Line and communications. They will clear dugouts and continue trench boarding.

1 section of each Field Company R.E. will work at Company Headquarters.

2. The 227th Field Company R.E. will work on Reserve Line and communications up to it, including THIEPVAL ROAD and on works in rear area. Working parties will be arranged direct by O.C. 227th Field Coy R.E. with the Brigade in support (H.Q. PAISLEY DUMP).

3. 1 Company of 13th Gloucester Regt remains employed on tramways, and 1 on roads and hutting, and metalling and clearing THIEPVAL ROAD.

4. Additional working parties for THIEPVAL ROAD can be obtained from C.R.E. and for carrying parties and other works.

[signature]

Lieut-Colonel R.E.
C.R.E. 39th Division.

Nov 4th 1916.

B.

SECRET

H.Q. 39TH DIVISION R.E. OPERATION ORDER NO. 6.

12/11/16.

1. (a) The Operations referred to in H.Q. 39th Div R.E. Operation Order No. 5 and amendments, will now be carried out by stages.
Operation Order No. 5 will hold good except for minor alterations given in this Order.
(b) On "Z" day the 19th and 39th Divisions of the II Corps will capture the line R.21.a.5.7 - R.20.b.8.9 - R.14.c.2.1 - R.13.b.4.6.-MILL at R.13.a.2.7 and the crossing at Q.18.b.85.40.
The V Corps will seize the general line of the BEAUCOURT ROAD and SERRE.
(c) In certain eventualities a further stage may be taken at a later hour on "Z" Day but more probably on "Z" plus 2 day.

2. (a) The main objective of the 39th Division is the HANSA LINE from R.14.c.2.1 to R.13.b.4.6; and on the capture of this objective a line roughly parallel to it facing East North East will be consolidated and held.
The 39th Division will also occupy the MILL at R.13.a.2.7. and the crossing at Q.18.b.85.40.
(b) The dividing line between the 19th and 39th Divisions is the line R.19.d.9.9. to R.14.c.2.1.
(c) The outline Time Table of the 63rd Division will be communicated to those concerned later.

3. O.C. 227th Field Company R.E. will arrange to keep in touch with Bde.Hd.Qrs. at PASSERELLE DE MAGENTA either personally or by orderly on "Z" day.

4. O.C. 13th Gloucester R. will withdraw all outlying working parties, except those with C.R.E. and the patrol of 1 Officer and 25 men on the tramway.

5. Field Companies will parade as strong as possible, leaving only the minimum number of men actually required for pumping and for guards on surplus baggage and stores.

6. Units will not load up their pontoons till ordered but keep bridging wagons to send up materials for consolidation of ST.PIERRE DIVION if ordered.

7. Headquarters of 116th Infantry Brigade will be at PASSERELLE DE MAGENTA.
Headquarters of 117th Infantry Brigade will be at AUTHUILLE NORTH BLUFFS.
Headquarters of 118th Infantry Brigade will be at PAISLEY DUMP.

8. 2 lorries from C.R.E's dump will be placed at disposal of O.C. 13th Glouc. R. at Q.35.c.8.4. at Zero plus ½ hour for road metalling.

ACKNOWLEDGE

Lieut-Colonel R.E.
C.R.E. 39th Division.

Copies issued at 11 a.m. to:-

225 F/Coy R.E.	116th Inf Bde.
227 F/Coy R.E.	117th Inf Bde.
234 F/Coy R.E.	118th Inf Bde.
13th Glouc. R.	Divl. Headquarters.
War Diary ½	File.

SECRET 29.10.16.

H.Q. 39TH DIVISION R.E. OPERATION ORDER No. 5.

Reference attached Sketch Map.
and 1/10,000 Map, Sheet 57D NE & SE.

1.(a). The Reserve Army will make a general attack on the line PYS - SERRE at Zero hour on November 1st (Z day).

(b). The II Corps is to attack Northwards and to capture MIRAUMONT, the line of the MIRAUMONT - BEAUCOURT SUR ANCRE Road, to South of the BOIS D'HOLLANDE and thence South Westwards, the crossings over the R.ANCRE.

(c). The V Corps is attacking Eastwards North of the ANCRE with a view to seizing the line BEAUREGARD DOVECOTE (L.28.c½) - SERRE (inclusive).

2. (a). The main objective of the 39th Division is the line of the River ANCRE from R.8cc.2.0 to Q.24.b.1.3 and the crossings at THE MILL (R.13.a.2.7) and BRIDGE ROAD (Q.18.b.85.40). This objective is to be gained by Zero plus 1 hour 40 minutes.

(b). The dividing line between the 19th Division and the 39th Division is the line R.19.d.9.9 - R.14.c.2.1 - R.8.c.3.3.

(c). The dividing line between the 39th Division and the 63rd Division is the line of the River ANCRE.

3. (a). The attack will be carried out by the 118th Infantry Brigade reinforced by one Battalion from each of the 116th and 117th Infantry Brigades and assisted by a subsidiary attack by 1 Battalion o f the 117th Infantry Brigade.

(b). The area of attack of the 39th Division will be divided into 5 subsidiary objectives.:-

Objective A.	Group of trenches R.19.b.9.7. R.19.b.9.6 - 6.4 - 2.4 - 5.6. and the line R.19.a.6.3 - R.19.c.3.8 - R.19.c.1.6.	To be captured by Zero plus 4 mins.
Objective B.	Line of SERB ROAD from R.13.d. 6.9 - R.19.a.6.8 - 4.5. - 0.4 - Q.24.b.9.0 - 95.00 - Q.24.d. 8.7.	To be captured by Zero plus 18 minutes.
Objective C.	The line of the GRANDCOURT - ST.PIERRE DIVION - HAMEL Road from R.13.b.3.5 to Q.24.b.1.1.	To be captured by Zero plus 28 minutes.

4. (a). O.C. 225th Field Company R.E. will place one section at disposal of 118th Infantry Brigade to assist in the consolidation of streng points in the HANSA LINE.

O.C. 225th Field Company R.E. will ask instructions from the 118th Infantry Brigade forthwith.

(b). 227th Field Company R.E. with its vehicles will be in reserve about W.5.a.7.8 ready to move forward via HAMEL and repair the HAMEL - ST PIERRE DIVION - GRANDCOURT Road.

(c). 225th Field Company R.E. (less 1 section) and 234th Field Company R.E. will remain their bivouacs ready to move at half an hour's notice.

(d). the 13th Gloucester Regt. (Pioneers) will be in Divisional Reserve about Q.35.c.8.4 and will be prepared to move forward with 6 G.S. wagons loaded with road metal, to repair the HAMEL - ST.PIERRE DIVION - GRANDCOURT Road.

5. Three Tanks have been allotted to the 39th Division and will move as shewn on the map (copy attached).

6. Steps will be taken to ensure that every man has his iron ration and water bottle filled, before proceeding to assembly positions.

7. All prisoners of war will be sent to 118th Infantry Brigade Headquarters at PAISLEY DUMP and thence to 39th Division Prisoners Cage at Q.35.d.4.8.

8. 39th Divisional Headquarters R.E. remain at W.7.b½3.1.

9. ZERO hour will be notified later.

10. ACKNOWLEDGE.

sd L.E.HOPKINS, Lt-Col R.E.
C.R.E., 39th Division.

Copies issued to:-
225th Field Coy. R.E.
227th do.
234th do.
13th Gloucester Regt.
H.Q. 39th Division (2).
118th Infantry Brigade.
File.
War Diary (2).

44/B

C

REPORT ON R.E. COOPERATION IN CONNECTION WITH THE OPERATIONS OF 39th DIVISION OF NOV. 10th - 14th.

PRELIMINARY WORK.

Before the 25th October a good deal of work had been done in digging assembly trenches notably a trench dug from R.19.c.3. to R.19.c.8.6. and from R.19.d.6.5. extending two thirds of the way across the SCHWABEN REDOUBT. But after the postoonements and for some days before the attack, the attempt to dig unrevetted assembly trenches had been definitely abandoned. The ground was then everywhere a waste of shell craters which were full of mud or water, and working parties arrived on their work too exhausted to dig, and any work unless trenchhoarded and revetted at once would, after a few hours of rain and shell fire, become untraceable.

The work of forming trench board routes up to the front line was then pushed on. Two routes were completed, one from PAISLEY DUMP to the rear face of the SCHWABEN REDOUBT with a branch to point 86 and 39 partly finished, and a second route from the THIEPVAL road at R.25.c.7.0. up to the old German front line and RIPLEY STREET and GRANDCOURT road to meet the first route at the SCHWABEN.

Without these routes the assembly of troops would have been almost impossible, and all the Field Companies deserve great credit for getting them through while neighbouring divisions, I believe, had not succeeded in doing so.

Over 4000 yards of trenchboarding was laid by the Field Companies in R.25 and R.19. The 234th Field Company R.E. did a great deal of setting out of marker cairns and tape lines for the assembly, and they also conducted parties of Infantry Officers round these marks for several days before the attack.

The road through THIEPVAL was cleared and a track 16 feet wide prepared. This road had been entirely destroyed by shell fire and about 5000 infantry in all were employed in the work, which had to be carried out at night, and was constantly interrupted by shell fire. The 13th Gloucester Regt did the work in the middle of October, where the shelling of THIEPVAL was almost continual, and small parties only could be used, and the 227th Field Company supervised the infantry parties clearing the worst portion of the road during the 2nd week of November.

Another preliminary work which was of considerable value was the tramway up PAISLEY VALLEY. This work was extended from R.30.d.6.4. to R.25.b.2.9. about 1000 yards and a connection was laid from LANCASHIRE DUMP to SOUTH CAUSEWAY about 1000 yards in length. The existing line was put in good order and sidings were put in every 400 yards, and the greater part of the line was ballasted. 38 trucks werecollected and repaired and the traffic was organised and controlled by a party of 25 men. A great deal of material was sent up by this line and the greater part of our wounded were evacuated by it on November 13th.

The construction of the line in R.25.a. was interrupted by much shell fire and the Officer Commanding the Pioneer Company deserves great credit for the arrangements he made and for personally pushing through this work.

The tracks to be followed by tanks were marked out with white tapes by the 225th Field Company and obstacles removed along them.

A forward dump of R.E. materials was prepared by the 13th Gloucéster Regt at R.25.a.8.1 containing 20,000 sandbags, 500 picks and 500 shovels, 200 concertina wires, 500 screw pickets, 250 coils barbed wire etc.

3. OPERATIONS OF NOVEMBER 1916.

One section of the 225th Field Company under 2/Lt. Holley was detailed to proceed with the 1/1 Herts Regt. with in the attack of the morning of the 13th. 2/Lt Holley carried out his duties with credit and his report as follows speaks for itself.

"Acting on instructions from the C.O. 1/1 Herts Regt. my section proceeded to the Bank at R.19.b.7.5. to R.19.b.7.7. and searched for dugouts marked on Operation Trench map. This squad was unsuccessful in their search and the C.O. Herts therefore ordered them to find any dugouts in Bank R.19.a.8.8. to R.19.b.1.9. 4 splinter proofs were found and cleared.
The remaining 18 men and myself proceeded to the HANSA LINE between R.13.d.6.9. and R.13.b.3.5. where the following works were carried out:-

Dugout marked M.G. cleared and to take 50 men
" " Bn H.Q. " " 20 men
" at R.13.b.3.8. " " 20 men
" at R.13.b.5.2. partially cleared to take 15 men, but work could not be finished as the dugout was urgently needed for garrison purposes. A firebay 12' long was also constructed to command The Valley of the Ancre. This had to depart from standard owing to crumbling nature of the ground where the O.C. garrison desired it to be constructed."

The 227th Field Company and the 13th Gloucester Regt were detailed to assemble at LANCASHIRE DUMP at W.5.a.7.3. at ZERO hour on morning of 13th November and await instructions to move forward and clear the HAMEL ST PIERRE DIVION road. This road across the river had previously been reconnoitred by Capt Wood R.E. who reported very few obstructions in that area. These obstructions were cleared at the end of October by 225th Field Company R.E. and they also reconnoitred the road again on November 12th and reported no obstructions, except for the trenches at Q.24.a.2.6.

The 227th Field Company had previously prepared and brought up with them materials for constructing any small timber bridges which might be required.

At 9.30 a.m. the G.O.C. ordered the R.E. and Pioneers to move forward and repair the road. They proceeded by platoons to Q.24.a.3.5 where O.C. 227th Field Company went forward to reconnoitre. On his return one Company Pioneers was put on to clear the road from Q.24.a.0.5.50 to Q.24.a.3.5, most of them being employed on the trenches, breastworks, and dugouts, which were part of the British line at the level crossing. Half a Company cleared the road across the river, 1½ Companies were on the portion from Q.24.a.6.0. to b.2.2. and 1 Company thence to ST PIERRE DIVION.

The R.E. were employed on wire cutting and clearing trees and on clearing the breastworks about the level crossing. From noon to 3 p.m. work was held up by shelling which caused some casualties among the Pioneers, but by 5.30 p.m. the road was open to Q.24.b.2.2. with a pathway on to ST PIERRE DIVION. The road was used at night by infantry transport.

Capt Egerton R.E. examined the road up to the HANSA LINE and reported that the portion Q.24.b.2.2 up to ST PIERRE DIVION was entirely destroyed by shell fire, and would take several thousand men and several hundred tons of stone to repair. This road is at river level and all shell holes full of water.

Beyond ST PIERRE DIVION the road improves and could be easily repaired, and near the HANSA LINE it is not much damaged.

Capt. Egerton R.E. deserves great credit for getting this work done satisfactorily, and for his excellent reconnaissances.

One of the Pioneer Companies was, on completion of their road work, sent forward to dig a supporting trench from R.13.c.6.8 across to the HANSA LINE facing North. This would have formed a less vulnerable front line than the Salient formed by the HANSA LINE and MILL trench, in the event of the Division on the BEAUCOURT bank being forced to fall back.

At 5.45 p.m. the remainder of 225th Field Company was sent up to carry on the trench. As all the officers of the Company, except 2/Lt Dibden were down with influenza or dugout fever, the duty of taking up the half company devolved on Lt Dibden who had only recently joined the company, and had been commissioned only in July. 2/Lt Dibden took his men up and carried out the work in spite of considerable shell fire.

He reported completing 300 yards of trench, 90 yards of which was 5 feet deep and remainder 3 feet. He was assisted part of the time by a party of the 1/1 Camb. Regt.

2/Lt Dibden deserves credit for the manner in which he performed his duties.

Lieut-Col R.E.
C.R.E. 39th Division.

Nov 17th 1916.

SECRET

HQ. 39th DIV. R.E. OPERATION ORDER No. 7.

23.11.16.

Reference 1/20,000 Map, Sheet 28.
and Trench Maps.

1. The 39th Division is to relive the 5th Belgian Division on the front C.7.c.05.60 to B.6.c.05.50 (Trench A.6 inclusive) by 12 m.n. Nov.30th/Dec 1st.

2. (a) The souþhern boundary of the new section is:-

CANAL BANK B.12.d.8.7 - Road junction B.12.d.3.4 - along road to Road Junction B.17.b.9.2 - Road Junction B.16.a.4.10 - South of road to Road Junction B.15.a.½.7 - B.9.c.0.0. - B.8.d.4.3. - B.8.c.6.0 - B.14.a.3½.7 to North of road to Road Junction A.18.d.3.8½. - Bridge A.16.b.6.8½. along road to A.10.a.3.5 - Cross Roads A.9.a.1.4½. - Southern and Western Edges of Wood A.8.b. and thence as shown on billeting map.

(b) The Northern boundary (between the VIII Corps and the 5th BELGIAN Division) is :-

B.6.c.½.5 (junction of trenches A.6 and A.7) - BOYAU DE LA CHAPELLE (inclusive to VIII Corps) - road at D.5.d.7.1 - junction of trenches 0.5 and 0.6 at B.11.a.7.7 - road at B.11.a. 2.6½.-cross roads at B.10.b.1.3½.- BOYAU DE BOESINGHE at B.9.b.8.0 - road at B.9.a.2.3½. - B.8.b.6.3½. - B.8.b.6.0 to B.8.c.0.9 - road junction at B.7.c.5.7½.-along north side of road to road junction at A.12.c.5.2 thence along west side of road to road junction A.18.d.3.8½.

3. (a) The 118th Infantry Brigade (less 1 Battalion) is to relieve the French 79th Territorial Regiment and one Battalion of the French 80th Territorial Regiment on the 29th and 30th November and night 30th Nov/1st Dec. on the above front under arrangements to be made direct between Brigadier-General FINCH HATTON, C.M.G., D.S.O. Commanding 118th Infantry Brigade and Lieut-Colonel. MORIN PONS, Commanding 79th Territorial Regiment (Headquarters at FERME DU BLEUET B.10.c.2.2).

(b) The Brigadier-General Commanding 118th Infantry Brigade will detail one Battalion to be attached to 114th Infantry Brigade (Headquarters C.25.d.2.4) 38th Division (Headquarters ST.SIXTE A.1.d.2.3).

(c) Moves will take place in accordance with the March Table.

(d) On completion of relief on the night Nov.30th/Dec.1st The Command of the Section will pass to Brigadier-General Commanding 118th Infantry Brigade, and the 118th Infantry Brigade will come under the Command of G.O.C. 38th Division, and will be disposed as follows :-

(1) Brigade H.Q. - ELVERDINGHE CHATEAU.

(2) 1 Battalion front line, H.Q. BOESINGHE CHATEAU.

(3) 1 Battalion Support, H.Q. FERME DU BLEUET (B.10.c.3.4.).

(4) 1 Battalion lent to 38th Division to replace 10th Welsh R.

(5(1 Battalion in L Defences H.Q. MACHINE GUN FARM.
1 Company ELVERDINGHE½
2 Companies L.8 (garrison of L.10 to be found by these companies).

2 Platoons L.2.
2 Platoons L.4.

(6)	Machine Gun Company	) In the area West of ELVERDINGHE) now occupied by the Reserve
(7)	Stokes Mortar Battery	) Battalion of the 79th French) Regiment. Billets to be allotted
(8)	234th Field Coy. R.E	) by A.A. & Q.M.G. 39th Division.

(9) Advanced Dressing Station - FERME 1889 (Road junction B.9.c.½.2½.)

Remainder of Field Ambulance, if required, in the area West of ELVERDINGHE.

4. (a) The 234th Field Coy. R.E. will be attached to the 118th Infantry Brigade under the orders of C.R.E. 38th Division.

(b) The O.C. 234th Field Coy. R.E. will take over from Lieut-Colonel BONNET, Royal Begian Engineers (at DE WIPPE CABARET) the programme of work (both administrative and tactical) under construction and proposed in the new Section, paying special attention to all work in connection with drainage.

5. Completion of relief will be reported by wire to C.R.E. 39th Division and repeated to C.R.E. 38th Division.

6. 39th Divisional Headquarters and C.R.E. Headquarters remain at ESQUELBECQ. 38th Division Headquarters is at ST.SIXTE.

7. ACKNOWLEDGE.

sd. L.E.Hopkins, Lt-Col R.E.
C.R.E. 39th Division.

Copies issued to
234th Field Coy. R.E.
C.R.E. 38th Division.
H.Q. 39th Division.
War Diary.

120/B. E

SECRET

O.C.225th Field Coy R.E.

Your Company will take over from 151st Field Company R.E. of 38th Division in line on 1/12/16.

Their H.Q. and horse ~~lines~~ and wagon lines are at A.28.central, Sheet 28.

Send advance party there as early as possible on 1/12/16. Main body to be at same place by 4 p.m. Sappers of 3 sections to be ready to march another 5 miles that evening.

You will come under orders of C.R.E. 38th Division as soon as you report at A.28.central.

Hand over present work on Camps to respective Camp Commandants.

You will continue to draw rations from same dump until further orders.

Report completion of move to this office.

sd. C.H.Egerton, Capt R.E.
A/C.R.E. 39th Division.

30/11/16.

Copies to C.R.E.38th Div.
C.E. 8th Corps.
"Q" 39th Div.
"G" 39th Div.
War Diary.

SECRET.

29.10.16.

H.Q. 39TH DIVISION R.E. OPERATION ORDER NO. 5.

Reference attached Sketch Map.
and 1/10,000 Map, Sheets 57D NE & SE.

1. (a). The Reserve Army will make a general attack on the line PYS - SERRE at Zero hour on November 1st (Z day).

(b). The II Corps is to attack Northwards and to capture MIRAUMONT, the line of the MIRAUMONT - BEAUCOURT SUR ANCRE Road, to South of the BOIS D'HOLLANDE and thence South Westwards, the crossings over the R.ANCRE.

(c). The V Corps is attacking Eastwards North of the ANCRE with a view to seizing the line BEAUREGARD DOVECOTE (L.28.c) - SERRE (inclusive).

2. (A). The main objective of the 39th Division is the line of the River ANCRE from R.8.c.2.0 to Q.24.b.1.3 and the crossings at THE MILL (R.13.a.2.7) and BRIDGE ROAD (Q.18.b.85.40). This objective is to be gained by Zero plus 1 hour 40 minutes.

(b). The dividing line between the 19th Division and the 39th Division is the line R.19.d.9.9 - R.14.c.2.1 - R.8.c.3.3.

(c). The dividing line between the 39th Division and the 63rd Division is the line of the River ANCRE.

3. (a). The attack will be carried out by the 118th Infantry Brigade reinforced by one Battalion from each of the 116th and 117th Infantry Brigades and assisted by a subsidiary attack by 1 Battalion of the 117th Infantry Brigade.

(b). The area of attack of the 39th Division will be divided into 3 subsidiary objectives:-

Objective A.	Group of trenches R.19.b.9.7. R.19.b.9.6 - 6.4 - 2.4 - 5.6. and the line R.19.a.6.3 - R.19.c.3.8 - R.19.c.1.6.	To be captured by Zero plus 4 mins. ~~18~~
Objective B.	Line of SERB ROAD from R.13.d.6.9 - R.19.a.6.8 - 4.5 - 0.4 - Q.24.b.9.0 - 95.00 - Q.24.d.8.7.	To be captured by Zero plus 18 minutes.
Objective C.	The line of the GRANDCOURT - ST.PIERRE DIVION - HAMEL Road from R.13.b.3.5 to Q.24.b.1.1.	To be captured by Zero plus 28 minutes.

4. (a). O.C. 225th Field Coy R.E. will place one section at disposal of 118th Infantry Brigade to assist in the consolidation of strong points in the HANSA LINE.

O.C. 225th Field Coy R.E. will ask instructions from the 118th Infantry Brigade forthwith.

(b). 227th Field Coy R.E. with its vehicles will be in reserve about W.5.a.7.8 ready to move forward via HAMEL and repair the HAMEL - ST.PIERRE DIVION - GRANDCOURT Road.

(c). 225th Field Coy R.E. (less 1 section) and 234th Field Coy R.E. will remain in their bivouacs ready to move at half an hour's notice.

(d). The 13th Gloucester Regt (Pioneers) will be in Divisional Reserve about Q.35.c.8.4 and will be prepared to move forward with 4 G.S. wagons loaded with road metal, to repair the HAMEL - ST.PIERRE DIVION - GRANDCOURT Road.

5. Three Tanks have been allotted to the 39th Division and will move as shewn on the map (copy attached).

6. Steps will be taken to ensure that every man has his iron ration and water bottle filled, before proceeding to assembly positions.

4

Sheet 2.

7. All prisoners of war will be sent to 118th Infantry Brigade Headquarters at PAISLEY DUMP and thence to 39th Division Prisoners Cage at Q.35.d.4.8.

8. 39th Division Headquarters R.E. remain at W.7.b.3.1.

9. ZERO hour will be notified later.

10. ACKNOWLEDGE.

Lieut-Col R.E.
C.R.E. 39th Division.

Copies issued to:-
225 Field Coy R.E.
227th "
234th "
13th Gloucester Regt.
H.Q. 39th Div. (2).
File. 118 INF BDE

OPERATION TRENCH MAP
St Pierre Divion

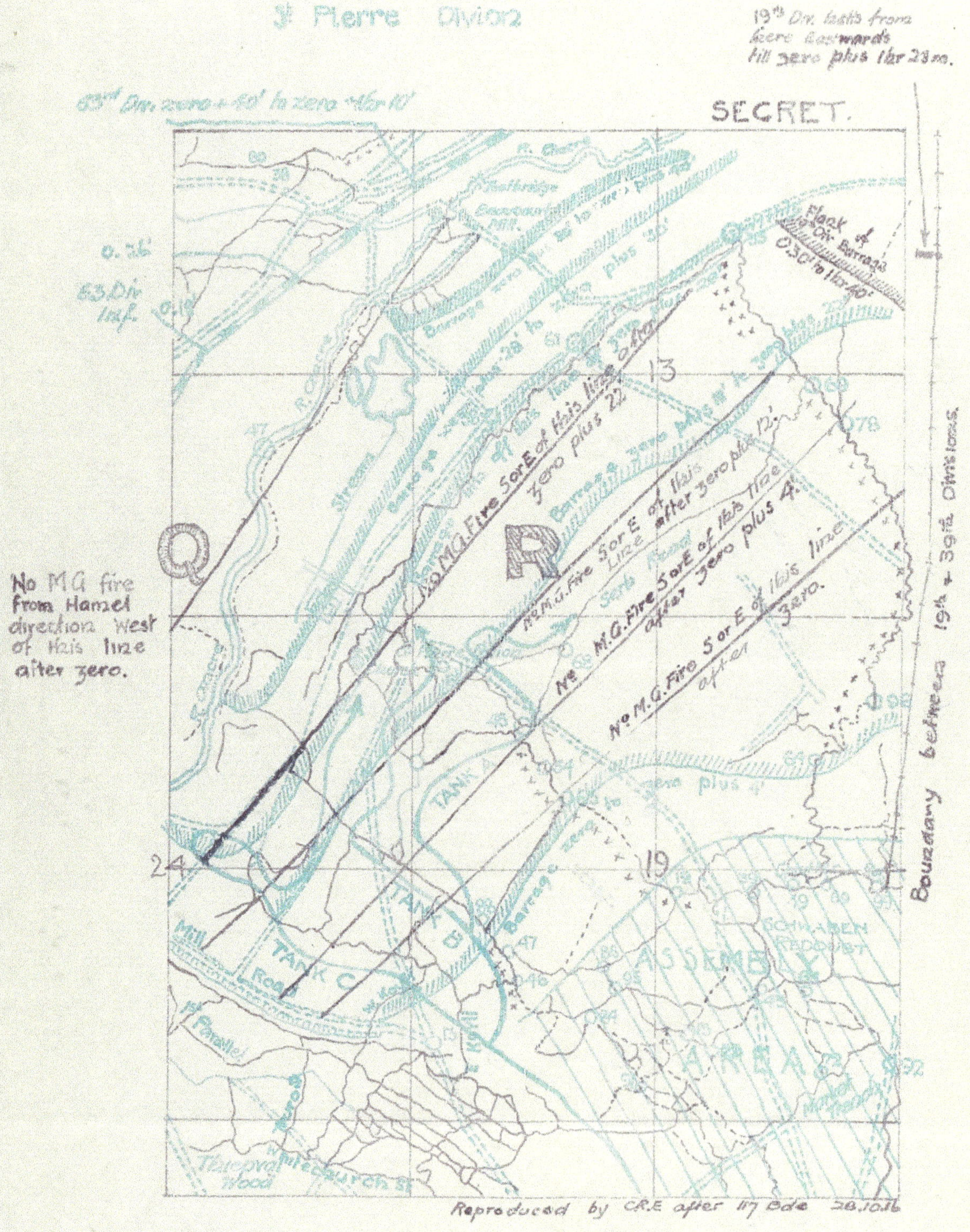

SCALE 1:10,000.

REFERENCE

Principle Artillery Barrage Lines
Tank Routes
Limits of M.G. FIRE. ALL M.G. Fire on 39 Div. Area of Attack will cease at zero plus 25'.

4

SECRET

H.Q. 39TH DIVISION R.E. OPERATION ORDER NO. 6.

12/11/16.

1. (a) The Operations referred to in H.Q. 39th Div R.E. Operation Order No. 5 and amendments, will now be carried out by stages.
Operation Order No. 5 will hold good except for minor alterations given in this Order.
(b) On "Z" day the 19th and 39th Divisions of the II Corps will capture the line R.21.a.5.7 - R.20.b.8.9 - R.14.c.2.1 - R.13.b.4.6.-MILL at R.13.a.2.7 and the crossing at Q.18.b.85.40.
The V Corps will seize the general line of the BEAUCOURT ROAD and SERRE.
(c) In certain eventualities a further stage may be taken at a later hour on "Z" Day but more probably on "Z" plus 2 day.

2. (a) The main objective of the 39th Division is the HANSA LINE from R.14.c.2.1 to R.13.b.4.6; and on the capture of this objective a line roughly parallel to it facing East North East will be consolidated and held.
The 39th Division will also occupy the MILL at R.13.a.2.7. and the crossing at Q.18.b.85.40.
(b) The dividing line between the 19th and 39th Divisions is the line R.19.d.9.9. to R.14.c.2.1.
(c) The outline Time Table of the 63rd Division will be communicated to those concerned later.

3. O.C. 227th Field Company R.E. will arrange to keep in touch with Bde.Hd.Qrs. at PASSERELLE DE MAGENTA either personally or by orderly on "Z" day.

4. O.C. 13th Gloucester R. will withdraw all outlying working parties, except those with C.R.E. and the patrol of 1 Officer and 25 men on the tramway.

5. Field Companies will parade as strong as possible, leaving only the minimum number of men actually required for pumping and for guards on surplus baggage and stores.

6. Units will not load up their pontoons till ordered but keep bridging wagons to send up materials for consolidation of ST.PIERRE DIVION if ordered.

7. Headquarters of 116th Infantry Brigade will be at PASSERELLE DE MAGENTA.
Headquarters of 117th Infantry Brigade will be at AUTHUILLE NORTH BLUFFS.
Headquarters of 118th Infantry Brigade will be at PAISLEY DUMP.

8. 2 lorries from C.R.E's dump will be placed at disposal of O.C. 13th Glouc. R. at Q.35.c.8.4. at Zero plus ½ hour for road metalling.

ACKNOWLEDGE ✓

1 Copy to AQ.

[signature]
Lieut-Colonel R.E.
C.R.E. 39th Division.

Copies issued at a.m. to:-

225 F/Coy R.E.	116th Inf Bde.
227 F/Coy R.E.	117th Inf Bde.
234 F/Coy R.E.	118th Inf Bde.
13th Glouc. R.	Divl. Headquarters.
War Diary ½	File.

Vol 10

CONFIDENTIAL.

W A R D I A R Y

F O R

39th Divisional R.E.

FROM 1st December TO 31st December 1916.

CONFIDENTIAL.

Vol

W A R   D I A R Y

FOR

HEADQUARTERS 39TH DIVISIONAL R.E.

FROM 1st December 1916 TO 31st December 1916.

Instructions regarding War Diaries and Intelligence Summaries are contained in F. S. Regs., Part II. and the Staff Manual respectively. Title pages will be prepared in manuscript.

WAR DIARY
or
INTELLIGENCE SUMMARY.
(Erase heading not required.)

Army Form C. 2118.

H.Q. 39 DIV. R.E.

Place	Date	Hour	Summary of Events and Information	Remarks and references to Appendices
	DEC.			
ESQUELBECQ	1.	MORNING.	A/C.R.E. visited site of rifle-range at FORET DE TOURNEHEM.	
		AFTER-NOON	A/C.R.E. attended VIII Corps Conference. — Weather - Fine. W.W.G.	
	2	MORNING.	A/C.R.E. visited 227 Fd. Co. R.E.	
		AFTER-NOON	A/C.R.E. attended VIII Corps Conference. — Weather - Fine + cold. W.W.G.	
	3.		A/C.R.E. visited rifle-range, at FORET DE TOURNEHEM, with Major TANNER of 2nd Army H.Q.rs — Weather - Fine + cold. W.W.G.	
	4.		A/C.R.E visited new Div. Laundry at WORMHOUDT - Weather cold + unsettled W.W.G.	
	5.		A/C.R.E. visited rifle-range with Major TANNER of 2nd Army H.Qrs. Weather cold + unsettled W.W.G.	
	6.		A/C.R.E. ~~visited~~ with Major ~~Lord~~ DUNMORE, G.S.O.2., visited the 39th DIV. SCHOOLS at VOLKERINGHOVE. Weather. Unsettled + cloudy. W.W.G.	
	7.		A/C.R.E. visited new DIV. LAUNDRY at WORMHOUDT. Weather. Showery. W.W.G. C.R.E. returned from leave + A/C.R.E. returned to his unit.	
	8.		C.R.E. visited old DIVL. LAUNDRY at WORMHOUDT. Weather. Showers at intervals W.W.G.	
	9.		C.R.E. visited C.R.E. 38th DIV. and made arrangements for taking over. Orders to move issued to 227 Fd. Co. R.E. Weather. Showers at intervals. W.W.G.	A

W.W. Gillespie [illegible]
ADJT. 39TH DIV. R.E. for CRE

Instructions regarding War Diaries and Intelligence Summaries are contained in F. S. Regs., Part II. and the Staff Manual respectively. Title pages will be prepared in manuscript.

WAR DIARY
or
INTELLIGENCE SUMMARY.
(Erase heading not required.)

Army Form C. 2118.

H. Q. 39 DIV. R.E.

Place	Date	Hour	Summary of Events and Information	Remarks and references to Appendices
	DEC			
ESQUELBECQ	10		C.R.E. visited II Army rifle range FORET DE TOURNEHEM. Weather - Unsettled.	W.W.G.
"	11.		C.R.E. prepared handing over of work in Corps Reserve Area to C.R.E. 38 DIV.	W.W.G.
ST. SIXTE BELGIUM.	12.		C.R.E. proceeded to COUVENT DES TRAPPISTES at STE. SIXTE, BELGIUM to take over work from C.R.E. 38th DIV. + visits trenches of new sector.	W.W.G.
	13.		C.R.E. takes over R.E. work from C.R.E. 38 DIV. + visits trenches of sector.	W.W.G.
	14.		39 DIV. H.Q. moved to STE. SIXTE. + opened at 11 A.M. C.R.E. employed in office work.	W.W.G.
	15.		C.R.E. employed in going over Office Work.	W.W.G.
	16.		C.R.E. employed in going over office work.	W.W.G.
	17.		C.R.E. visited C.E. VIII Corps. and Div. R.E. PARK. at PESELHOEK.	W.W.G.
	18.		C.R.E. visited trenches.	W.W.G.
	19.		C.R.E. attended Board of Enquiry at VIII Corps H.Q. to investigate circumstances leading to men being gassed after blowing up of 'camouflet' ~~at~~ in BRIELEN Sector.	W.W.G.
	20.		C.R.E. attended to Office Work.	
	21.		C.R.E. attended to Office Work.	
	22.		C.R.E. + D.A.Q.M.G., 39 Div. visited trenches.	W.W.G.
	26.		C.R.E visited trenches.	W.W.G.

W.W. Gillespie LtRE.
ADJT. 38TH DIV. R.E. ~~for~~ for C.R.E.

T2134. Wt. W708–776. 500000. 4/15. Sir J. C. & S.

Instructions regarding War Diaries and Intelligence Summaries are contained in F. S. Regs., Part II. and the Staff Manual respectively. Title pages will be prepared in manuscript.

WAR DIARY
or
INTELLIGENCE SUMMARY.
(Erase heading not required.)

Army Form C. 2118.

H.Q. 39 DIV. R.E.

Place	Date	Hour	Summary of Events and Information	Remarks and references to Appendices
	DEC.			
ST. SIXTE.	26.		C.R.E. visited trenches W.W.G.	
BELGIUM	28.		— ditto — W.W.G.	
	30.		— ditto — W.W.G.	
	31.		C.R.E. visited DIV. R.E. PARK. at PESELHOEK. W.W.G.	

W.W. Gillespie Lt R.E.
ADJT. 39TH DIV. R.E.
for C.R.E.
2 1/17.

HEADQUARTERS 39TH DIV. R.E. OPERATION ORDER No. 8.

(A)

Map Sheet 28 1/40,000 BELGIUM & PART OF FRANCE.

9/12/16.

1. The 39th Division is to relieve the 38th Division, commencing 11th December.
The 115th Infantry Brigade and 123 Field Co.R.E. will be attached to 39th Division in the left section.

2. Till further orders the 123, 225 and 234 Field Cos. R.E. will carry on with the work now in their charge. 123 Field Co.R.E. in the right Brigade area, 234 Field Co.R.E. in the left Brigade area, and 225 Field Co.R.E. in the Reserve Area.

3. The 227th Field Co.R.E. will relieve the 124 Field Co.R.E. in the centre section (117 Brigade area) by 9 p.m. on Dec. 13th.

4. The 227 Field Co.R.E. will march from LEDRINGHEM to billets at A.15.b.5.9 on December 12th and move Headquarters and 3 sections to CANAL BANK C.19.c.2.3. on evening of Dec. 13th.

5. O.C. 227 Field Co.R.E. will take an advance party of 2 Officers and 6 N.C.Os. and men to go over the trenches; they will proceed direct to CANAL BANK dugouts on Dec. 12th.

6. Arrangements will be made by O.C. 227 Field Co.R.E. to carry on works without a break.

7. Receipts will be given for all trench stores, tools and materials, maps, plans &c, muster sheets of local labour.

8. C.R.E. 38th Division will replace any 38th Division R.E. labour in PESELHOEK Workshops with men from the 123, 225, and 234 Field Cos.R.E.

9. Lieut. Morgan R.E. will remain in charge of PESELHOEK Worhshops. Lieut. Reece & Interpreter VANDAMME will report to him for orders on Dec. 13th.

10. Headquarters 39th Divl. R.E. will open at ST.SIXTE on December 14th at 11 a.m.

11. O.C. 227 Field Co.R.E. will hand over billets at LEDRINGHEM and work on Laundry at WORMHOUDT to a N.C.O. from 38th Division on Dec. 13th and will leave a N.C.O. and 10 men for the work on Divisional School at VOLKERINCKHOVE till further orders.

12. Report completion of reliefs and moves by wire to C.R.E.

13. ACKNOWLEDGE.

M.M. Pellingen [?] Lt. R.E.
ADJT. 39TH DIV. R.E.
for Lt-Col R.E.
C.R.E. 39th Division.

Copies issued to
- C.R.E. 38th Div. (4)
- 227 Field Co.R.E. (1)
- Headquarters 39th Div. (2).
- War Diary (2)
- File. (1).

Vol XI

C O N F I D E N T I A L.

WAR DIARY.

for

39th DIVISION R.E.

from

JANUARY 1st 1917 to JANUARY 31st 1917.

C O N F I D E N T I A L.

WAR DIARY

for

HEAD QUARTERS 39th DIVISION.R.E.

from

JANUARY 1st 1917 to JANUARY 31st 1917.

Instructions regarding War Diaries and Intelligence Summaries are contained in F. S. Regs., Part II. and the Staff Manual respectively. Title pages will be prepared in manuscript.

WAR DIARY
or
INTELLIGENCE SUMMARY.
(Erase heading not required.)

Army Form C. 2118.

H.Q. 39 DIV. R.E.

Place	Date	Hour	Summary of Events and Information	Remarks and references to Appendices
	JAN 1917			
ST SIXTE BELGIUM	3		C.R.E visited R.E. Yard. PESELHOEK.	WWG
	4		C.R.E. visited trenches.	WWG
	5		C.R.E. visited trenches.	WWG
	9.		C.R.E. visited trenches.	WWG
			39 Div. Secret Order No 89 received detailing moves of units of Division 12th/17th January [illegible] Fd. Coys. to move on 12th 13th + 14th insts. to YPRES area. C.R.E. Orders No 9. issued in accordance.	A
	10		C.R.E. visited Div. Schools VOLKERINCKHOVE.	WWG
	12.		C.R.E proceeded to HAMHOEK to take over R.E. work in YPRES area from C.R.E. 55 DIV. + visited trenches of new area.	WWG
	13.		C.R.E. 38 DIV took over present area from C.R.E. 39 Div.	WWG
	14.		C.R.E. 38 DIV visited trenches of present area with C.R.E. 39 DIV.	WWG
	15.		DIV. HD. QRS. moved from ST SIXTE to HAMHOEK. Closed at former + opened at latter at 10 A.M.	WWG
HAMHOEK BELGIUM.	16.	MORN.	C.R.E. 39th DIV. visited trenches in new area.	WWG
		AFTN.	C.R.E. attended Corps Conference concerning general routine + trench warfare	

W.W. [illegible] ADJT. 39TH DIV. R.E. for C.R.E.

T2134. Wt. W708-776. 500000. 4/15. Sir J. C. & S.

Instructions regarding War Diaries and Intelligence Summaries are contained in F. S. Regs., Part II. and the Staff Manual respectively. Title pages will be prepared in manuscript.

WAR DIARY or INTELLIGENCE SUMMARY.

(Erase heading not required.)

Army Form C. 2118.

H.Q. 39 DIV. R.E.

Place	Date	Hour	Summary of Events and Information	Remarks and references to Appendices
HAMHOEK	18		C.R.E. visited trenches.	
BELGIUM	20		C.R.E. visited trenches.	
	21		C.R.E. indisposed. Unable to attend to duty, under M.Os. orders. Lt. H M S MEARES 227 F/Co. R.E. reported for duty as Acting Adjutant. Severe frost.	
	22		C.R.E. indisposed.	
	23.		C.R.E. better - attended to business in his room.	
	24.		C.R.E. attended Office. Adjt. (Lt. W.M. GILLESPIE R.E.) went on a Course to 116 Inf Bde as Staff learner. Capt. W. MACKESY R.E. 227 F/Co. reported Heavy Branch, M.G.C., Bermicourt.	
	25.		C.R.E. attended Corps Conference. A/Adjt. to bed under M.Os. orders.	
	26.		C.R.E. visited site of New Div. Baths WORMHOUDT with AA+QMG and inspected work at 39th Div. Schools, being carried on by Lt. Macrae, 227 Co. R.E. A/Adjt. indisposed.	
	27.		C.R.E. visited F/Coy. Hdqrs YPRES and trenches. A/Adjt. indisposed.	
	28.		C.R.E. attended to office work. A/Adjt. indisposed. Major J.C.I. WOOD withdrawn from 234 F/Co. after handing over command of Coy to Lieut. W.H. KIRBY R.E. Major Wood temporarily attached C.R.E. Hdqrs.	
	29.		CRE visited MGE's in West Lane + up to BIRR Cross Road + Hellfire Corner with Corps M.G. Officer.	

[signature] Lt. Col. R.E. CRE 39 Div

T2134. Wt. W708-776. 500000. 4/15. Sir J. C. & S.

Instructions regarding War Diaries and Intelligence Summaries are contained in F. S. Regs., Part II. and the Staff Manual respectively. Title pages will be prepared in manuscript.

WAR DIARY
or
INTELLIGENCE SUMMARY.
(Erase heading not required.)

Army Form C. 2118.

Place	Date	Hour	Summary of Events and Information	Remarks and references to Appendices
HAMHOOK	30.		Severe frost has now continued since 21st and the ground is frozen 18ins deep, no earthwork or wiring is possible owing to hard ground great trouble keeping pumps going to clear deep dugouts. orders issued to deal with this. Some snow in evening + less frost.	1
	31		slight thaw in sun in day time.	
			orders issued for guidance to infantry interested in making CT.s + patrolling trenches + drains attached	
			8 lorries of wiring material sent up nightly to forward dumps since 28th.	
			A platoon of Pioneers put on to make fascines at St Sixte on 29th.	
			Copy of letter re concrete work in relation to dugouts is attached	47/C 31/1

Headquarters,
39th Division.

DISTRIBUTION OF WORK IN RIGHT DIVISION AREA.

1. RIGHT BRIGADE AREA.

225th Field Coy.R.E.

1 Section assisting infantry in reclaiming front line and wiring it, and maintaining all C.Ts and trenches in use or occupied and in charge of Bridges round YPRES, and electric lighting and water supply from Moat.

2 Sections on M.G.E's etc, under C.R.E. Dug-outs in MENIN ROAD etc.

1 Section on Workshops at rear billet.

1 Company Pioneers deepening MUDDY LANE to 6 feet depth from CAMBRIDGE ROAD upwards and reclaiming MUD TRENCH, and maintaining and patrolling drains.

2. LEFT BRIGADE AREA

234th Field Coy.R.E.

1 Section assisting Infantry reclaiming front line and CAMBRIDGE ~~XXXX~~ TRENCH and maintaining all C.Ts and trenches used or occupied; also in charge of Canal Bridges and electric lighting, and thickening up JOHN STREET and wiring.

2 Sections on M.G.E's and deep dug-outs etc, under C.R.E.

1 Section on workshops ets, at back billet.

1 Company Pioneers completing Strand extensionto Front Line and maintaining and extending drains.

3 The Infantry Brigades in line will obtain R.E. materials through the Field Companies who will be supplied with transport from Divisional Ammunition Column for carrying to forward dumps.

4. The repair of ST JEAN AND POTIJZE road will be undertaken with Belgian labour attached to 234th Field Coy.R.E.

5. The Pioneers Companies working in forward ares as detailed above, will be under orders of O.C. Field Coy in Brigade Area. They will detail carpenters if necessary to assist in making up their materials in the Field Coy workshop. They will not be moved from work detailed above, without reference to C.R.E.

6. Field Companies will arrange with Brigades for necessary permanent loading parties at their dumps, and for carrying parties for their work.

7. Brigades with help of Field Coys C.O. will submit at once programme of special works they propose to complete during their tour in the line, e.g. wire, reclaiming trenches as outlined above, programme should state exact location of work and number of yards to be done. Brigades will make their own arrangements for maintenance and repair parties, and for carrying parties for R.E.works.

8. RESERVE BRIGADE AREA.

227th Field Coy. R.E.

1 Section at Divisional Schools.
1 Section on Artillery work.
1 Section on Camps and Horse Standings.
1 Section on Workshopx.

1 Company Pioneers - ½ at Divisional Schools & Laundries.
½ on Divisional work in rear Camps.

1 Company Pioneers on "X" Line and rear drainage, up to old "X" line.

9. 227th Field Coy will provide materials for Pioneers working on "X" Line and Camps.

10. 2 Lorries per Field Coy for carrying materials, they will rendezvous daily at Corps Park at 9 a.m.

11 Field Companies and Artillery will indent on C.R.E. by 7 p.m. for next day's requirements and C.R.E. will allot the stores available for the Division equally between the Field Companies and Artillery.

12 Pioneers will detail patrols, who patrol all drains daily.

Jan 13th 1917.

(sd) L.E.Hopkins.
Lt-Col.R.E.
C.R.E. 39th Division.

473/B.

O.C. 225th Field Coy.R.E.
O.C. 234th Field Coy.R.E.

Please arrange with Brigades for parties for maintenance of Duckboards and drainage of C.Ts as follows;-

WEST LANE. 2 men RED CHATEAU to SOUTH LANE.
2 men SOUTH LANE toBECK STREET.
2 men BECK STREET to FRONT LINE.
3 men BECK STREET & MUDDY LANE.

PICCADILLY 2 men new "X" line to PICCADILLY switch.
2 men PICCADILLY switch to Front Line.

HAYMARKET. 2 men POTJZE road to BELLEWARDE BECK.
2 men BELLEWARDE BECK to Front line.

GARDEN ST. 2 men.

NEW JOHN ST.2 men.

Each party will keep trenchboards repaired,and drains clear.

Each party will have written orders what are their duties,where to get materials and tools (saw,hammer,shovel, nails,slats).

Party will report to O.C. Field Coy daily that work is all correct,at 5 p.m.or will inform if extensive repairs are wanted and how many men will be required.

Jan 15.1917

(sd) L.E.Hopkins.
Lt.-Col.R.E.
C.R.E. 39th Division.

225th Field Coy. R.E.

One Officer and platoon of the Pioneer Coy, in the Right Brigade Area will attend to drains in your Brigade area in front of "X" line. The Officer will report to you daily Each party will patrol its beat daily.

Each man requires a shovel and gum boots. Gauge readings will be reported daily.

When trenches are flooded, they should report when and where and how deep. They will clear all blocks and when there are no blocks they will improve their drains.

They will report when they require assistance.

Drains.	Party.
BELLEWAARDE BEEK. HAYMARKET to OUTPOST FARM.	4 men.
Drain from I.4.c.7.1 to I.10.d.5.4. with branches into SOUTH LANE.	2 men
Branches from BECK STREET & MUD LANE into the BELLEWAARDE BEEK.	2 men
Drains from CAMBRIDGE TRENCH & the gully in BELLEWAARDE BEEK between PICCADILLY & RAILWAY.	2 men
Drains from front line into BELLEWAARDE BEEK between PICCADILLY & HAYMARKET.	4 men
Drain behind Front line, HAYMARKET to the gully.	2 men
Remainder of Platoon will work as a party where drains specially need improvement.	

Please communicate these instructions to the Officer in command. of the Company.

Any corrections to map should be reported to C.R.E. and patrols adjusted.

Jan 17.1917.

(sd) L.E.Hopkins
Lt-Col.R.E.
C.R.E. 39th Division.

DIVISIONAL PROGRAMME OF WORK.

INSTRUCTIONS FOR No 4 PARTY.

EXTENSION CAMBRIDGE TRENCH NORTH FROM PICCADILLY.

This trench will be constructed 4 feet deep below ground and 4' 6" above ground using the 4 feet type of "U" frame with corrigated iron sheets below, and 4 feet revetting hurdles above ground.

There will be a traffic trench behind along the existing road drain, and firebays in front.

The corrugated iron shelters will be placed in the back trench 12" above the trench boards. The "U" frames will be placed 2' 6" apart. The work will be carried out in the following manner;-

Where the site is in view of German lines, the R.E. party of, 1 N.C.O and 6 men will set up a screen of camouflage material about 50 yards long and 6 yards from the existing drain; they will clear the drain from PICCADILLY till the required depth of 4 feet in the drain can be obtained, and then block the road-side drain above the work to prevent water flowing along it to where the work ~~the work~~ is ging on. They will see that anchorage wires and pickets are fixe d in the parapet and traverses, the ends of wires being attached to small pickets along the edges of the trenches where they can be found when wanted.

Ancherage wires to be 4 strands of plain wire twisted together.

Lieut-Col.R.E.
C.R.E. 39th Division.

Jan.19.1917.

(C O P Y)

A Table of Work on following lines will be prepared by Infantry Officer in charge.

Day.	Time.	Inf. Party.	Operations.
1st day.	9 am.	1 Inf. Off i/c of work with 1 R.E. Off & a few men	Visits site of work and sets out trace of 1 firebay and 2 traverses. R.E. party erect screens and see to drainage.
	4.30pm	60 men (carrying party)	Rendezvous MENIN GATE. Proceed to R.E. dump MENIN Road, pick up and carry up to work 20 "U" frames (4ft.), 10 trenchboards, 40 sheets Corr. Iron, 20 strong pickets (3ft long & 4"dia) and anchorage wires, 1 Baby Elephant complete (dug-out), and with help of 2 R.E's fix anchorage. They must take a written order for material.
2nd day.	8 am.	1 Off & 12 Inf.	Rendezvous at MENIN GATE and proceed to trench "A-B" which they excavate to a depth of 3 ft, throwing earth in front, leaving site for Baby Elelphant clear.
	12 noon	12 more Inf 4 men.	Complete excavation. Prepare the Baby Elephant for erection and trenchboards for foundations of it.
	4 pm.	3 men	Excavate site for baby elephant.
	4.30pm	60 men (carrying party)	Rendezvous at MENIN GATE, proceed to R.E. Dump and take up to site of work 16 "U" frames, (4ft), 8 trench boards, 20 revetting frames (4' x3') 30 sheets corrug, iron 160 feet of 4" x 2" timber.
	8 pm.	7 men	Lay trenchboards as floor for baby elephant and erect dug-out and cover with earth.
3rd day	8 am.	1 Off & 12 Inf & 2 R.E.	Proceed to work and set "U" frames & Corr, Iron and fix trench boards in back trench; R.E. see that they are correctly graded for which purpose they take Field Level & hammer & nails for fixing trench boards
	12 noon	6 Inf.	Start excavating firebay trench throwing earth over dug-out behind.

Day.	Time.	Inf .Party.	Operations.
3rd Day.	4 pm.	6 Inf. 18 "	Complete excavating Firebay. Erect and anchor back all the revetting frames on the front side of firebay & traverses.
	8 pm.	25 men	Remove screen and excavate borrow pit 20 ft in front & throw up parapet against the revetting frames.
	12 pm.	25 men	Continue of parapet earthing up from borrow pit.
4th Day.	8 am.	6 men	Fix "U" framing in the firebay and place revetting.
	12 noon	6 men	Fix trenchboarding and complete the revetting by adjusting earth at back.
	4 pm.	10 men	Fix revetting frames round the island traverse.
	4.30.pm.	30 men	Start carrying up as on first day.
	8 pm.	25 men	Continue earthing up the parapet and island traverse.
5th day.	8 am.	10 men	Make sandbag parados in front of dug-out entrance.
	12 noon.	12 men 12 men	Start first task as on second day above) on the next firebay previously set out " second " " " " " ") and prepared.
	4.30 pm.	25 men	Complete earthing up parapet of first bay.
	4.30 pm.	30 men	Complete carrying up as on first day.

INSTRUCTIONS FOR DEEPENING MUDDY LANE.

Commence at the East side of CAMBRIDGE ROAD where there is a drain which runs down to BELLEWAARDE BEEK. Start the first frame here so that the trench boards are 4½ feet below the general level of the ground deepening the draim down to the BEEK enough to allow this. The "U" Frames should be of the 6 feet type as sketch;-

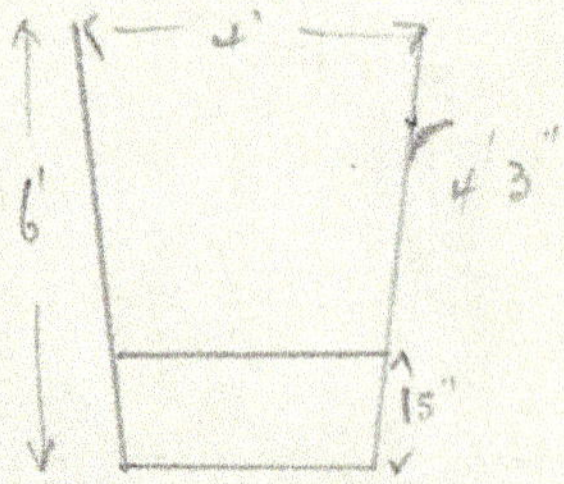

They will be placed 28 6" apart,centre to centre and each succeeding frame will be placed by Masons level ½" higher than the last (working towards the front line); a gauge for the purpose will be supplied to the parties as sketch;-

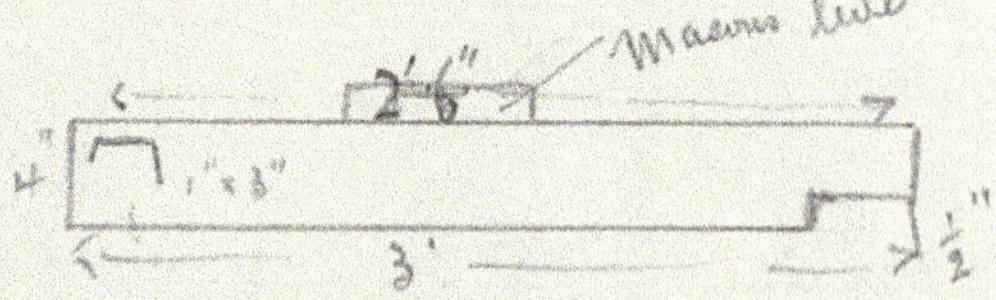

The work of sapping will be carried on continuously day and night in four reliefs.

Table of tasks,materials and parties.

Hour of arrival on work.	Materials.	Officers & Men	Task
6 a,m.	1 Trenchboard 2 "U" frames 4 sheets C.I. 3ft. long. 4 Revetting frames 3 ft. 4"nails,wire, 10.	1 Officer 6 diggers & revetters 6 carriers.	Excavate 60 c.f. and set 1 "U" frame Earth to be filled in bags used for revetting above the frames.
12 NOON.	Nil.	6 diggers & revetters.	Excavate 60 c.f. set 1 "U" frame & trench boards.
_ P.M.	2 Trenchboards. 4 "U" Frames 4 sheets C.I. 6 ft. 4 revetting panels 6 ft. 10. 4" nails.	1 Officer 6 diggers & revetters. 10 Carriers.	Excavate 120 c,f. set 2 "U" frames & 1 trench board.

12 mid)

Hour of arrival on work.	Materials	Officers & Men	Task.
12 mid-night.	Nil.	6 diggers	Excavate 120 c.f. set 2 "U" frames & 1 trench board

INSTRUCTION IN CONSOLIDATION.

Experience on the ANCRE proves that;-

1. A deep dug-out is the only form of strong point of value in continued bombardments. Therefore from strong points round captured deep dug-outs, several entrances are necessary as it is difficult to keep them open.

2. In conjunction with deep dug-outs fire positions are chosen for men and Lewis guns in the adjacent shell holes or depressions where there have been trenches.

3. It is inadvisable to throw up works under enemy observation, as they only attract artillery fire and expose to the enemy the exact position of troops, at which he can only otherwise guess.

If work can be done without attracting attention, it will probably be a matter of connecting up shell craters. Any trenches so dug will take the form shown in the drawing which is a post for 25 men.

The first task, which is carried out by the garrison, who are to hold the post, is a simple fire trench 3 feet deep with the earth thrown up on both sides. It is made zig zag on plan to obtain distribution of fire and men can fire in front or in rear. The flanks are defended by Lewis Guns. The work is done with the aid of shovels and sandbags, which are the only tools or materials available with the most advanced troops in an attack, for which this post is designed.

No R.E. or Pioneers will be there to assist you, and you will probably get no assistance at night, as all labour will be employed on trenches and dug-outs just behind you, under the protection afforded by your post, and in a position behind the crest out of view of the enemy.

Siting of these trenches will usually be where all the enemy artillery positions can be fully observed i,e, well in front of the crest overlooking enemy valleys. They will form a line of observation less well sited for resistance than a trench, which will be dug just behind the crest of the position.

This does not mean that the line of observation will be less well defended, but merely that it is necessary to hold such a line, although from a purely infantry point of view, a more retired line is more favourable for defence.

As soon as the first fire trench is completed the fire-bays can be deepened to 7 feet and a 7 feet trench carried round the traverses.

WIRING. Unless the captured position is to be held for some time, wiring will probably not be necessary or at least only certain areas will be wired which it is desired to deny to the enemy, and which would be avoidable at moment of our advance. For this purpose barbed wire Concertinas will be brought up at night and set out where required.

Jan. 28th 1917.

(sd) L.E.Hopkins.
Lt-Col.R.E.
C.R.E. 39th Division.

O.C. 225th Field Coy.R.E.
O.C. 234 th --do-

PUMPS FOR DUG-OUTS.

In continuation of previous instructions the common R.E. Lift & Force Pump is not suitable for this purpose.

The Wilcox, Semi Rotary will be used 2" size bolted to wall of dug-out and with screw iron piping for suction and delivery, the whole lagged with straw to prevent freezing, and provided with a cock to empty pipes which come to the surface.

1.2.17

(sd) L.F.Hopkins
Lt-Col.R.E.
C.R.E. 39th Division.

Head Quarters "G"
39th Division.

There has often been a great waste of labour and materials on M.G.E's and in this area alone I constructed in May and June 1916, three very strong emplacements which were carefully sited by proper authority and which are now abandoned.

I think it would be advisable to try and fix in a general way, what is practivable from an Engineering point of view, in the way of protection for Machine Guns and Crews, so that Machine Gun Officers may realise the difficulties.

As regards dug-outs, the deep tunnelled dug-out is the only form of prot ection from heavy artillery and should be practically always used unless there is difficulty with water.

Protection with concrete against anything over 5.9" is not possible, and nothing less than 3 feet of concrete or double two feet walls, will stop, even a 5.9". This means that a dug-out or emplacement will be 7 feet high above the floor and therefore a site must be chosen where the amount of cover can be obtained..

The smallest dug-out possible, strong enough to stop a 5.9" shell will contain 70 wagon loads of material and therefore it is not practicable to construct anything of this kind unless there is a tramway or road within 100 yards of the site. A design for a small concrete shelter is attached.

Any concrete work will not set hard enough to stand a 5.9" shell in less than two months at the earliest.

The use of concrete as protection against smaller shells is not worth the labour. The walls will need to be two feet thick and therefore a large amount of materialis required. Protection can be much more easily obtained by means of earth with a concrete burster. A design for an emplacement of this kind is attached.

Acting on these principles, a large number of concrete emplacemenets were sited and made in this area by the XIV Corps, near the Roads and Railways and Farm Buildings, known by their old numbers as 2a, 5d, in the railway bank, 10d at Dragoon Farm, 7d at Potijze and a number at St, Jean, Kaie, Salient and the ramparts. It is now proposed to site strong concrete shelters at I.10.1, I.10.2, I.11.6 in each case some distance from roads or railways, and I don't think it is a practical prpposition to use the labour necessary to make strong concrete shelters at these sites.

I.10.1 and I.10.2 should be resited near roads or d ep dug-outs should be made for them. I.11.6 can be got down deep enough with natural drainage; with 6 feet of earth cover and a burster of bricks from Witteport Farm, a satisfactory shelter can be obtained.

31.1.17

(sd) L.E.Hopkins.
Lieut-Col.R.E.
C.R.E. 39th Division

O.C. 225th Field Coy.R.E.
O.C. 234th Field Coy. R.E.

PUMPS AND PUMPING DEEP DUG-OUTS.

---

1. Before handing over to Machine Gunners, pumps should be fixed and provided with iron discharge pipes, well protected from frost and with cocks to empty them.

2. A sump is required to hold 4 hours soakage,

3. If the pumping is continuous spare pumps must be always ready, equal to the number in use.

4. The pumps provided must be able to cope with the water, pumping not more than half the time.

5. If machine gunners do not provide enough men to pump, it should be reported at once to Brigade.

6. Before handing over to machine gunners, written orders as to number of pumps to be used, number of men required and number of hours to be pumped daily, must be posted at the pump.

7. An R.E. party sufficiently strong to maintain all the pumps (and not less than one fitter and one plumber per two pumps) will be detailed by the Field Company, to the sole use only of maintaining the pumps in running order.

8. If Petrol pumps are installed a permanent driver is required to be detailed by Brigade, and no spare petrol may be stored in the dug-out. Only the petrol in the tank to be permitted in the dug-out.

(sd) L.E.Hopkins.
Lt-Col.R.E.
C.R.E. 39th Division.

Vol 12

W A R   D I A R Y

---of---

C. R. E., 39th D I V I S I O N .

From February 1st 1917.

To February 28th 1917.

------0------

Instructions regarding War Diaries and Intelligence Summaries are contained in F. S. Regs., Part II. and the Staff Manual respectively. Title pages will be prepared in manuscript.

WAR DIARY
or
~~INTELLIGENCE SUMMARY.~~
(Erase heading not required.)

Army Form C. 2118.

39 Div HQ. RE.

Place	Date	Hour	Summary of Events and Information	Remarks and references to Appendices
	February			
HAMHOEK	1.		CRE visited 116 Brigade lines in morning + Field Co YPRES in afternoon + work on Bellewaarde Beek in evening.	
	2.		Hard frost continues. Adjutant went to Dunkerque about materials. 12° Fahr	
	3.		CRE went round Kaie Salient + YPRES defences.	
	4.		CRE went round YPRES defences. Frost continues. 10° Fahr. Work only possible on wiring + deep dugouts.	
	4.			
	5.			
	6.		CRE went round Railway Wood area + Kaie Salient. Adjutant went to Dunkerque to purchase materials	
	7		Frost less severe. CRE visited Wieltje area + YPRES with Div M.G.O.	
	8.		CRE visited Div Schools at Volkerinhove + laundry at Wormhoudt. Very cold again.	
	9.		CRE examined proposed bridge over canal + over YPRES moat also Camouflage screen near ECOLE	
	10		CRE visited all works of 227th Field Co from YPRES to K Camp. Signs of Thaw at night. Cloudy + warmer.	
	11		Warmer. Temperature about 32° in shade	

[illegible signature]
Lt Col RE

T2134. Wt. W708–776. 500000. 4/15. Sir J. C. & S.

Instructions regarding War Diaries and Intelligence Summaries are contained in F. S. Regs., Part II. and the Staff Manual respectively. Title pages will be prepared in manuscript.

WAR DIARY
or
INTELLIGENCE ~~SUMMARY~~.
(Erase heading not required.)

Army Form C. 2118.

HQ/RE/39 Divn/.

Place	Date	Hour	Summary of Events and Information	Remarks and references to Appendices
HAMHOEK	February 12		Wrote note on "Consolidation"	
	13		CRE visited YPRES + HALFMOON TRENCH + POTIJZE. Thawing slightly in sun but frost in evening.	
	14.		Sharp frost again all day. Warm in sun.	
	15.		Preparing handing over papers. CRE + adjt visited St Sixte + Proven. Div^l Train frost in shade all day. Warm sun.	
	16.		Went round trenches with CRE 55 Div. Adjutant went round back area with adjutant 55. Div. Thaw set in	
	17.		wind veered from East where it had been since Jan 21st to S by W. 225 F^d Co marched to Ledringhem	
ESQUELBECQ	18		Handed over to 55th Div + moved by car to Reserve area.	
"	19.		Rode to Div Schools Volkerinckhove with G802 adjutant visited 225 F^d Co + Div^l Schools + Bollezeele, Foggy + wet.	
"	20.		CRE visited 23 Div CRE at Reninghelst + arranged relief. Adjutant also visited Reninghelst. Wet + cold.	
	21.		CRE By car to YPRES + went round trenches with CRE 23 Div. 227 Field Co marched to Herzeele.	

T2134. Wt. W708–776. 500000. 4/15. Sir J. C. & S.

Instructions regarding War Diaries and Intelligence Summaries are contained in F. S. Regs., Part II. and the Staff Manual respectively. Title pages will be prepared in manuscript.

WAR DIARY
or
~~INTELLIGENCE SUMMARY.~~
(Erase heading not required.)

Army Form C. 2118.

HQ 39 Div RE

Place	Date	Hour	Summary of Events and Information	Remarks and references to Appendices
	February			
Esquelbec	22.		arranging orders for relief	
	23.		CRE visited CE II Army & Div'l Schools Volkerinkhove & 225 Field Co.	
			Adjutant visited Dunkerk to pay bills & buy stores.	
	24		CRE remained at Esquelbec.	
	25.		nil.	
	26.		CRE & adjt rode to Volkerinckhove and inspected work at Div'l schools.	
RENINGHELST	27		Div HQ. moved to Reninghelst & relieved 23 Div. CRE went to YPRES in afternoon & visited Field Cos & Pioneers	
"	~~[illegible]~~			
"	28		CRE went round right brigade trenches with Major Hammonds.	

[signature]
Lt. Col. R.E.
C.R.E. 39TH DIVISION.

T2134. Wt. W708-776. 500000. 4/15. Sir J. C. & S.

S E C R E T.

Headquarters "G"
C.R.E. 55th Division.
O.C. 225th Field Co y.R.E.
O.C. 227th -do-
O.C. 234th -do-
O.C. 13th Glouester Regt.

The following are the probable arrangements for relief by 55th Division;-

(1) Feb,15th.423rd Co,R.E. arrives BRANDHOEK and relieves 225th Co,in YPRES at 9-pm at night of 15/16th. 225th Co,marches back to BRANDHOEK.

Feb,16th.225th Co,entrains at POPERINGHE with transport at 10-am and proceeds to WATTEN,marching thence to HOULE by road.
422nd Coy arrives EDWARDHOEK and relieves 234th Coy in YPRES at 9-pm on night of 16/17th. 234th Coy marches back to EDWARDHOEK.

Feb,17th 234th Coy ehtrains at POPERINGHE with transport at 10-am andproceeds to WATTEN billets at WATTEN.

Feb,18th.227th Coy relieves 419th Coy at 12 noon in BOESINGHE Sector and 419th Coy relieves 227th Goy in VLAMERTINGHE at 4-pm same day.

(2) 225th and 234th Compnies will send billeting parties to WATTEN & HOULE on day before their move.

(3) Advance parties of 423rd and 422nd Companies will arrive day before relief to arrange for carrying on work.

(4) O.C. 227th Field Coy,will obtain from 419th Coy a list of work in progress and will arrange to carry on work without a break.

(5) Companies will give relieving Companies a list of work in progress,and proposed,with brief notes on them,and send a copy to C.R.E. 39th Division, the day before relief.

amended

(6) The 13th Gloucester Regt,will berelieved by Pioneers of the 55th Division,who will arrive at BRANDHOEK Feb,17th,morning and relieve Companies at 9-pm on night of 17/18th.
13th Gloucesters will remove to reserve area,morning of the 18th.

sd/L.E.Hopkins.R.E.
Lieut-Col.R.E.
C.R.E. 39th Division.

11.2.17.

"A" Form. Army Form C. 2121.

MESSAGES AND SIGNALS. No. of Message............

Prefix.......... Code..........m. Office of Origin and Service Instructions.	Words	Charge	This message is on a/c of: .... Service. (Signature of "Franking Officer.")	Recd. at..........m. Date.......... From.......... By..........
	Sent At..........m. To.......... By..........			

TO { all concerned.

* Sender's Number	Day of Month	In reply to Number	AAA
212/C-2	12.		

amend arrangements for relief as follows aaa 423 Company will relieve 234 Company on 15/16 and 422 Company will relieve 225 Co on 16/17

From CRE 39 DW
Place
Time

The above may be forwarded as now corrected. (Z)

Censor. Signature of Addressor or person authorised to telegraph in his name.

* This line should be erased if not required.

(A1) . Ltd., London — W.14542/M.41. 150,000 Pads. 12/15. Form C.2121.

S E C R E T.

H.Q. 39th DIVISION R.E. OPERATION ORDER No.10.

14.2.17.

1. The 55th Division will relieve the 39th Division in the Right Divisional Sector; the 39th Division will move into the VIII Corps Area Reserve Area.

Relief will commence on February 15th 1917 and be completed by the 18th February 1917 on which date Divisional Headquarters opens at ESQUELBECQ at 11-am.

2. Feb,16th. The 423rd Field Company R.E. will relieve the 225th Field Company R.E. in the Right Brigade Sector on the night of 16/17th at 9-pm.

The 225th Field Company R. . will march back from YPRES to BRANDHOEK after relief.

Advanced parties of the 423rd Field Company R.E. will arrive the day before relief to take over work.

3. Feb,17th. The 225th Field Company R.E. will march to LEDRINGHEM via WATOU,HOUTKERQUE,HERZEELE,WORMHOUDT. Two lorries will report at 7-am to convey blankets and surplus stores.

O.C. 225th Field Company R.E. will detail one Officer and 2 O.R. to go in advance on lorries to arrange Billets at LEDRINGHEM.

The 225th Field Company R.E. can be billeted in the adjoining Farms of M.AMIEUX and BLONDE at LEDRINGHEM.

Refilling point will be communicated later.

4. Feb,17th. The 13th Gloucester Regiment will be relieved by 1/4 South Lancashire Regiment at 12-noon.

The 13th Gloucester Regiment will move to ZEGGERS-CAPPEL under orders from General Staff 39th Division.

Advanced parties of the 1/4 South Lancashire Regiment will arrive on the 16th to take over work in hand.

5. Feb,18th Headquarters 39th Division R.E. will open at ESQUELBECQ at 11-am.

The 227th Field Company R.E. relieves the 419th Field Company R.E. at 6-pm in HILL TOP Sector and the 419th Field Company R.E relieves the 227th Field Company R.E. in VLAMERTINGHE at 11-am.

O.C. 227th Field Company R.E. will obtain from O.C. 419th Field Company R.E. a list of work in progress and will arrange to carry on without a break

Back billets 419th Field Company R.E. A.28 Central sheet No.28.

Forward billets 419th Field Company R.E. C.25 a.9.1.

6. The 234th Field Company R.E. will be relieved by the 422nd Field Company R.E. on or about the 20th inst.

Orders for this relief will be issued at a later date.

The 234th Field Company R.E. will be under orders of the C.R.E 55th Division from 11-am on the 18th

7. The following receipts will be obtained from O.C of the incoming Field Companies;-

(a) Billets and Dug-outs handed over in a clean condition.
(b) For all secret maps and plans.
(c) For trench stores,area stores and R.E. materials.
(d) Motor Cycles with equipment as taken over from Companies of the 38th Division.

8. Companies will give relieving Companies a list of work in progress and proposed,with brief notes on them and send a copy to the C.R.E. 39th Division the day before relief.

9. Report completion of relief to Headquarters 39th Division R.E.

10. Acknowledge.

A M Chears

ADJT. 39TH DIV. R.E.

for Lieut.-Col. R.E.
C.R.E. 39th Division.

Copies to;-	Headquarters 39th Division.	2
	C.R.E. 55th Division.	1
	C.R.E. 38th Division.	1
	O.C. 225th Field Company R.E.	1
	O.C. 227th Field Company R.E.	1
	O.C. 234th Field Company R.E.	1
	O.C. 13th Gloucester Regiment.	1
	War Diary	2
	File	1.

SECRET.

HEADQUARTERS 39TH DIVL.R.E.OPERATION ORDER NO.11.

1. February 20th.

The 234th Field Coy R.E is to be relieved by the 422nd Field Coy R.E. Times of relief to be settled by C.R.E., 55th Division.
234th Field Coy R.E. will move from YPRES to Back Billet A.28.d.5.3. upon completion of relief.

2. February 21st.

234th Field Coy R.E. will proceed at 8 a.m. with all transport from POPERINGHE to WINNEZEELE via WATOU and DROGLANDT.

3. 2 lorries will report at 7 a.m. at Billet (A.28.d.5.3) to remove blankets, surplus stores etc.

4. O.C. 234th Field Coy will detail an advance party, consisting of 1 officer and 4 O.R. to accompany lorries to WINNEZEELE. This officer will arrange necessary billets and transport lines with the MAIRE.

5. Refilling point will be wired later.

6. The completion of move to WINNEZEELE will immediately be wired to this office.

7. ACKNOWLEDGE.

Feb. 19th 1917.

Copies issued to:-
C.E.VIII Corps.
H.Q.39th Div (2)
C.R.E.,55th Div.
234th Field Coy R.E.
War Diary (2)
File.

Capt & A/Adj R.E.
for C.R.E., 39th Division.

SECRET.

HEADQUARTERS 39TH DIVL.R.E.OPERATION ORDER NO.12.

Feb 20th 1917.

1. 227th Field Coy R.E. is to be relieved on Feb 20th 1917. Times of relief to be settled by C.R.E., 38th Division.

2. Feb 21st. 227th Field Coy R.E. will proceed from CHEESE MARKET STATION, POPERINGHE at 2.30 p.m. to HERZEELE.
Transport will proceed to HERZEELE via WATOU and HOUTKERQUE

3. O.C. 227th Field Coy R.E. will arrange necessary billets and transport lines with the Town Major, HERZEELE.

4. 2 lorries will call for blankets and surplus kit to A.28.central as soon as necessary arrangements for train can be made. Rearguard consisting of 1 N.C.O. and 2 men will remain behind to guard stores. The N.C.O. will be instructed to proceed to Town Major's Office, HERZEELE, thence to 227th Field Coy Billet.~~as-seen~~

5. Each man will carry one blanket in the train.

6. Refilling point will be wired later to c/o Town Major, HERZEELE

7. Completion of move will be reported to C.R.E.,39th Division immediately by wire.

8. ACKNOWLEDGE.

H. W. Skene

Capt & A/Adj R.E.,
for C.R.E., 39th Division.

Copies issued to:-
C.E., VIII Corps.
H.Q. 39th Division.
C.R.E.,38th Division.
O.C. 227th Field Coy R.E.
War Diary.
File.

SECRET.

HEADQUARTERS 39TH DIVL. R.E. OPERATION ORDER No.13.

Feb. 21st 1917.

1. The 39th Divl. R.E. relieves the 23rd Divl. R.E. in accordance with the following orders.

2. 22nd February.

(a) 234th Field Co.R.E. will move with all transport from A.28.d.5.3. at 8.30 a.m. to Camp at H.14.a.central, 23rd Divl.area.

(b) O.C. 234th Field Co. R.E. to arrange for return trip of necessary transport to remove baggage and surplus stores to H.14.a.central.

(c) Refilling point will be wired later.

(d) 225th Field Co. R.E. Inspection party, consisting of 3 officers and 6 N.C.Os. will proceed to Rue de Lille, YPRES (I.8.c.central) to the billets of the 128 Field Co.R.E., and will inspect the works in progress.

(e) This party will be conveyed to VLAMERTINGHE and back by lorry, leaving LEDRINGHEM Church at 8 a.m.

3. 23rd February.

Advance party of 234 Field Co. R.E., consisting of 1 officer & 3. O.R. will proceed to H.13.d.9.5. at 9 a.m., to take over back billet H.13.d.9.5. and work in hand from O.C. 102 Field Co. R.E. This party will carry 24 hours rations and remain at H.13.d.9.5. until arrival of 234 Field Co. R.E.

4. 24th February.

(a) 234 Field Co. R.E. will move into Camp H.14.d.9.5. and take over from the 102 Field Co.R.E. at 11.a.m.

(b) 225 Field Co.R.E. Lorry will leave LEDRINGHEM Church at 2 p.m. to take advanced working party to YPRES to carry on work from 128 Field Co. R.E. This party will take 48 hours rations.

(c) 2/Lt. F.B.Whittall, 13th Bn. Gloster Regt. will report to C.R.E., 23rd Division, at RENINGHELST at 12 noon to take over all stores in R.E.Dump at H.13.d.9.2.

5. 25th February.

(a) 225 Field Co. R.E. will proceed by train vicinal from WORMHOUDT to POPERINGHE (times will be notified later). Thence by road to Rue de Lille, YPRES, and relieve 128 Field Co. R.E. in Right Brigade Area at 9 p.m.

(b) 225 Field Co. R.E. Transport will proceed from LEDRINGHEM at 8 a.m. by road to OUDERDOM, H.13.d.9.5., via WORMHOUDT, HOUDE, HERZEELE, HOUTKERQUE and POPERINGHE, and take over back billet and transport lines occupied by 128 Field Co. R.E.

(c) 225 Field Co.R.E. 2 lorries will report to 225 Field Co. R.E. LEDRINGHEM Church at 9 a.m. to convey stores and surplus kit to OUDERDOM H.13.d.9.5. 1 officer and 3 O.R. will proceed by these lorries to make necessary arrangements.

(d) 227th Field Co. R.E. 1 lorry will report at HERZEELE at 2 p.m. to take advanced working parties to YPRES (Rue de Lille) to carry on work from 101 Field Co. R.E.

6. 26th February.

(a) 227th Field Co. R.E. dismounted men will proceed by train vicinal from HERZEELE to POPERINGHE. Time of departure will be notified later. Thence by road to Rue de Lille, YPRES, to relieve 101 Field Co. R.E. in Left Brigade Area at 9 pm.

(b) 227th Field Co.R.E. transport will proceed from HERZEELE at 9 a.m. to OUDERDOM, H.13.d.9.5., via HOUTKERQUE, WATOU, POPERINGHE, and take over back billet and transport lines from 101 Field Co. R.E. at 1 p.m.

(c) 227th Field Co.R.E. 2 lorries will report at HERZEELE Church at 9 a.m. to take surplus stores to OUDERDOM.

(d) Os.C. 225th & 227th Field Coys R.E. will arrange with Os.C. 128 and 101 Field Co. R.E., the strength of advanced parties required to carry on work without a break on night of relief.

7. All maps, plans and orders dealing with work in progress, also trench stores and R.E.material will be taken over and receipts given for same.

8. O.C. Field Co. R.E. will note that the Motor Cycle taken over (if any) is complete with all spares. The missing accessories must be carefully noted and receipt for mawhine given accordingly.

9. Refilling points will be notified later.

10. Headquarters, 39th Divl. R.E., will open at RENINGHELST al 11 a.m. on 27th inst.

11. ACKNOWLEDGE.

Capt. A/ADjt. R.E.
for C.R.E., 39th Division.

Copies issued to :-

C.E., VIII Corps.
Headquarters, 39th Division.
C.R.E., 23rd Division.
C.R.E., 55th Division.
O.C., 225th Field Co.R.E.
O.C., 227th do.
O.C., 234th do.
War Diary.
File.
H.Q., 39th Div. Train.
O.C., 39th Div. Sig. Co.R.E.

SECRET

AMENDMENTS TO H.Q.39TH DIV R.E.OPERATION ORDER NO.11.

Para (1) For Feb 20th read Feb 21st.

Para (2) For Feb 21st read Feb 22nd.

Para (3) After "7 a.m." insert 22nd inst.

Copies issued to
C.E.8th Corps. War Diary
C.R.E. 55th Div. File.
O.C.234 Field Coy.
H.Q.39th Div.
Feb 20th 1917

Capt & A/Adj R.E.
for C.R.E.,39th Division.

War Diary

SECRET.

HEADQUARTERS, 39th DIVISIONAL R.E., OPERATION ORDER No.15.

Feb. 22nd 1917.

1. Reference 39th Division Order No.94, the 39th Division is being transferred to the X Corps and will take over front at present held by the 23rd Division.

2. The 13th (Pioneer) Bn. Gloucestershire Regt., will relieve the 9th South Staffs Pioneers on the evening of Feb. 25th & 26th.
Forward Billets, RAMPARTS, YPRES, I.14.b.2.3.
Horse Lines, H.14.a.40.

3. Each Company will take over works now carried on by the Company relieved.

4. The distribution of the Companies will be as follows :-

1 Coy. with Tunnelling Co. R.E.
1 Coy. on Tramways.
1 Coy. in Right Brigade Area.
1 Coy. in Left Brigade Area.

5. The C.O.13th Bn. Gloster Regt., will arrange details for relief with C.O., 9th South Staffs. Regt., Movements will be carried out in accordance with ~~attached~~ time table, forwarded to C.O.13th Bn. Gloster Regt. under my No.394/C of 22nd inst.

6. Inspection party of 13th Bn.Gloster Regt., will proceed to YPRES on 23rd inst., and go round works in hand.

Advanced working parties will be sent on 24th inst., to carry on all urgent works in hand without a break.

7. All plans, secret maps and orders dealing with work in progress, also Trench Stores and R.E. material, will be taken over and receipts given for same.

8. Completion of relief will be notified by wire to Headquarters, 39th Divl. R.E.

9. Headquarters, 39th Divl. R.E., will open at RENINGHELST at 11 a.m. on 27th inst.

10. ACKNOWLEDGE.

[signature]
Capt. & A/Adjt. R.E.
for CR.E., 39th Division.

Copies sent to :-
C.E., VIII Corps.
H.Q., 39th Division. (2)
C.R.E., 23rd Division.
C.O., 13th Bn. Gloster Regt.
O.C., 39th Div. Sig.Co.R.E.
C.O., 39th Div.Train.
War Diary (2).
File.

Vol 13

CONFIDENTIAL.

W A R D I A R Y

O F

39th DIVISIONAL R. E.

From March 1st 1917.

To March 31st 1917.

---0---

C O N F I D E N T I A L .
))))))))))))))))))))))))))))))))))

W A R D I A R Y .

O F

HEADQUARTERS, 39th DIVISIONAL R. E.

From March 1st 1917.

To March 31st 1917.

.....oooOooo.....

Instructions regarding War Diaries and Intelligence Summaries are contained in F. S. Regs., Part II. and the Staff Manual respectively. Title pages will be prepared in manuscript.

WAR DIARY
or
~~INTELLIGENCE SUMMARY.~~
(Erase heading not required.)

Army Form C. 2118.

HQ 39 Div RE

Place	Date	Hour	Summary of Events and Information	Remarks and references to Appendices
RENINGHELST March	1.		CRE went round left brigade trenches + got out programme of work	
"	2		CRE + adjt visited RE Park	
do	3		CRE visited YPRES twice + RE Park. Dont at night.	
do	4		CRE visited the culvert on Menin Road with GSO2 + Battalion	
			Armoured Headqrs in Vince Street + Dormy House	
do	5.		CRE visited YPRES + inspected roads + dumps on South side of	
			the town.	
	6.		CRE visited trenches with GSO2. in connexion with dumps at Zillebeke	
	7.		CRE visited Kruisstraat + back area + Canadian Tunnelling Coy	
	8.		CRE went on leave Major Hammonds officiated.	
			Major Hammonds took over	[initials]
"	9		A/CRE went round camps accompanied by Adjutant. Visited 2nd Can Tunnelling Coy	[initials]
"	10		A/CRE went round trenches (portions of both Brigades) Visited Tramway Major	[initials]
"	11		A/CRE visited RE dump and 234th Coy. Inspected horselines of 225th + 227th Coys	[initials]
"	12		A/CRE visited Right Brigade trenches with Capt ARGENT and the Adjutant RE.	
			Also visited the RE dump.	[initials]

[signature]
LT. COL. R.E.
C.R.E. 39TH DIVISION

T2134. Wt. W708-776. 500000. 4/15. Sir J. C. & S.

Instructions regarding War Diaries and Intelligence Summaries are contained in F. S. Regs., Part II. and the Staff Manual respectively. Title pages will be prepared in manuscript.

WAR DIARY
or
~~INTELLIGENCE SUMMARY.~~
(Erase heading not required.)

Army Form C. 2118.

HQ 39 Div RE,

Place	Date	Hour	Summary of Events and Information	Remarks and references to Appendices
RENINGHELST	13/3/17		Rain in night. Visit from Corps Mg. Officer.	[initials]
"	14/3/17		CRE went to French tramway conference.	[initials]
"	15/3/17		A/CRE sick	[initials]
"	16/3/17		A/CRE attended to office work.	[initials]
"	17/3/17		A/CRE visited trenches in right Bde front and H.Q. Fd Coys. Pioneers in YPRES	[initials]
"	[illegible]		& went to conference at CE. Xth Corps in morning.	
"	18/3/17		Adjutant visited camp work. A/CRE visited Fd Coy Horse lines	[initials]
"	19/3/17		A/CRE visited YPRES and met OC Fd Coys, tramway officer & staff capt. re. tramway and road control	[initials]
"	20/3/17		Lt Col Hopkins returned from leave by car from Boulogne arriving 7.30 pm	
	21/3.		Major Hammond rejoined 225th Fd Co. CRE visited proposed Div HQ at [illegible] with [illegible]	
	22.2.		CRE went to Divisional school Volkerinkove to inspect work. Adjutant went to Dunkirk to pay bills & purchase materials	
	23.2.		CRE went to Field Cos Pioneers & Brigades in YPRES.	

[signature]
Lt. Col. R.E.
C.R.E. 39th Division

T2134. Wt. W708-776. 500000. 4/15. Sir J. C. & S.

Instructions regarding War Diaries and Intelligence Summaries are contained in F. S. Regs., Part II. and the Staff Manual respectively. Title pages will be prepared in manuscript.

WAR DIARY
or
~~INTELLIGENCE~~ SUMMARY.
(Erase heading not required.)

Army Form C. 2118.

HQ 39 Div RE

Place	Date	Hour	Summary of Events and Information	Remarks and references to Appendices
	March			
RENINGHELST				
"	24			
"	25		CRE inoculated for Paratyphoid.	
"	26		CRE sick	
"	27		do	
"	28		CRE. attended office work.	
"	29		CRE went to trenches. visited Halfway Ho + Ritz St + Dormy House	
"	30		CRE attended Tramway Board at ABEELE	
"	31		CRE + Adjt went to Div Schools Volkerinckove.	
"	April 1.			

[signature]
LT. COL. R.E.
C.R.E. 39TH DIVISION

Ap 1.

T2134. Wt. W708-776. 500000. 4/15. Sir J. C. & S.

Vol 14

Confidential

War Diary

of

Headquarters 39th Divisional R.E.

From April 1st, 1917.

To April 30th, 1917.

Army Form C. 2118.

WAR DIARY
or
~~INTELLIGENCE SUMMARY.~~
(Erase heading not required.)

Instructions regarding War Diaries and Intelligence Summaries are contained in F. S. Regs., Part II. and the Staff Manual respectively. Title pages will be prepared in manuscript.

HQ 39 Div RE

Place	Date	Hour	Summary of Events and Information	Remarks and references to Appendices
Reninghelst	April			
	1.		CRE visited YPRES in morning & with adjutant to Hellfire Corner & Zillebeke at night	
	2.		Heavy fall of snow at night & following morning.	
	3.		Prepared programme of work for Left Brigade area.	
	4.		—	
	5.		CRE visited new camps of Field Cos. 225 Field Co transport moves to Vlamertinghe.	
	6.		CRE To YPRES in morning with GSO I 227 + 234 Field Cos moved transport to Vlamertinghe.	
	7		CRE to YPRES & trenches at town examined work in progress & proposed with OC Pioneers 225 Field Co marched to billets near Houtkerque. after handing over work in trenches to 128th Fd Co + 234th Fd Co.	
	8.		CRE to YPRES in evening to set out new CT from Sallyport to Ecole very fine but cold with frost at night. Handed over notes & papers referring to Right brigade area to Lt Col Rooke CRE 23 Division.	
	9.		CRE & adjutant visited proposed new dump at Brandhoek.	
	10		Capt Argent joined to take over duties of adjutant. CRE inspected tramway to Zillebeke. Heavy snowstorms at intervals during day. Capt Meares went on ten days leave.	

[signature] Lt Col RE

T2134. Wt. W708—776. 500000. 4/15. Sir J. C. & S.

Instructions regarding War Diaries and Intelligence Summaries are contained in F. S. Regs., Part II. and the Staff Manual respectively. Title Pages will be prepared in manuscript.

WAR DIARY
or
INTELLIGENCE SUMMARY
(Erase heading not required.)

Army Form C. 2118

HQ 39 Div RE

Place	Date	Hour	Summary of Events and Information	Remarks and references to Appendices
RENINGHELST	11		CRE to YPRES with GSO I to inspect new CTs.	
	12.		CRE visited VIII Corps Head Qrs + new Divl Head Qrs with AA&QMG	
	13.		CRE visited 234 Field Co. issued orders for relief of 234 + 227 Field Cos by 128th Fd Co of 23 Division	
	14.		CRE + adjutant visited work at Divisional schools + 225 Field Co at Waton	
	15.		CRE visited new Divisional camp with GOC. Rain all day	
	16		CRE rode to Camp D. Fine + warm. 227 + 234 Field Cos moved out of YPRES on night of 15/16 to back billets at Vlamertinghe + Brandhoek	
	17.		227 Field Co moved to Canal Bank Dugouts in the HILLTOP section. CRE + adjt went round front line trenches	
	18.		CRE visited new Divisional Head Qrs. rain all day	
	19		CRE went round trenches with OC Pioneers. very wet + cold.	
	20th		CRE went round trenches with GSO 1.	
	21st		CRE visited new camp in morning + 225 Field Co + Divisional schools in afternoon	
	22nd		Capt Meares adjt returned from leave. CRE visited front line work at night	

H. Hallett
Lt Col RE CRE 39 Div

1875 Wt. W593/826 1,000,000 4/15 J.B.C. & A. A.D.S.S./Forms/C. 2118.

Instructions regarding War Diaries and Intelligence Summaries are contained in F. S. Regs., Part II. and the Staff Manual respectively. Title Pages will be prepared in manuscript.

WAR DIARY
or
~~INTELLIGENCE SUMMARY~~
(Erase heading not required.)

Army Form C. 2118

39 Div H.Q. RE.

Place	Date	Hour	Summary of Events and Information	Remarks and references to Appendices
RENINGHELST	23.		CRE visited trenches Capt Argent rejoined his company.	
"	24		CRE.	
"	25.		CRE went round front line with CE VIII Corps. + visited Pioneers + 227 Field Co	
"	26		CRE went to Canal Bank with Major Marston + visited new Camp.	
"	27		CRE + Adjt. prepared estimate of work for offensive operations	
"	28.		CRE. visited front line works with OC Pioneers. Adjt visited new camp.	
"	29		~~CRE~~	
D Camp.	30.		CRE visited front line with GSO I Head Qrs. moved to D Camp.	

[signature]
Lt Col RE
CRE 39 Divn

1875 Wt. W593/826 1,000,000 4/15 J.B.C. & A. A.D.S.S./Forms/C. 2118.

SECRET.

HEADQUARTERS, 39th DIVL. R. E.

OPERATION ORDER No.16.

1. (a). The 39th Division will be relieved in the Right Subsection of their present front (from trench I.30.1 to I.30.9., both inclusive) by 23rd Division on the night 6/7th April.

(b). The boundary between the 23rd and 39th Divisions will be the line ST.PETER'S ST. - ZILLEBEKE ST. - THE PROMENADE, all inclusive to the 23rd Division, but the 39th Division will have the use of ZILLEBEKE STREET.

ZILLEBEKE BUND is allotted to 23rd Division.

(c). The command of the Right Subsection will pass to G.O.C. 23rd Division at 6 a.m. on April 9th.

2. 225th Field Co. R.E., are to be relieved by two sections from 128th Field Co. R.E.,23rd Division, and by two sections of 234th Field Co. R.E., 39th Division, on the evening of the 6th inst.

O.C., 225th Field Co. R.E. will hand over all work in hand south of line ST.PETER'S ST. - ZILLEBEKE ST. - THE PROMENADE to O.C., 128th Field Co. R.E.23rd Division and all work in hand north of this line to O.C. 234th Field Co. R.E.

Advance party of 1 officer 3 O.R. of 128th Field Co. R.E. will arrive at YPRES on 5th inst. at time to be notified later to go round work in progress with O.C. 225th Field Co. R.E.

O.C. 234th Field Co. R.E. will arrange to go round work to be taken over from 225th Field Co., on the 5th inst., - arrangements to be made between Officers concerned, direct.

All transport of 225th Field Co. R.E. will be clear of their present lines ny noon on the 5th inst. and move to new lines in VLAMERTINGHE at H.9.a.6.5.

Headquarters 225th Field Co. R.E., will move from YPRES to VLAMERTINGHE after handing over to 128th & 234th Field Companies on evening of the 6th inst.

3. (234th Field Co. R.E. Hdqrs., and two sections will relieve Hdqrs., and two sections of 225th Field Co. R.E. in accordance with para. 2. O.C., 234th Field Co. R.E., will take over Hdqrs. 225th Field Co. and billets for two sections.

Transport of 234th Field Co. will be clear of their present lines by 12 noon 6th inst., and move to new lines in BRANDHOEK at G.12.d.2.4.

One section (complete) of 234th Field Co. will proceed with 118th Infantry Brigade on the 5th inst., to HOUTKERQUE. This section will be under the orders of G.O.C. 118th Brigade and will be rationed by 118th Brigade from 6th inst. inclusive. Further orders will be issued as soon as received from 118th Brigade.

One section 234th Field Co. (Lieut. Davis') will remain at 39th Divl. Schools until further notice.

4. Transport of 227th Field Co. R.E.will be clear of their present billet by noon 6th inst., and proceed to new lines at BRANDHOEK at G.12.d.2.4. These lines and hutting accommodation will be shared equally by 227th & 234th Field Coys. R.E.

5. All maps, plans, secret ducuments in possession of 225th Field Co. R.E. will be handed over to Os.C. 234th & 128th Field Companies.

6. Receipt will be obtained from incoming Companies that billets and lines handed over are in a clean condition.

7. Completion of moves will be notified by wire.to this office.

8. A C K N O W L E D G E.

(sd) L.E.HOPKINS, Lt.Col.R.E.

4. 4. 17. C. R. E., 39th Division.

AMENDMENT TO 39th DIV. R.E. ORDER No.16.

Para. 3.

The Section of 234th Field Co. R.E. will not proceed to HOUTKERQUE AREA with 118th Infantry Brigade as stated.

(Sd) L. E. HOPKINS, Lt. Col.R.E.

4. 4. 17.

C. R. E., 39th Division.

SECRET.

HEADQUARTERS, 39th DIVL. R. E.

OPERATION ORDER No.17.

1.(a) 225th Field Co. R.E. will proceed by road on the 7th inst. at 8.30 a.m. from F.9.a.6.5. to HOUTKERQUE via POPERINGHE and WATOU.
(b) An officer will proceed on Motorcycle on the 6th inst., to arrange billets with Town Major, HERZEELE.
(c) Two lorries will report to O.C. 225th Field Co. R.E. at 8 a.m. on the 7th inst. to take surplus baggage to HOUTKERQUE.

2. 227th Field Co. R.E. will move from C.12.d.2.4. to F.9.a.6.5. and take over lines from O.C. 225th Field Co. R.E. at 8.30 a.m. on the 7th inst. They will move into these Lines as soon as the 225th Field Co. is clear.

3. Receipt will be obtained from incoming Companies that billets and Lines are handed over in a clean condition.

4. Completion of all moves will be notified to this office by wire as soon as possible.

5. ACKNOWLEDGE.

[signature]

Lieut. Col. R.E.,
C. R. E., 39th Division.

5. 4. 17.

Copies to :-

H.Q., 39th Division.(2)
O.C., 225th Field Co. R.E.
" 227th Field Co. R.E.
" 234th Field Co. R.E.
" 39th Div. Sig. Co. R.E.
War Diary. (2)
File.

HEADQUARTERS, 39th DIV. R.E.

OPERATION ORDER No.18.

1. One complete section of 225th Field Co. R.E., will relieve Lieut. P.W.DAVIS, R.E., and complete section of 234th Field Co.R.E. now working at 39th Divl. Schools, VOLKERINCKHOVE, on the 10th inst.

2. Upon completion of relief, Lieut. Davis and Section will rejoin the 234th Field Co. R.E., at G.12.d.4.4. (Sheet 28).

3. One lorry will report to Lieut. Davis at 39th Divl. Schools at 10 a.m. on the 10th inst., to convey his dismounted men with their surplus stores to G.12.d.4.4.

4. Mounted men of this section of 234th Field Co. R.E., will proceed by road on the 10th inst., to rejoin their Company.

Lieut. Davis will accompany this party. He will arrange to halt for the night at STEENVOORDE.

Two days rations for men and feeds for animals will be carried.

Lieut. Davis will report to Town Major, STEENVOORDE, for billets.

5. All work in hand and plans of same will be taken over by relieving officer of 225th Field Co. R.E.

6. Completion of move will be notified by wire to this office.

7. A C K N O W L E D G E.

[signature] Capt.
for Lieut. Col. R.E.,
C. R. E., 39th Division.

7. 4. 17.

Copies to :- F.Q., 39th Division. (2)
Commandant, 39th Div.Schools.
O.C., 225th Field Co. R.E.
O.C., 234th Field Co. R.E.
O.C., 39th Div. Sig. Co.R.E.
Lieut. P.W.DAVIS, R.E.
O. i/c. 39th Div. R.E.Park.

SECRET.

HEADQUARTERS, 39th DIVISIONAL R.E.

OPERATION ORDER No.19.

----

1. (a) 39th Division will be transferred to the VIII Corps on the 16th April and will be relieved by the 23rd Division in the HDDGE Sector on the night of the 15th/16th April.

(b) The 39th Division will take over from the 55th and 38th Divisions the front from PRATT STREET C.22.c.7.1. (inclusive) to Trench C.14.4. (inclusive) on the night of the 17th/18th April.

2. Details of relief will be issued later.

3. ACKNOWLEDGE.

Lieut. Col. R.E.
C.R.E., 39th Division.

12. 4. 17.

Copies to :-
~~H.Q., 39th Division. (2)~~
O.C. 225 Field Co. R.E.
" 227 do.
" 234 do.
" 39th Div. Sig. Co.R.E.
O. i/c. 39th R.E.Park.
~~2/Lt. L.A.Dibdin, 39th Div. Schools.~~
War Diary (2).

Secret

HEADQUARTERS?, 39th DIVL. R. E.

OPERATION ORDER No. 20.

----

1. The 227th & 234th Field Companies, R.E., will be relieved on the night of the 15th/16th April and will hand over the line and billets to the 128th Field Co.R.E. by 9 p.m. on the 15th inst.

2. The 227th Field Co. R.E., will march back to their Back billet at VLAMERTINGHE, H.9.a.6.5.

3. The 234th Field Co. R.E., will march to billets situated at H.7.a.2.1. Their Transport Lines remain as at present.

4. Officers of the 128th Field Co. R.E., will report to go over the work in hand at times to be arranged between the Os.C., 128th, 227th & 234th Field Companies.

5. All maps, plans, secret documents, details of works in hand or proposed, R.E.Stores, etc., will be handed over to the O.C., 128th Field Co. R.E.

6. Receipts will be obtained from the incoming Company that billets are handed over in a clean condition.

7. Completion of moves will be notified by wire to this office.

8. A C K N O W L E D G E.

[signature]

13. 4. 17.

Lieut. Col. R.E.,
C. R. E., 39th Division.

Copies to :-

H.Q., 39th Division. (2)
C.R.E., 23rd Division.
O.C., 225th Field Co. R.E.
O.C., 227th Field Co. R.E.
O.C., 234th Field Co. R.E.
O.C., 128th Field Co. R.E.
O.C., 39th Div. Sig. Co. R.E.S.
O. i/c. R.E.Park.
War Diary. (2)
File.

SECRET.

HEADQUARTERS 39TH DIVL. R.E.OPERATION ORDER NO. 22.

---

1. The 39th Division will take over the CENTRE SECTOR of the line consisting of the present Left Battalion of the 55th Division and the present Right Battalion of the 38th Division on the night of the 17th/18th April.

2. The 227th Field Co.R.E. will take over the work in this Sector from the 123rd Field Co.R.E. (38th Division) and the 423rd Field Co.R.E. (55th Division).
Headquarters 123rd Field Co.R.E. CANAL BANK.
Headquarters 423rd " " " RUE DE DIXMUDE.

3. The 227th Field Co.R.E. will send Officers and N.C.O's to go round the works in hand on the 16th and 17th inst at times to be arranged with Os.C. Coys.

4. The 227th Field Co.R.E. Headquarters and dismounted men will move to the forward billets of the 123rd Field Co.R.E. on the evening of the 17th inst.
An advance party will be sent to take over the billets.

5. The 227th Field Co.R.E. Transport will move to the Horse lines and Billet of the Field Co.R.E. at A.28.c.7.5 on the afternoon of the 17th inst.

6. The 234th Field Co.R.E. will take over the Transport Lines and Billets at A.28.b.1.4 from the Field Co.R.E. on the afternoon of the 17th inst.

7. The O i/c R.E.Park will take over the Workshops, billets, R.E. Stores &c from the 423rd Field Co.R.E. situated at A.28.d.5.2. on the afternoon of the 17th inst and will move in with all the Sappers, & Infantry at present attached to the C.R.E.

8. Pioneers, 13th Gloucester Regt.

Headquarters & Transport & 1 Coy. will move to HOSPITAL FARM B.19.d.1.0.
2 Companies to Billets in CANAL BANK.
1 Company to BOLLEZEELE to Billets to be notified later.
All on the day and night of the 17th inst.

9. C.O.13th Gloucester Regt will send officers to go round the works in hand of the Pioneers in the area to be taken over. Their location can be obtained by enquiry at the billets of the 123rd and 423rd Field Coys.R.E. mentioned in (2).

10. O.C.Field Coys will see that the billets and Transport Lines vacated are left clean and in good order. If handed over to another unit a certificate to that effect must be obtained. If no unit takesthem over, a list of Area Stores left to be sent to the Area Commandant.

11. Report completion to this office by wire.

12. ACKNOWLEDGE.

15/4/17

[signature]
Lt-Col R.E.
C.R.E., 39th Division.

Copies to:- H.Q.39th Div (2).
C.R.E.38th & 55th Div.
O.C. 227th & 234th Field Coys R.E.
C.O.13th Glouc Regt. O.C. 39th Div.Sig.Co.R.E.
O i/c 39th R.E.Park. War Diary (2) File.

Vol 15

CONFIDENTIAL.

WAR DIARY.

OF - HEADQUARTERS,
39th. DIVISIONAL. R.E.

From:- May. 1st. 1917.

To:- May.31st. 1917.

Instructions regarding War Diaries and Intelligence Summaries are contained in F. S. Regs., Part II. and the Staff Manual respectively. Title Pages will be prepared in manuscript.

WAR DIARY
or
~~INTELLIGENCE SUMMARY~~
(Erase heading not required.)

Army Form C. 2118

HQ 39 Div RE

Place	Date	Hour	Summary of Events and Information	Remarks and references to Appendices
D Camp A 30 b 2 7	1 to 3.		Fine hot weather cold at night.	
	3.		Capt Bell. OC 39 Signals gazetted acting Major	
	4.			
	5.		CR went round trenches with CRE. 225 Field Co relieved 227 in Canal Bank	
	6		227 Field Co moved to Holque by train for training	
	7		Lt PW DAVIS 234 Fld Co reported slightly wounded at duty.	
	8		CR & CRE went round trenches up to Belge Trench. Some rain.	
			Work on new trenches proceeding very well but supply of material short owing to failure of train service from Poperinghe to YPRES due to shell fire	
	11.		Lt MacLauchlan of 225 Field Co blew up Canadian Tunnels successfully	
	12.		CRE inspected 227 Field Co at Holque.	
	13.		Report submitted on employment of Pioneers & RE in attack	
	19.		Bellingham trench begun. Lt Holley 225 F Co wounded.	
	20-22		Bellingham trench completed.	
	23.		Armytage trench reconnoitred.	
	24		Major Garland wounded. by MG fire in thigh.	
	25.		Arrangements & orders for Armytage trench completed.	

M MacPherson
Lt Col
CRE 39 Div

1875 Wt. W593/826 1,000,000 4/15 J.B.C. & A. A.D.S.S./Forms/C. 2118.

Instructions regarding War Diaries and Intelligence Summaries are contained in F. S. Regs., Part II. and the Staff Manual respectively. Title Pages will be prepared in manuscript.

WAR DIARY
or
~~INTELLIGENCE SUMMARY~~
(Erase heading not required.)

Army Form C. 2118

HQ 39 Div RE.

Place	Date	Hour	Summary of Events and Information	Remarks and references to Appendices
	26.		Armytage Trench successfully dug about 900 yds long and 4 ft deep 120 yds revetted with U frames. much drainage work done and Finch Street + Garden St. CTs extended 350 yds altogether up to Armytage about 250 RE 450 Pioneers + 300 Infantry employed besides covering party.	
	27.		Hopkins Trench reconnoitred + set out.	
	28		Hopkins Trench dug. 1200 yds long + 18 in deep.	
	29 to 31		Improvement + extension of trenches continued.	

June 4th

[illegible]
Lt Col RE
CRE 39 Div

1875 Wt. W593/826 1,000,000 4/15 J.B.C. & A. A.D.S.S./Forms/C. 2118.

WO 95/16

C O N F I D E N T I A L.

W A R   D I A R Y.

of the Headquarters, 39th. Divisional Royal Engineers.

From:- June 1st. 1917.

To:- June 30th. 1917.

WAR DIARY
or
~~INTELLIGENCE~~ SUMMARY
(Erase heading not required.)

Army Form C. 2118

Instructions regarding War Diaries and Intelligence Summaries are contained in F. S. Regs., Part II. and the Staff Manual respectively. Title Pages will be prepared in manuscript.

June .17. HQ 39 Divn RE

Place	Date	Hour	Summary of Events and Information	Remarks and references to Appendices
BORDER CAMP	1.		2nd Lt Halliday joined from 1st Field Squadron.	
	2		HORNBY TRENCH dug 750 yds + 18" deep.	
	10.		Weather turned cold + cloudy after long spell of dry hot weather	
	13.		2nd Lt Halliday killed.	
	14.		CRE 51st Divn went round trenches	
	15.		Handed over Wieltje sector to 55th Divn	
	17.		51st Divn RE took over work in Lancashire Farm sector.	
"	26th		Lt Col HOPKINS DSO left the divn to report to the War Office. Major D.H. HAMMONDS M.C. RE. took over the work as acting CRE.	[illegible]
"	27th		A/CRE went round front trenches and visited field companies. Work of digging HORNBY trench interfered with by heavy rain.	[illegible]
"	28th		A/CRE visited Canal bank with CE XVIIIth Corps to fix new site for divisional dump and to decide on positions for dugout accommodation.	[illegible]
"	29th		Issued work orders and visited site of new Div camp. Visited Canal bank and inspected work of 86th Fd Coy (11 Div) attached.	[illegible] [illegible]
"	30th		Got out new Div programme of work.	[illegible]

D.H. Hammonds
Major RE

1875 Wt. W593/826 1,000,000 4/15 J.B.C. & A. A.D.S.S./Forms/C. 2118.

WO 95/2587

C O N F I D E N T I A L .

W A R D I A R Y .

-o-o-o-o-o-o-o-o-o-o-o-o-o-

HEADQUARTERS 39TH. DIVISIONAL ROYAL ENGINEERS.

From:- 1st. July 1917.

tO:- 31st. July 1917.

-o-o-o-o-o-o-o-o-o-o-o-o-o-o-o-

Instructions regarding War Diaries and Intelligence Summaries are contained in F. S. Regs., Part II. and the Staff Manual respectively. Title Pages will be prepared in manuscript.

WAR DIARY
or
~~INTELLIGENCE SUMMARY~~
(Erase heading not required.)

Army Form C. 2118

Place	Date	Hour	Summary of Events and Information	Remarks and references to Appendices
BORDER CAMP	1/7/17		A/CRE visited Pioneer – Fd Coy HQrs and inspected line of proposed PITTSBURG tramway and other works. Heavy shelling in front area. HORNBY trench flooded out.	MB
"	2.7.17		Lt Col. H.J. Couchman MCRE assumed duties of CRE vice Lt Col. L.E. Hopkins DSO. RE left for ~~[illegible]~~ England on 26th inst vide	
C. Camp	3.7.17		Division H.Q. moved to C Camp. CRE and Major Hammonds visited trenches. Lt P.W. Davis 234 Field Coy admitted Hospital wounded. CE held conference CRES at their H.Q.	
	4.7.17		CRE visited trenches	
	6.7.17		CRE held conference with Company Commanders 48 Div; CO 5 Batt Sussex Regt was also present	
	7.7.17		Lt Fogerty rejoined 227 Field Coy from Hospital	
	9.7.17		CRE & Adj visited Div dump & Pills box Rd. 5 Sussex took over work from 6 E YORKS Pioneers	
	10.7.17		CRE visited trenches	
	11.7.17		CRE visited trenches	
	12.7.17		3 Fld Coys 474 475 477 48 Divn commenced work under CRE 39 Divn	
	14.7.17		CRE visited trenches, found same fair condition	
	15.7.17		CRE visited trenches, rather wet.	

Instructions regarding War Diaries and Intelligence Summaries are contained in F. S. Regs., Part II. and the Staff Manual respectively. Title Pages will be prepared in manuscript.

WAR DIARY
or
INTELLIGENCE SUMMARY
(Erase heading not required.)

Army Form C. 2118

Place	Date	Hour	Summary of Events and Information	Remarks and references to Appendices
C. Camp A 30 d.0.0 Sh 28 NW				
	18/7/17		Lt J F C Fogerty wounded, Lt T W R Haycraft wounded at duty. Canal bank shelled fairly heavily with gas shells	
	20/7/17		CRE visited trenches with CRE 48 Divn. Adj to Hazebrouck buying stores	
	21/7/17		CRE visited trenches. Conference at CE office. CRE, Major Hammond & Major Munster attended.	
	23/7/17		CRE visited trenches inspected forward roads. Heavy shelling of Canal Bank with gas shells night 22/23	
	24/7/17		CRE visited trenches in afternoon	
	25/7/17		Conference at Div H.Q. Very wet	
	26/7/17		CRE visited trenches	
	28/7/17		CRE visited trenches. Lt Fogerty rejoined 227 for duty	
	29/7/17		CRE visited trenches. Hd Qrs moved back into camp G 5 b 1.9 sheet 28 NW. Heavy thunderstorm and rain	
	30/7/17		Fine but poor observation	
	31/7/17		Details of 5 Army Offensive in which the Divn took part not yet to hand (see app. [illegible])	Hammond Lt Col RE ADJT. 39TH DIV. R.E. 3/8/17

1875. Wt. W593/826 1,000,000 4/15 J.B.C. & A. A.D.S.S./Forms/C. 2118.

1x

Copy No. 17

SECRET.

HEADQUARTERS 39TH DIVISIONAL R.E.ORDER NO.32.

July 10th, 1917.

1. The 474th, 475th and 477th Field Companies R.E., 48th Division at present working under orders of C.R.E., 39th Division, will move from "I" Camp on 11th inst as follows:-

3 sections of 474th Field Coy. R.E. to CANAL BANK (I.1.b.8.7) and take over accommodation from 86th Field Coy. R.E; this move will be completed by 11 p.m.

1 section of 475th Field Coy. R.E. plus 3 sections of 477th Field Coy. R.E. to billets in L.8 which will be handed over by Labour Coy. (Lieut.Manisty); move to be completed by 10 p.m.

Headquarters plus 1 section of 474th Field Coy R.E.
Headquarters plus 3 sections of 475th Field Coy R.E.
Headquarters plus 1 section of 477th Field Coy R.E.
will move to A.22.central on the 11th inst; move to be completed by 8 p.m. Billets at A.22.central as arranged between C.R.E. 48th Division and Headquarters XVIII Corps.

2. O.C., 474th, 475th and 477th Field Coys. will take over work from O.C. 86th Field Coy. R.E. and 6th Batt.East Yorks Regt and carry out programme of work as arranged at Conference with C.R.E., 39th Division on 6th inst.

This work will be carried on by the above mentioned units from the 12th inst (inclusive).

3. Men marching to and from CANAL BANK in daylight will move at intervals of not less than 200 yds in parties of 4.

4. Wagons or lorries containing R.E. material can proceed to CANAL BANK in daylight.

No material will be dumped on roadside within 300 yds either side of Road RED HART ESTAMINET.

5. Box respirators will invariably be carried East of VLAMERTINGHE.

6. All secret maps, etc. in connection with work will be handed over by O.C. 86th Field Coy and C.O. 6th East Yorks R.

7. Receipts will be obtained by incoming companies that billets handed over are in a clean condition.

8. Completion of relief will be notified by wire to this office.

9. ACKNOWLEDGE.

H M Simeons [signature]
Capt & Adj R.E.
for C.R.E., 39th Division.

Copies issued at 8 p.m. to

~~1 & 2~~	~~H.Q.39th Div.~~	8	~~O.C.86th Fd.Coy.~~	~~14.A.P.M.~~
~~3~~	~~C.R.E., 48th Div.~~	9	~~G.O.6th E.Yorks~~ R.	15.C.R.A.
~~4~~	~~C.E., XVIII Corps.~~	10	~~O.C.225th Fd.Coy.~~	~~16.A.D.M.S.~~
5	O.C., 474th Fd.Coy	~~11~~	~~O.C.227th Fd.Coy.~~	17 War Diary.
6.	O.C., 475th Fd.Coy	~~12~~	~~O.C.234th Fd.Coy.~~	18
7.	~~O.C., 477th Fd.Coy~~	~~13~~	~~O.C.,39th Signals.~~	19 File.
				~~20 RE Park~~
				~~21 CRE 5th Div~~

1K

Copy No.

SECRET.

HEADQUARTERS;39th.DIVISIONAL R.E. ORDER NO.33.

July 10th.1917.

1. 5th.Battalion R.Sussex Regt.(Pioneers) will be billeted in "Z" Camp,and will send one Platoon forward (or more if accommodation is available) to billet on Canal Bank (West) in Dug-outs either side of Bridge 2,as arranged between C.O.,5th.R. Sussex Regt., (Pioneers) and C.O.,6th.East Yorks Regt.(Pioneers) today. This Platoon will continue work on PITTSBURG Plank Road - working by night.

2. Lorries will report to C.O.,5th.R.Sussex Regt.(Pioneers) "Z" Camp,at 7.30 a.m. daily commencing 12th.instant.to take 210 men to REIGERSBURG CHATEAU for work on PITTSBURG Plank Road. The Lorries will be available at 4 p.m.REIGERSBURG CHATEAU for return journey.

3. Accommodation for 3 Companies 5th.Battn.,R.Sussex Regt., (Pioneers) will be found in CANAL BANK on evening of the 15th.inst. Details will be notified later.

4. Quantity of wire netting and canvas will be sent from Corps,R.E.Park daily to "Z" Camp for making Camouflage. C.O.,5th. R.Sussex Regt.(Pioneers) will employ as many men as possible on this work. Lieut.Reece,i/c of 39th.Divl.R.E.Park,will send 1 Sapper to "Z" Camp on the 12th.inst.,to shew these men what is required. Camouflage made will be collected later.

5. Dumps of Split pit props for Plank Road are at H.6.d.9.5. and on BOESINGHE - YPRES Road near AUCTION BRIDGE. There is also a large quantity of material at B.4.c. - any further material required will be indented through the C.R.E.,39th.Division.

6. ACKNOWLEDGE.

[signature]
Capt. & Adjt.,R.E.,
for C.R.E.,39th.Division.

Copies issued at p.m. to
1 & 2 H.Q.39th.Div.
3. C.R.E.48th.Div.
4. C.E.XVIIIth.Corps.
5. A.D.M.S.
6. O.C.,5th.R.Sussex Regt.(Pioneers).
7. O.C.,225th.Field Co.,R.E.
8. O.C.,227th.Field Co.,R.E.
9. O.C.,234th.Field Co.,R.E.
10. Lieut.Reece.

Copy No......

SECRET.

HEADQUARTERS,39th.DIVISIONAL R.E. ORDER No. 34.

14th.July 1917.

1. 225th.Field Co.,R.E.,will relieve 234th.Field Co.,R.E. on the 15th.instant.
On relief 234th.Field Co.,will move to "C" CAMP,and take over accommodation now occupied by 225th.Field Co.,R.E.

2. Details of relief will be arranged between O.C.,Companies concerned.

3. Owing to a Brigade relief little work will be possible on the night of 15th./16th.inst.
Arrangements must however be made to work on the following :-

Divisional Dump.
Right Brigade Dump.

4. The parties now found by 225th. & 234th.Field Companies for work at 39th.R.E.Park,will not be relieved,with the exception of 50 Infantry now found by 225th.Field Co.,for unloading trucks sent forward (vide para. 3 of this Office 417/F.of 7th. July 1917). This party will not be required on 15th.inst. and will be provided by 234th.Field Co.,on 16th.inst., and following days.

5. O.C.,234th.Field Co.,R.E.will hand over all work in hand, together with all maps,plans,secret documents,R.E.Stores, and a detailed list of contents of Dumps.

6. Men marching to and from CANAL BANK in daylight will move in parties of 4 at a distance of 100 yards apart.

7. Completion of relief will be notified by wire to this Office.

8. ACKNOWLEDGE.

Lieut.-Col.,R.E.,
C.R.E.,39th.Division.

Copies issued at ....to :-

1 & 2.H.Q.,39th.Div.	11. A.D.V.S.
3. A.P.M.	12. D.A.D.O.S.
4. C.R.A.	13. O i/c R.E.Park.
5.C.E.,XVIIIth.Corps.	14. AREA Commandant. (Canal Bank.)
6.225th.Field Co.,R.E.	15. C.R.E.,48th.Div.
7. 227th.Field Co.	16.)
8. 234th.Field Co.	17.) War Diary.
9. 39th.Signal Co.	18. File.
10. A.D.M.S.	

SECRET. Copy No. 13......

HEADQUARTERS, 39th. DIVISIONAL R.E. ORDER NO. 35.

22nd July 1917.

1. Sections of 474th, 475th, and 477th. Field Companies R.E. and 2 Companies of 5th. Royal Sussex Regt. (Pioneers) now in the CANAL BANK, will move on 24th/25th. to Camps in the vicinity of A.30 to be selected by 48th. Division. All moves will be completed by 10 a.m. 25th. inst.

2. On completion of move these Units will come under the Orders of Chief Engineer XVIII Corps.

3. It is essential that a full day and night's work is done on 24th day and 24th/25th. night.
Parties working by day on the 24th, and by night on 24th/25th., will move under Field Company and Battalion arrangements via BATH ROAD (from Bridge 2A.) or QUEENS ROAD (From Bridge 2.) to CHEMIN MILITAIRE (Plank Road) W. of VLAMERTINGHE, and thence by this road to A.30.

4. There will be no movement by march route, between the hours of 9.0.a.m. and 9.0.p.m.
Between these hours all movement will be in parties of not more than 4 at not less than a 100 yds distance.

5. The usual Progress Reports of work done on 24th./25th will be submitted to this Office by 8.0.a.m. on 25th inst.

7. Completion of relief will be notified by wire to this Office.

8. ACKNOWLEDGE.

[signature]

Lieut Colonel. R.E.

C.R.E. 39th Division.

Copies issued at 7.45 pm to:-

1 & 2. H.Q.39th Div.
3. C.E.XVIII Corps.
4. C.R.E. 48th. Division.
5. 474th. Field Coy.R.E.
6. 475th. " " "
7. 477th. " " "
8. 5th. R.Sussex Regt.(pioneers)
9. 39th. Divl.Signal Coy.R.E.
10. 39th. Divl.R.E.Park.
11. Area Commandant. (CANAL BANK)
12, 13 War Diary
14 File

Copy No....9

SECRET.

HEADQUARTERS, 39th. DIVISIONAL R.E. ORDER No. 36.

30th. July 1917.

Ref. Sheet 28. 1. 225th, 227th and 234th. Field Companies, 255th Tunnelling Company and 13th Battalion Gloucestershire Regt. (Pioneers) will march to CANAL BANK on night 30th/31st.

2. STARTING POINT. Road Junction A.30.d.1.9.

Order of march and times of passing Starting Point.	(225th. Field Coy. R.E.	11.[illegible].p.m.
	(227th. " " "	11.3.p.m.
	(234th. " " "	11.6.p.m.
	(255th. Tunnelling Coy.	11.10.p.m.
	(13th. Gloster Regt.	11.15.p.m.

ROUTE. Plank road to H.2.c.8.7. ---- BATH ROAD to CANAL BANK.

3. On arrival at CANAL BANK units will clear the line of march at once so as to avoid blocking units behind them

4. Units will observe the usual hourly halts from 10 minutes to the hour, to the hour.

5. Units will send an orderly with a watch to the C.R.E's Office at 7.30 p.m. tonight to get correct time.

6. ACKNOWLEDGE.

Copies to:-

1 & 2 H.Q. 39th. Division.
3. 225th. Field Coy. R.E.
4 227th. " "
5. 234th. " "
6. 255th. Tunnelling Coy.
7. 13th. Gloster Regt.
8. A.P.M.
9. WAR DIARY.
10. FILE.

Lieut- Colonel. R.E.

July 30th. 1917. C.R.E. 39th. Division.

A P E N D I X   "A".

SECRET.

INSTRUCTION NO.12.

(Issued in connection with 39th.Division Order No.125.)

GENERAL.

The 39th. Divisional R.E. and 13th.Gloucester Regiment will be employed as follows after zero hour on Z day.

225th. Field CO.R.E. on the construction of a cross country track;

For first line Transport from about C.22.a.1.9 across the hostile trenches (as shown on the map issued with 39th. Division Order No.125).

234th. Field CO.R.E. on the construction of strong points.

227th. Field Co.R.E. in Divisional Reserve.

255th. Tunnelling Co.R.E. on burying cable under 39th. Divisional Signal Co.R.E.

13th Gloucester Regiment (less 1 Company on Railway work) on the construction of a lorry route along BUFFS ROAD to its junction with the WIELTJE-ST.JULIEN Road and along the latter.

225th.Field Co.R.E. Cross country track.

2. (a) The 225th. Field Co.R.E. will assemble in the CANAL BANK and will send an Officerto report to G.S.O.3. at 39th.Divisional Advanced Report Centre (CANAL BANK C.25.d.3.2.) by Zero minus 1 hour. This Officer will be informed on the capture of the BLACK Line, when 225th. Field Co.R.E. will move forward to HAMPSHIRE FARM.

(b) "A" Co. 16th.Notts & Derby Regt. (Captain LORD) and "A" Co. 11th. R.Sussex Regt. (Captain ALLEN) will re-organise on the capture of the BLUE LINE and report to Major HAMMONDS R.E., Commanding 225th. Field Co.R.E. at HAMPSHIRE FARM at Zero plus 2 hours. Should the R.E. not have arrived, the Infantry Companies will wait there.

Each man of these Companies will bring one shovel with him.

(c) The cross country track will be constructed by the troops mentioned in this para. under the command of Major HAMMONDS, who will wire time of commencing work and hourly progress reports to 39th. Divisional Headquarters.

234th.Field Co.R.E., Strong Points (39th Division Order.

3. (a) The 234th Field Co.R.E. will assemble in the CANAL BANK and will detail one Officer and 5 N.C.O's and sappers to accompany the Headquarters of each Infantry Brigade, and one Officer to be at 39th.Divisional Advanced Report Centre (C.25.d.3.2.) at zero minus 1 hour.

(b) The duties of these Officers will be to inform O.C. 234th Field Co.R.E., through the Officer at 39th. Divisional Advanced Report Centre.

(i) When, to what point, and by what route the 234th Field Co. R.E., can advance.

(ii) The locality and amount of R.E. assistance required at any point, in the area of the Infantry Brigade to which they are attached, for the consolidation or the construction of strong points.

(c). R.E. Officers attached to 116th and 117th Infantry Brigades will reconnoitre the Valley of the STEENBEEK in their respective Infantry Brigade Areas and report by wire to the C.R.E. points where trestle bridges are required.

(d). The R.E. N.C.O's and sappers attached to 116th and 117th Infantry Brigades will be used to assist the Infantry to construct crossing places for Tanks over the STEENBEEK about C.12.c.2.1., C.12.c.0.6., C.11.b.2.7., and C.5.d.1.0.

(e). The 234th. Field Company will move forward by bounds , halting near Brigade Forward Stations and reporting its position to C.R.E. and Infantry Brigades at each halt.

The R.E. Officer at 39th.Divisional Advanced Report Centre will rejoin the 234th.Field Co.R.E. on the latter advancing.

(f) Infantry garrisons detailed for strong points will at once occupy these points on notification being received from the R.E. that they are ready.

227th.Field Co.R.E. Reserve.

4. The 227th. Field Co.R.E. will be in Divisional Reserve in the CANAL BANK and will be ready either to work in relief of the 225th.Field Co.R.E. or to bridge the STEENBEEK or for any other contingency.

The C.R.E. will detail parties from this Field Company to reconnoitre and repair wells and the water supply in the captured trenches.

255th.Tunnelling Co.R.E. Cable Burying.

5. (a) The 255th Tunnelling Co.R.E. parties will be withdrawn to PROVEN on completion of their [illegible] present tasks and will assemble in the CANAL BANK (with their attached Infantry) on Y/Z night under instructions to be issued.

(b) The 255th. Tunnelling Co.R.E. will detail an Officer to report to the 39th. Divisional Advanced Report Centre (C.25.d.3.2.) at Zero minus one hour. This Officer will be informed when the Company can move forward (on the Infantry advancing from the DOTTED BLUE LINE).

(c) On receiving instructions, 255th. Tunnelling Co.R.E. will move to the Battalion Headquarters at C.21.b.4.2 (BILGE TRENCH) where they will be met by an Officer and party to be detailed by O.C. 39th. Divisional Signal Co.R.E. They will then proceed to bury cable from C.21.b.4.2. to CORNER COT.

(d) The 255th. Tunnelling Co.R.E. will draw 500 shovels and 50 picks on arrival at the CANAL BANK on Y/Z night under instructions to be issued by the C.R.E.

13th Gloucestershire Regt. Lorry Route.

6. (a) The 13th. Bn.Gloucester Regt (less 1 Company on Railway work) will assemble in the CANAL BANK on Y/Z night and will send an Officer to report to 39th. Divisional Advanced Report Centre at Zero minus one hour. This Officer will be informed when the advance from the DOTTED BLUE LINE commences and the and the 13th. Gloucestershire Regiment can move forward.

(b) On receiving instructions, the 13th. Bn. Gloucestershire Regt less 2 Companies (one left in CANAL BANK as reserve and to provide reliefs) will move to the junction of ADMIRALS ROAD and BUFFS ROAD and continue the latter thence as a lorry route across NO MAN'S LAND and the captured trenches.

(c) O.C. 13th.Bn. Gloucestershire Regt will report by wire to C.R.E. hour at which work commences and hourly progress thereafter.

R.E.Dumps. 7. (a). The C.R.E. will arrange to form dumps of R.E. materials as follows:-

(i). At 39th. Divisional Dump, I.2.a.1.9.
(ii).Brigade R.E. Dumps, about C.21.c.4.4.
(iii).Forward R.E. Dump about C.22.a.3.7 (where the cross country track crosses the enemy front line.) This will be forward from the Divisional R.E.Dump as soon as the situation admits (see para.8).
(iv). Advance R.E.Dumps near CORNER COT and South-East corner of KITCHENERS WOOD (see para.8).
(v). Road metal and pit prop Dump near CROSS ROADS FARM.
(vi). The XVIII Corps Forward R.E. Dump will be formed near LA BELLE ALLIANCE.

(b) R.E. material from the Dump at C.22.a.3.7. will only be used for consolidation, etc: in and in front of the BLACK LINE.

R.E. material from the Dumps at CORNERCCOT and South East Corner of KITCHENER'S WOOD will only be used for consolidation etc., in front of the DOTTED GREEN LINE.

(c) The C.R.E. will arrange to organise the supply of material from any hostile Engineer Dumps that may be captured.

Transport. 8. (a) The C.R.E. will arrange to have 3 pontoon wagons loaded with R.E. material at the Divisional Dump (I.2.a.1.9.) by Zero hour. Teams for these wagons will be sent up on the capture of the BLACK LINE to take them to the Forward R.E.Dump at C.22.a.3.7.

(b) The C.R.E. will arrange for 2 pack trains (10 pack animals each) to carry R.E. material from the Forward R.E. Dump at C.22.a.3.7 to the advanced R.E. Dumps near CORNER COT and the South East corner of KITCHENER'S WOOD as soon as the situation admits.

(c) Three pontoon wagons will be loaded with material for trestle bridges at the Divisional Dump (I.2.a.1.9) by Zero hour, and will be sent forward under instructions to be issued by the C.R.E.

Bridges. 9. The 284th. Army Troops Coy.R.E. will be ~~responsible~~ responsible for the repair and maintenance of all wagon bridges over the CANAL under instructions to be issued by the C.R.E.

W A R   D I A R Y

F O R

Headquarters 39th Divl. R.E.

FROM 1st August to 31st August, 1917.

Instructions regarding War Diaries and Intelligence Summaries are contained in F. S. Regs., Part II. and the Staff Manual respectively. Title Pages will be prepared in manuscript.

WAR DIARY
or
INTELLIGENCE SUMMARY
(Erase heading not required.)

Army Form C. 2118

Place	Date	Hour	Summary of Events and Information	Remarks and references to Appendices
C Camp A30 c 0.0 sh 28	1/8/17		5th Army attacked hostile trenches on front 12 miles 39th Div formed right Div 18 Corps. 39 Div RE were employed as per appendices A and A2. Garvey 234 Fd Coy killed in action 31/7/17	App. "A" App A.2
	2/8/17		CRE visited German trenches	
	3/8/17		Adj - Capt Argent visited trenches, saw trench board track.	
	4/8/17		CRE visited trenches. Inspected trench board track and lorry road	
	5/8/17		CRE attended Conference at CE office. CE emphasised importance of road work.	
F23 C1.4 sh 28	6/8/17		CRE H.Q. moved out of C Camp to A23 C1.4 sh 28. CRE 48 took over. Move of Div H.Q. to Eberlecques cancelled orders issued H.Q. to stand to & be prepared to move to ECKE. Field Coys at work as usual, having taken over from Fd Coys 48 Div with exception of 227 Fd Coy who are resting.	
METEREN	8/8/17		Fd Coys moved to Reserve Area 10 Corps. H.Q. CRE joined Div H.Q. at METEREN	App. B.
	9/8/17		CRE & Adj visited CRE 41 Div & made preliminary arrangements re taking over.	

1875 Wt. W593/826 1,000,000 4/15 J.B.C. & A. A.D.S.S./Forms/C. 2118.

Army Form C. 2118

Instructions regarding War Diaries and Intelligence Summaries are contained in F. S. Regs., Part II. and the Staff Manual respectively. Title Pages will be prepared in manuscript.

WAR DIARY
or
INTELLIGENCE SUMMARY
(Erase heading not required.)

Place	Date	Hour	Summary of Events and Information	Remarks and references to Appendices
METEREN FRANCE	11/8/17		CRE went round line to be taken over from 41 Divn; with CRE 41 Divn. Fld Coys 39 Divn to relieve Fld Coys 41 Divn in accordance with appendix C attached	App C
	13/8/17		CRE visited CRE 41 made final arrangements re taking over. Adj visited 225 & 227 Fld Coys. Major Hammond proceeded on 10 days leave to England	
WESTOUTRE BELGIUM	15/8/17		Divn HQ moved to WESTOUTRE took over HQ from 41 Divn CRE and Adj visited Field Coys. Showery.	
	16/8/17		CRE visited trenches. Fine day, windy. 5th Army attacked hostile trenches. Major Murston to England, 10 days leave.	
	18/8/17		Major SH Joseph OC 227 Fld Coy killed in action. CRE, a/OC 225 and Adj. visited trenches. Fine. Lt Summerscales 225 Coy wounded	
	19/8/17		CRE & AAQMG visited Vierstraat baths & Camp. Adj. visited 227 & 234 Coys. CRE & Adj attended Major Josephs funeral at VIERSTRATT CEMETARY. Fine, windy. Ground drying up	
	20/8/17		CRE visited trenches today inspected Optic avenue & decided on scheme of drainage for same. Adj. visited 2nd Army workshops HAZEBROUCK re machine gun mountings Fine day.	
	22/8/17		CRE visited trenches, went round left with Capt Argent Adj saw Tramway officer in VOORMEZEELE re working of tramways	

Instructions regarding War Diaries and Intelligence Summaries are contained in F. S. Regs., Part II. and the Staff Manual respectively. Title Pages will be prepared in manuscript.

WAR DIARY
or
INTELLIGENCE SUMMARY
(Erase heading not required.)

Army Form C. 2118

Place	Date	Hour	Summary of Events and Information	Remarks and references to Appendices
	23 8/17		CRE visited trenches (right sector) with Captn Kirby 234 Fld Coy. looked at proposed route for new tramway. Fine. Windy	
	26 8/17		CRE visited trenches. Major D.H. Hammonds returned from leave. Lieut W. H. GILLESPIE rejoined from XVIII Corps & was attached to 225 Field Co.	
	27 8/17		Heavy Rain. Capt J.T. Argent 225 Fld Coy took over command 227 Coy	
	28 8/17		Strong Wind. Rain. Visit from CE X Corps (Vice Major S.H. Joseph killed in action)	
	29 8/17		~~Major J.T. Argent proceeded on 10 days leave to England~~. CRE attended Conference at CE X Corps HQ. Work South of Canal handed over to CRE 37 Div vide appendix attached	APP. D
	30 8/17		CRE visited trenches. Adj visited Div Schools with GSO II	
			Major J.T. ARGENT on leave to England. Capt G.M. ROSS acts for him.	
	31st		CRE. visited new Bde H.Q. VLAMERTINGHE.	

[illegible]
CRE 39 Div.

1875 Wt. W593/826 1,000,000 4/15 J.B.C. & A. A.D.S.S./Forms/C. 2118.

APPENDIX A

SECRET.

INSTRUCTION NO.12.

(Issued in connection with 39th Division Order No. 125.)

EMPLOYMENT OF R.E. AND PIONEERS.

GENERAL 1. The 39th Divisional R.E. and 13th Gloucester Regiment will be employed as follows after zero hour on Z day:-

225th Field Co. R.E. on the construction of a cross country track;

For 1st line Transport from about C.22.a.1.9 across the hostile trenches (as shown on the map issued with 39th Division Order No. 125).

234th Field Co. R.E. on the construction of strong points.

227th Field Co. R.E. in Divisional Reserve.

255th Tunnelling Co.R.E., on burying cable under 39th Divisional Signal Co. R.E.

13th Gloucester Regiment (less 1 Company on Railway work) on the construction of a lorry route along BUFFS ROAD to its junction with the WIELTJE-ST.JULIEN Road and along the latter.

225th Field Co. R.E. Cross country track.

2. (a) The 225th Field Co. R.E. will assemble in the CANAL BANK and will send an Officer to report to G.S.O.3 at 39th Divisional Advanced Report Centre (CANAL BANK C.25.d.3.2.) by Zero minus 1 hour. This Officer will be informed on the capture of the BLACK Line, when 225th Field Co. R.E. will move forward to HAMPSHIRE FARM.

(b) "A" Co. 16th Notts & Derby Regt. (Captain LORD) and "A" Co. 11th R.Sussex Regt. (Captain ALLEN) will re-organise on the capture of the BLUE LINE and report to Major HAMMOND, R.E., Commanding 225th Field Co. R.E., at HAMPSHIRE FARM at zero plus 2 hours. Should the R.E. not have arrived, the Infantry Companies will wait there.

Each man of these Companies will bring one shovel with him.

(c) The cross country track will be constructed by the troops mentioned in this para. under the command of Major Hammond, who will wire time of commencing work and hourly progress reports to 39th Divisional Headquarters.

234th Field Co. R.E., Strong Points (39th Division Order No. 125, para. 3 (f).

3. (a) The 234th Field Co. R.E. will assemble in the CANAL BANK and will detail one Officer and 5 N.C.O's and sappers to accompany the Headquarters of each Infantry Brigade, and one Officer to be at 39th Divisional Advanced Report Centre (C.25.d.3.2.) at zero minus 1 hour.

(b) The duties of these Officers will be to inform O.C. 234th Field Co. R.E., through the Officer at 39th Divisional Advanced Report Centre -

(i) When, to what point, and by what route the 234th Field Co. R.E., can advance.

(ii) The locality and amount of R.E. assistance required at any point, in the area of the Infantry Brigade to which they are attached, for the consolidation or the construction of strong points.

(c). R.E.Officers attached to 116th and 117th Infantry Brigades will reconnoitre the Valley of the STEENBEEK in their respective Infantry Brigade Areas and report by wire to the C.R.E. points where trestle bridges are required.

(d). The R.E. N.C.Os and Sappers attached to 116th and 117th Infantry Brigades will be used to assist the Infantry to construct crossing places for Tanks over the STEENBEEK about C.12.c.2.1., C.12.c.0.6, C.11.b.2.7., and C.5.d.1.0.

(e). The 234th Field Company will move forward by bounds, halting near Brigade Forward Stations and reporting its position to C.R.E. and Infantry Brigades at each halt.

The R.E. Officer at 39th Divisional Advanced Report Centre will rejoin the 234th Field Co.R.E. on the latter advancing.

(f). Infantry garrisons detailed for strong points will at once occupy these points on notification being received from the R.E. that they are ready.

227th Field Co.R.E. Reserve.

4. The 227th Field Coy R.E. will be in Divisional Reserve in the CANAL BANK and will be ready either to work in relief of 225th Field Co.R.E., or to bridge the STEENBEEK or for any other contingency.

The C.R.E. will detail parties from this Field Company to reconnoitre and repair wells and the water supply in the captured trenches.

255th Tunnelling Co.R.E. Cable Burying.

5. (a). The 255th Tunnelling Co.R.E. parties will be withdrawn to PROVEN on completion of their present tasks and will assemble in the CANAL BANK (with their attached Infantry) on Y/Z night under instructions to be issued.

(b). The 255th Tunnelling Co.R.E. will detail an Officer to report at 39th Divisional Advanced Report Centre (C.25.d.3.2.) at Zero minus one hour. This Officer will be informed when the Company can move forward (on the Infantry advancing from the DOTTED BLUE LINE).

(c). On receiving instructions, 255th Tunnelling Co.R.E will move to the Battalion Headquarters at C.21.b.4.2 (BILGE TRENCH) where they will be met by an Officer and party to be detailed by O.C. 39th Divisional Signal Co.R.E. They will then proceed to bury cable from C.21.b.4.2. to CORNER COT.

(d). The 255th Tunnelling Co.R.E. will draw 500 shovels and 50 picks on arrival at the CANAL BANK on Y/Z night under instructions to be issued by the C.R.E.

13th Gloucestershire Regt. Lorry Route.

6. (a). The 13th Bn Gloucestershire Regt (less 1 Company on Railway work) will assemble in the CANAL BANK on Y/Z night and will send an Officer to report to 39th Divisional Advanced Report Centre at Zero minus one hour. This Officer will be informed when the advance from the DOTTED BLUE LINE commences and the 13th Bn Gloucestershire Regiment can move forward.

(b).

(b). On receiving instructions, the 13th Bn Gloucestershire Regt less 2 Companies (one left in CANAL BANK as reserve and to provide reliefs) will move to the junction of ADMIRAL'S and BUFF'S ROAD and continue the latter thence as a lorry route across NO MAN'S LAND and the captured trenches.

(c). O.C., 13th Bn Gloucestershire Regt will report by wire to C.R.E. hour at which work commences and hourly progress thereafter.

R.E.Dumps. 7. (a). The C.R.E. will arrange to form dumps of R.E. material as follows:-

(i). At 39th Divisional Dump, I.2.a.1.9.
(ii). Brigade R.E.Dumps, about C.21.c.4.4.
(iii). Forward R.E.Dump about C.22.a.3.7 (where the cross country track crosses the enemy front line). This will be formed from the Divisional R.E.Dump as soon as the situation admits (see para 8).
(iv). Advance R.E.Dumps near CORNER COT and South-East corner of KITCHENER'S WOOD (see para 8).
(v). Road metal and pit prop dump near CROSS ROADS FARM.
(vi). The XVIII Corps Forward R.E.Dump will be formed near LA BELLE ALLIANCE.

(b). R.E.material from the Dump at C.22.a.3.7 will only be used for consolidation, &c. in and in front of the BLACK LINE.

R.E.material from the Dumps at CORNER COT and South-East Corner of KITCHENER'S WOOD will only be used for consolidation &c. in front of the DOTTED GREEN LINE.

(c). The C.R.E. will arrange to organise the supply of material from any hostile Engineer dumps that may be captured.

Transport. 8. (a). The C.R.E. will arrange to have 3 pontoon wagons loaded with R.E.material at the Divisional Dump (I.2.a.1.9) by Zero hour. Teams for these wagons will be sent up on the capture of the BLACK LINE to take them to the Forward R.E. Dump at C.22.a.3.7.

(b). The C.R.E. will arrange for 2 pack trains (10 pack animals each) to carry R.E.material from the Forward R.E. Dump at C.22.a.3.7 to the Advanced R.E.Dumps near CORNER COT and the South-East corner of KITCHENER'S WOOD as soon as the situation admits.

(c). Three Pontoon wagons will be loaded with material for trestle bridges at the Divisional Dump (I.2.a.1.9) by Zero hour, and will be sent forward under instructions to be issued by the C.R.E.

Bridges. 9. The 284th Army Troops Coy R.E. will be responsible for the repair and maintenance of all Bridges over the Canal under instructions to be issued by the C.R.E.

SECRET.

INSTRUCTION NO.12.

(Issued in connection with 39th Division Order No. 125.)

EMPLOYMENT OF R.E. AND PIONEERS.

GENERAL 1. The 39th Divisional R.E. and 13th Gloucester Regiment will be employed as follows after zero hour on Z day:-

225th Field Co. R.E. on the construction of a cross country track;

For 1st line Transport from about C.22.a.1.9 across the hostile trenches (as shown on the map issued with 39th Division Order No. 125).

234th Field Co. R.E. on the construction of strong points.

227th Field Co. R.E. in Divisional Reserve.

255th Tunnelling Co.R.E., on burying cable under 39th Divisional Signal Co. R.E.

13th Gloucester Regiment (less 1 Company on Railway work) on the construction of a lorry route along BUFFS ROAD to its junction with the WIELTJE-ST.JULIEN Road and along the latter.

225th Field Co. R.E. Cross country track. 2. (a) The 225th Field Co. R.E. will assemble in the CANAL BANK and will send an Officer to report to G.S.O.3 at 39th Divisional Advanced Report Centre (CANAL BANK C.25.d.3.2.) by Zero minus 1 hour. This Officer will be informed on the capture of the BLACK Line, when 225th Field Co. R.E. will move forward to HAMPSHIRE FARM.

(b) "A" Co. 16th Notts & Derby Regt. (Captain LORD) and "A" Co. 11th R.Sussex Regt. (Captain ALLEN) will re-organise on the capture of the BLUE LINE and report to Major HAMMOND, R.E., Commanding 225th Field Co. R.E., at HAMPSHIRE FARM at zero plus 2 hours. Should the R.E. not have arrived, the Infantry Companies will wait there.

Each man of these Companies will bring one shovel with him.

(c) The cross country track will be constructed by the troops mentioned in this para. under the command of Major Hammond, who will wire time of commencing work and hourly progress reports to 39th Divisional Headquarters.

234th Field Co. R.E., Strong Points (39th Division Order No. 125, para. 3 (f). 3. (a) The 234th Field Co. R.E. will assemble in the CANAL BANK and will detail one Officer and 5 N.C.O's and sappers to accompany the Headquarters of each Infantry Brigade, and one Officer to be at 39th Divisional Advanced Report Centre (C.25.d.3.2.) at zero minus 1 hour.

(b) The duties of these Officers will be to inform O.C. 234th Field Co. R.E., through the Officer at 39th Divisional Advanced Report Centre -

(i) When, to what point, and by what route the 234th Field Co. R.E., can advance.

(ii) The locality and amount of R.E. assistance required at any point, in the area of the Infantry Brigade to which they are attached, for the consolidation or the construction of strong points.

¢

(c). R.E.Officers attached to 116th and 117th Infantry Brigades will reconnoitre the Valley of the STEENBEEK in their respective Infantry Brigade Areas and report by wire to the C.R.E. points where trestle bridges are required.

(d). The R.E. N.C.Os and Sappers attached to 116th and 117th Infantry Brigades will be used to assist the Infantry to construct crossing places for Tanks over the STEENBEEK about C.12.c.2.1., C.12.c.0.6, C.11.b.2.7., and C.5.d.1.0.

(e). The 234th Field Company will move forward by bounds, halting near Brigade Forward Stations and reporting its position to C.R.E. and Infantry Brigades at each halt.

The R.E. Officer at 39th Divisional Advanced Report Centre will rejoin the 234th Field Co.R.E. on the latter advancing.

(f). Infantry garrisons detailed for strong points will at once occupy these points on notification being received from the R.E. that they are ready.

227th Field Co.R.E. Reserve.

4. The 227th Field Coy R.E. will be in Divisional Reserve in the CANAL BANK and will be ready either to work in relief of 225th Field Co.R.E., or to bridge the STEENBEEK or for any other contingency.

The C.R.E. will detail parties from this Field Company to reconnoitre and repair wells and the water supply in the captured trenches.

255th Tunnelling Co.R.E. Cable Burying.

5. (a). The 255th Tunnelling Co.R.E. parties will be withdrawn to PROVEN on completion of their present tasks and will assemble in the CANAL BANK (with their attached Infantry) on Y/Z night under instructions to be issued.

(b). The 255th Tunnelling Co.R.E. will detail an Officer to report at 39th Divisional Advanced Report Centre (C.25.d.3.2.) at zero minus one hour. This Officer will be informed when the Company can move forward (on the Infantry advancing from the DOTTED BLUE LINE).

(c). On receiving instructions, 255th Tunnelling Co.R.E will move to the Battalion Headquarters at C.21.b.4.2 (BILGE TRENCH) where they will be met by an Officer and party to be detailed by O.C. 39th Divisional Signal Co.R.E. They will then proceed to bury cable from C.21.b.4.2. to CORNER COT.

(d). The 255th Tunnelling Co.R.E. will draw 500 shovels and 50 picks on arrival at the CANAL BANK on Y/Z night under instructions to be issued by the C.R.E.

13th Gloucestershire Regt. Lorry Route.

6. (a). The 13th Bn Gloucestershire Regt (less 1 Company on Railway work) will assemble in the CANAL BANK on Y/Z night and will send an Officer to report to 39th Divisional Advanced Report Centre at zero minus one hour. This Officer will be informed when the advance from the DOTTED BLUE LINE commences and the 13th Bn Gloucestershire Regiment can move forward.

(b).

(b). On receiving instructions, the 13th Bn Gloucestershire Regt less 2 Companies (one left in CANAL BANK as reserve and to provide reliefs) will move to the junction of ADMIRAL'S and BUFF'S ROAD and continue the latter thence as a lorry route across NO MAN'S LAND and the captured trenches.

(c). O.C., 13th Bn Gloucestershire Regt will report by wire to C.R.E. hour at which work commences and hourly progress thereafter.

R.E.Dumps. 7. (a). The C.R.E. will arrange to form dumps of R.E. material as follows:-

(i). At 39th Divisional Dump, I.2.a.1.9.
(ii). Brigade R.E.Dumps, about C.21.c.4.4.
(iii). Forward R.E.Dump about C.22.a.3.7 (where the cross country track crosses the enemy front line). This will be formed from the Divisional R.E.Dump as soon as the situation admits (see para 8).
(iv). Advance R.E.Dumps near CORNER COT and South-East corner of KITCHENER'S WOOD (see para 8).
(v). Road metal and pit prop dump near CROSS ROADS FARM.
(vi). The XVIII Corps Forward R.E.Dump will be formed near LA BELLE ALLIANCE.

(b). R.E.material from the Dump at C.22.a.3.7 will only be used for consolidation, &c. in and in front of the BLACK LINE.

R.E.material from the Dumps at CORNER COT and South-East Corner of KITCHENER'S WOOD will only be used for consolidation &c. in front of the DOTTED GREEN LINE.

(c). The C.R.E. will arrange to organise the supply of material from any hostile Engineer dumps that may be captured.

Transport. 8. (a). The C.R.E. will arrange to have 3 pontoon wagons loaded with R.E.material at the Divisional Dump (I.2.a.1.9) by Zero hour. Teams for these wagons will be sent up on the capture of the BLACK LINE to take them to the Forward R.E. Dump at C.22.a.3.7.

(b). The C.R.E. will arrange for 2 pack trains (10 pack animals each) to carry R.E.material from the Forward R.E. Dump at C.22.a.3.7 to the Advanced R.E.Dumps near CORNER COT and the South-East corner of KITCHENER'S WOOD as soon as the situation admits.

(c). Three Pontoon wagons will be loaded with material for trestle bridges at the Divisional Dump (I.2.a.1.9) by Zero hour, and will be sent forward under instructions to be issued by the C.R.E.

Bridges. 9. The 284th Army Troops Coy R.E. will be responsible for the repair and maintenance of all Bridges over the Canal under instructions to be issued by the C.R.E.

A/A.2.

WORK OF FIELD COMPANIES AND PIONEER BATTALION

ON JULY 31st.1917.

On the afternoon and evening of July 29th the three Field Companies and Pioneer Battalion (less one Company previously detached for work under A.D.L.R.) had to be withdrawn from their billets in the CANAL BANK to make room for the Infantry assembly. These Units marched back to the CANAL BANK during the night July 30th/31st arriving about 2 a.m. This move was unavoidable. It had the advantage of giving these units a rest on July 30th and the disadvantage of depriving them of rest immediately before Zero hour (3.50 a.m.)

Each Unit sent an Officer to the Advanced Divisional Report Centre in the CANAL BANK shortly before Zero to keep in touch with the situation.

At about 6 a.m. the 225th Field Coy.R.E. under Major HAMMONDS M.C. and the 13th.Gloucestershire Regiment (less ½ coy.) under Major HOWMAN were able to move forward to their appointed tasks viz: the continuation of a track for guns and pack transport beyond ADMIRALS ROAD and the repair of BUFFS ROAD respectively.

The work of these units proceeded uninteruptedly though both suffered several casualties from shell fire. Two ~~of these~~ men were killed by a mine exloding at about 11 a.m. close to the point where CALIFORNIA RESERVE crosses the road. One of the victims is reported to have been seen tugging at some wire with his pick shortly before the explosion.

By 12 noon the main overland track had been cleared for transport over the German front line system (CALF TRENCH, SUPPORT and RESERVE) and for pack to the road beyond OBLONG FARM, while two side tracks off the main route had been clear-ed to the areas previously chosen for forward 18 pounder positions. BUFFS ROAD was clear up to the German front line wire.

By 3 p.m. the pack track was clear nearly to ALBERTA, and BUFFS ROAD through to its junction with the WIELTJE - ST. JULIEN ROAD.

Work was continued on this track and road during the evening by 227th.Field Coy.R.E. and the remaining half company of the 13th. Gloucestershire Regt.. These parties suffered no casualties. By 1a.m. the overland track was passable for wheeled transport to within 150 yds of ALBERTA.

Owing to the rain, however, the track soon became a sea of mud impassable for transport and passable with difficulty for pack.

In addition to work on the track small parties were detailed from 225th. Field Company R.E. to search for wells in captured trenches. Four wells were found and samples taken; but only one (at RACECOURSE FARM) was subsequently found to be fit for drinking (two scoops).

The remaining Field Company (234th) had been detailed to construct four strong points, two in and close behind the GREEN LINE, one at ST.JULIEN and one at ALBERTA.

Three R.E. Officers from this Company were detailed to accompany the three Infantry Brigades Headquarters to reconnoitre sites for strong points, and advise O.C. Company generally where R.E. assistance was required.

Reports from these Officers and from O.C. 234th.Field Coy.R.E. are attached, and it will be seen that this Field Company was able to do practically no work. The reasons for this do not come into the scope of this narrative.

Three pontoon wagons had been loaded up with R.E. stores prior to Zero to be sent forward as soon as possible to the vicinity of the German front line. Capt ARGENT 225th. Field Company R.E. who was in charge of these wagons moved off from MACHINE GUN FARM at 6.30 a.m., parked his wagons East of the CANAL and reconnoitred the road forward. Finding ADMIRALS ROAD blocked and the transport track not yet passable up to our old front line he reported by telephone and was ordered to dump the stores near the junction of ADMIRALS and BUFFS ROAD. This was done. One wagon was hit by a shell but though badly damaged was brought back. Capt ARGENT then took up a load of Artillery Bridges for the transport track.

At 2.45.p.m. the pack track being reported through to KITCHENERS WOOD I ordered the pack train forward. This consisted of 20 animals under Capt ROSS 227th. Field Coy.R.E. Stores were loaded up at HAMMONDS CORNER and taken to S. Corner of KITCHENERS WOOD. Two trips were made and the following stores carried.

Wire	60 coils.
Pickets. (long)	260.
Pickets. (short)	80.
Shovels.	320.
Sandbags.	500.

The first load was dumped at 7.30.p.m.

In addition to these stores 234th. Field Company took with them 26 mules loaded with wire and pickets for their strong points. This was dumped at VAN HEULE FARM.

During the day the Field Companies and Pioneer Battalion suffered the following casualties (including attached Infantry).

	Killed.	Wounded.	Missing.
225th.Field Coy.R.E.	3.O.R.	12 O.R.	
227th.Field Coy.R.E.		1.O.R.	
234th.Field Coy.R.E.	1Off.& 6.O.R.	22.O.R.	3.O.R.
13th.Gloster.Regt.	1Off.& 4.O.R.	23.O.R.	

10. 8. 17

[signature] Lt Col RE
CRE 39 Div

WORK OF FIELD COMPANIES AND PIONEER BATTALION
ON JULY 31st 1917.

On the afternoon and evening of July 29th the three Field Companies and Pioneer Battalion (less one Company previously detached for work under A.D.L.R.) had to be withdrawn from their billets in the CANAL BANK to make room for the Infantry assembly. These Units marched back to the CANAl BANK during the night July 30th/31st arriving about 2 a.m. This move was unavoidable. It had the advantage of giving these units a rest on July 30th and the disadvantage of depriving them of rest immediately before Zero hour (3.50 a.m.).

Each unit sent an officer to the Advanced Divisional Report Centre in the CANAL BANK shortly before Zero to keep in touch with the situation.

At about 6 a.m. the 225th Field Coy. R.E. under Major HAMMONDS, M.C. and the 13th Gloucestershire Regt½ (less ½ Coy) under Major HOWMAN were able to move forward to their appointed tasks viz the continuation of a track for guns and pack transport beyond ADMIRALS ROAD and the repair of BUFFS ROAD respectively.

The work of these units proceeded uninteruptedly though both suffered several casualties from shell fire. Two men were killed by a mine exploding at about 11 a.m. close to the point where CALIFORNIA RESERVE crosses the road. One of the victims is reported to have been seen tugging at some wire with his pick shortly before the explosion.

By 12 noon the main overland track had been cleared for transport over the German front line system (CALF TRENCH, SUPPORT and RESERVE) and for pack to the road beyond OBLONG FARM, while two side tracks off the main route had been cleared to the areas previously chosen for forward 18 pounder positions. BUFFS ROAD was clear up to the German front line wire.

By 3 p.m. the pack track was clear nearly to ALBERTA, and BUFFS ROAD through to its junction with the WIELTJE - ST.JULIEN ROAD.

Work was continued on this track and road during the evening by 227th Field Coy. R.E. and the remaining half company of the 13th Gloucestershire Regt. These parties suffered no casualties. By 1 a.m. the overland track was passable for wheeled transport to within 150 yds of ALBERTA.

Owing to the rain, however, the track soon became a sea of mud impassable for transport and passable with difficulty for pack.

In addition to work on the track small parties were detailed from 225th Field Company R.E. to search for wells in captured trenches. Four wells were found and samples taken; but only one (at RACECOURSE FARM) was subsequently found to be fit for drinking (two scoops).

The remaining Field Company (234th) had been detailed to construct four strong points, two in and close behind the GREEN LINE, one at ST.JULIEN and one at ALBERTA.

Three R.E. Officers from this Company were detailed to accompany the three Infantry Brigade Headquarters to reconnoitre sites for strong points, and advise O.C. Company generally where R.E. assistance was required.

Reports from these Officers and from O.C. 234th Field Coy. R.E. are attached, and it will be seen that this Field Company was able to do practically no work. The reasons for this do not come into the scope of this narrative.

Three pontoon wagons had been loaded up with R.E. atores prior to ZERO to be sent forward as soon as possible to the vicinity of the German front line. Capt. ARGENT, 225th Field Company R.E. who was in charge of these wagons moved off from MACHINE GUN FARM at 6.30 a.m., parked his wagons East of the Canal and reconnoitred the road forward. Finding ADMIRALS ROAD blocked and the transport track not yet passable up to our old front line he reported by telephone and was ordered to dump the stores near the junction of ADMIRALS and BUFFS Road . This was done. One wagon was hit by a shell but though badly damaged was brought back. Capt. ARGENT then took up a load of Artillery Bridges for the transport track.

At 2.45 p.m. the pack track being reported through to KITCHENERS WOOD I ordered the pack train forward. This consisted of 20 animals under Capt. ROSS, 227th Field Company R.E. Stores were loaded up at HAMMONDS CORNER and taken to S. Corner of KITCHENERS WOOD. Two trips were made and the following stores carried.

Wire.		60 coils.
Pickets.	(long)	260
"	(short)	80
Shovels.		320
Sandbags.		500

The first load was dumped at 7.30 p.m.

In addition to these stores 234th Field Company took with them 26 mules loaded with wire and pickets for their strong points. This was dumped at VAN HEULE FARM.

During the day the Field Companies and Pioneer Battalion suffered the following casualties (including attached Infantry).

	Killed.	Wounded.	Missing.
225th Field Coy. R.E.	3 O.R.	12 O.R.	
227th Field Coy. R.E.		1 O.R.	
234th Field Coy. R.E.	1 Off. 6 O.R.	22 O.R.	3 O.R.
13th Gloucestershire R.	1 Off. 4 O.R.	23 O.R.	

Lieut-Colonel R.E.
C.R.E., 39th Division.

August 10th, 1917.

Copy No...11.....

SECRET.

HEADQUARTERS, 39th.DIVISIONAL. R.E. ORDER NO.38.

Ref. 1/40000 Sheet 27 & 28. Tuesday Aug.7th.1917.

1. Field Companies and Pioneer Battalion will move to BERTHEN Area on August 8th. 1917 as follows. .

Dismounted men by train from VLAMERTINGHE.

Time of departure of train will be notified later.

Detrain at CAESTRE.

Transport and mounted details by march route.

STARTING POINT Cross Road RENINGHELST G.34.d.3.9.

Order of march and Time of passing Starting point.	) 225th.Field Coy.R.E.	10.35.a.m.
	) 13th.Glosters.	10.40.a.m.
	) 227th.Field Coy.R.E.	10.45.a.m.
	) 234th.Field Coy.R.E.	10.50.a.m.

ROUTE. RENINGHELST - WESTOUTRE - MONT VIDEIGNE - SCHAEXKEN.
Between RENINGHELST and SCHAEXKEN the whole Column will be under the Command of Capt ARGENT 225th. Field Coy.R.E.

2. Billets have been allotted as follows:-

225th.Field Coy.	X.10.b.5.7.	6 Tents, Billets 1 Officer and 130 O.R's.
	X.4.c.4.3.	Billets 4 Officers and 75 O.R's.
227th. " "	R.32.d.0.9.	Billets for 100 O.R's.
	R.32.c.2.3.	3 Tents & billets for 60 O.R's.
234th. " "	Q.34.b.4.4.	Billets 120 O.R's.
	Q.35.c.4.3.	Billets 44 O.R's.
13th. Gloucestershire Regt(Pioneers).		
	R.34.a.5.9.	3 Tents.Billets for 2 Officers & 200 O.R's.
	R.28.d.central.	2 Tents.Billets for 1 Officer & 150 O.R's.
	R.28.c.4.8.	2 Officers.
	R33.b.8.0.	9 Tents.Billets for 150 O.R's.
	R.26.d.3.4½.	20. O.R's.
	R.26.d.2.5.	50. O.R's.

Headquarters Infantry Brigades are at:-

116th. Infy Bde.	X.16.c.1.6.
117th. " "	X.1.d.2.2.
118th. " "	Q.35.b.3.1.

3. Location of H.Q. Divl.R.E. will be notified later.

4. ACKNOWLEDGE.

J. K. Couchman
Lieut.-Colonel.R.E.
C.R.E. 39th. Division.

7.8.17.

APPENDIX B

HEADQUARTERS. 39th.DIVISIONAL. R.E.ORDER NO.38.

Copies issued at 12 noon to:-

1. "G" 39th.Div.
2. "Q" 39th.Div.
3. 225th. Field Co.R.E.
4. 227th. Field Co.R.E.
5. 234th. Field Co.R.E.
6. 13th. Glosters.(Pioneers)
7. 39th. Divl. Train.
8. S.S.O.
9. A.P.M.
10.& 12. WAR DIARY.
13. FILE.

Copy No...12...

SECRET.

HEADQUARTERS, 39th.DIVISIONAL. R.E. ORDER NO.38.

Ref. 1/40000 Sheet 27 & 28. Tuesday Aug.7th.1917.

1. Field Companies and Pioneer Battalion will move to BERTHEN Area on August 8th. 1917 as follows.

Dismounted men by train from VLAMERTINGHE.

Time of departure of train will be notified later.

Detrain at CAESTRE.

Transport and mounted details by march route.

STARTING POINT Cross Road RENINGHELST G.34.d.3.9.

Order of march and Time of passing Starting point.	) 225th.Field Coy.R.E.	10.35.a.m.
	) 13th.Glosters.	10.40.a.m.
	) 227th.Field Coy.R.E.	10.45.a.m.
	) 234th.Field Coy.R.E.	10.50.a.m.

ROUTE. RENINGHELST - WESTOUTRE - MONT VIDEIGNE - SCHAEXKEN.
Between RENINGHELST and SCHAEXKEN the whole Column will be under the Command of Capt ARGENT 225th. Field Coy.R.E.

2. Billets have been allotted as follows:-

225th.Field Coy.	X.10.b.5.7.	6 Tents, Billets 1 Officer and 130 O.R's.
	X.4.c.4.3.	Billets 4 Officers and 75 O.R's.
227th. " "	R.32.d.0.9.	Billets for 100 O.R's.
	R.32.c.2.3.	3 Tents & billets for 60 O.R's.
234th. " "	Q.34.b.4.4.	Billets 120 O.R's.
	Q.35.c.4.3.	Billets 44 O.R's.
13th. Gloucestershire Regt(Pioneers).	R.34.a.5.9.	3 Tents.Billets for 2 Officers & 200 O.R's.
	R.28.d.central.	2 Tents.Billets for 1 Officer & 150 O.R's.
	R.28.c.4.8.	2 Officers.
	R33.b.8.0.	9 Tents.Billets for 150 O.R's.
	R.26.d.3.4½.	20. O.R's.
	R.26.d.2.5.	50. O.R's.

Headquarters Infantry Brigades are at:-

116th. Infy Bde.	X.16.c.1.6.
117th. " "	X.1.d.2.2.
118th. " "	Q.35.b.3.1.

3. Location of H.Q. Divl.R.E. will be notified later.

4. ACKNOWLEDGE.

7.8.17.

H. Couchman
Lieut-Colonel.R.E.
C.R.E. 39th. Division.

APPENDIX C

Copy No...14...

SECRET.

HEADQUARTERS. 39th.DIVISIONAL. R.E.ORDER.NO.39.

Sunday. 12.8.17.

1. Field Companies and Pioneer Battalion 39th. Division will relieve Field Companies and Pioneer Battalion of the 41st. Division on 13th, 14th, and 15th. Aug. as under.

(a) 234th. Field Coy.R.E. will relieve 228th. Field Coy. on 13th.Aug and will work in Right Brigade Area.

(b) 225th. and 227th. Field Companies relieve 233rd. and 237th. Field Coy. respectively on 14th Aug. and will work in Left Brigade Area and back area respectively.

(c) 13th. Glosters (less 1 coy.) relieve 19th.Bn. Middlesex Regt. (Pioneers) on 15th. Aug. and will work as already detailed.

2. Dismounted men will move by bus to HALLEBAST CORNER H.32.d.8.0. thence to camps by march route.

Times of busses for Field Companies have been issued, those for Pioneer Battalion will follow.

All movement East of LA CLYTTE will be in bodies not larger than 1 Section R.E. or 1 Platoon.

3. Locations of Units will be as follows.

	Camp.	Transport Lines.
225th.Field Coy.R.E.	N.6.d.1.1.	N.2.c.7.3.
227th. " " "	N.12.a.3.9.	N.2.c.5.9.
234th. " " "	N.6.c.6.1.	N.2.c.3.2.
13th. Glosters.	N.11.b.4.3.	N.2.c.1.3.

Advance parties will be sent to take over accommodation to arrive by 9 a.m. on day of relief.

4. Work in hand will be reconnoitred before hand under arrangements already notified.

Receipts will be given for any maps, plans or secret documents, etc taken over.

5. Completion of relief will be notified to this Office by wire.

6. ACKNOWLEDGE.

G. M. Means
Capt & Adjt. R.E.

Aug.12th. 1917.

for C.R.E. 39th. Division.

Copies issued at.......to:-

1. "G" 39th. Div.
2. "Q" " "
3. O.C. 225th.Field Coy.
4. O.C. 227th. " "
5. O.C. 234th. " "
6. C.O. 13th. Glosters.
7. C.E. X Corps.
8. C.R.E. 41st. Div.
9. O.C. 39th.Divl.Sigs.
10. A.P.M.
11. A.D.M.S.
12. D.D.V.S.
13. 39th.Divl.Train.
14 & 15. WAR DIARY.
16. FILE.

Copy No....15....

SECRET.

HEADQUARTERS. 39th.DIVISIONAL. R.E.ORDER.NO.39.

Sunday. 12.8.17.

1. Field Companies and Pioneer Battalion 39th. Division will relieve Field Companies and Pioneer Battalion of the 41st. Division on 13th, 14th, and 15th. Aug. as under.

(a) 234th. Field Coy.R.E. will relieve 228th. Field Coy. on 13th.Aug and will work in Right Brigade Area.

(b| 225th. and 227th. Field Companies relieve 233rd. and 237th. Field Coy. respectively on 14th Aug. and will work in Left Brigade Area and back area respectively.

(c) 13th. Glosters (less 1 coy.) relieve 19th.Bn. Middlesex Regt. (Pioneers) on 15th. Aug. and will work as already detailed.

2. Dismounted men will move by bus to HALLEBAST CORNER H.32.d.8.0. thence to camps by march route.

Times of busses for Field Companies have been issued, those for Pioneer Battalion will follow.

All movement East of LA CLYTTE will be in bodies not larger than 1 Section R.E. or 1 Platoon.

3. Locations of Units will be as follows.

	Camp.	Transport Lines.
225th.Field Coy.R.E.	N.6.d.1.1.	N.2.c.7.3.
227th. " " "	N.12.a.3.9.	N.2.c.5.9.
234th. " " "	N.6.c.6.1.	N.2.c.3.2.
13th. Glosters.	N.11.b.4.3.	N.2.c.1.3.

Advance parties will be sent to take over accommodation to arrive by 9 a.m. on day of relief.

4. Work in hand will be reconnoitred before hand under arrangements already notified.

Receipts will be given for any maps, plans or secret documents? etc taken over.

5. Completion of relief will be notified to thid Office by wire.

6. ACKNOWLEDGE.

G. Mcmeans
Capt & Adjt. R.E.

Aug.12th. 1917.

for C.R.E. 39th. Division.

Copies issued at.......to:-

1. "G" 39th. Div.
2. "Q" " "
3. O.C. 225th.Field Coy.
4. O.C. 227th. " "
5. O.C. 234th. " "
6. C.O. 13th. Glosters.
7. C.E. X Corps.
8. C.R.E. 41st. Div.
9. O.C. 39th.Divl.Sigs.
10. A.P.M.
11. A.D.M.S.
12. D.D.V.S.
13. 39th.Divl.Train.
14 & 15. WAR DIARY.
16. FILE.

Appendix D

"D".

SECRET.

G.772.

O.C., 225th Field Company R.E.
O.C., 227th Field Company R.E.
O.C., 234th Field Company R.E. 13th Gloucestershire Regt.

37th Division are taking over Right Brigade Sector on 29th/30th. South Divisional Boundary will run, then, as follows :- along CANAL (inclusive to 37th Division) to I.33.c.9.8, thence by north edges of BOIS CONFLUENT and BOIS CARRE to cross roads N.10.b.8.4, thence as at present.

On August 29th 234th Field Coy. R.E. and 13th Gloucestershire Regt. will be prepared to show relieving units of 37th Division all work now in hand in Right Brigade Area.

On relief, the following will be the allotment of work.

225th Field Coy.R.E.	Left Battalion area.
234th Field Coy.R.E.	Right Battalion area.
227th Field Coy.R.E.	Back area.
1 Coy. Pioneers.	OAF AVENUE up to Reserve Line.
" "	IMPERIAL AVENUE up to Reserve Line.
" "	CATERPILLAR TRACK.
" "	Tramways.

Details of work will be issued separately to all concerned.

Map showing proposed system of Defence is attached (not to 227th Coy). The trenches shown in green are dependent on further operations,

sd. H.J.Couchman, Lt-Col R.E.
C.R.E., 39th Division.

August 28th, 1917.

"D".

S E C R E T.

G.772.

O.C., 225th Field Company R.E.
O.C., 227th Field Company R.E.
O.C., 234th Field Company R.E. 13th Gloucestershire Regt.

37th Division are taking over Right Brigade Sector on 29th/30th. South Divisional Boundary will run, then, as follows :- along CANAL (inclusive to 37th Division) to I.33.c.9.8, thence by north edges of BOIS CONFLUENT and BOIS CARRE to cross roads N.10.b.8.4, thence as at present.

On August 29th 234th Field Coy. R.E. and 13th Gloucestershire Regt. will be prepared to show relieving units of 37th Division all work now in hand in Right Brigade Area.

On relief, the following will be the allotment of work.

225th Field Coy.R.E.	Left Battalion area.
234th Field Coy.R.E.	Right Battalion area.
227th Field Coy.R.E.	Back area.
1 Coy. Pioneers.	OAF AVENUE up to Reserve Line.
" "	IMPERIAL AVENUE up to Reserve Line.
" "	CATERPILLAR TRACK.
" "	Tramways.

Details of work will be issued separately to all concerned.

Map showing proposed system of Defence is attached (not to 227th Coy). The trenches shown in green are dependent on further operatiohs,

sd. H.J.Couchman, Lt-Col R.E.
C.R.E., 39th Division.

August 28th, 1917.

C.E.Xth Corps 975.

Xth Corps G.S.

With reference to my letter No.975 dated 13/11/17. forwarding copies, in triplicate, of reports on work done by R.E and Pioneers of various Divisions during recent operations - I forward herewith, in triplicate, a corrected front page of the report submitted by the C.R.E.39th Division.

2. The following alteration is also necessary on page 2, para iv, last line, for 'long' read 'large'.

A.T. Shakespear
Captain, R.E.
for Chief Engineer, Xth Corps.

Headquarters.
Xth Corps.
17.11.17.

39 CRE

Vol 19

WAR DIARIES

OF

39TH DIVL R.E.

FROM 1ST

TO 30TH SEPTEMBER 1917

W A R   D I A R Y

O F

HEADQUARTERS 39TH DIVL. R.E.

FROM 1st SEPTEMBER TO 30th SEPTEMBER 1917.

Instructions regarding War Diaries and Intelligence Summaries are contained in F. S. Regs., Part II. and the Staff Manual respectively. Title Pages will be prepared in manuscript.

WAR DIARY
or
~~INTELLIGENCE SUMMARY~~
(Erase heading not required.)

Army Form C. 2118

H. Q. R.E. 39th Div — Sept 1917

Place	Date	Hour	Summary of Events and Information	Remarks and references to Appendices
WESTOUTRE	1st		CRE & Adjt to see CRE 24th Div about taking over work in SHREWSBURY FOREST Sector.	
			CRE 37th Div & CRE 19th Div visited CRE re work in KLEIN ZILLEBEKE Sector.	
	2nd		39th Div took over SHREWSBURY FOREST Sector from 24th Div. on night 2/3rd	
	3rd		CRE. to Trenches with O.C. 225th Co to reconnoitre crossings over Railway cutting in Div' area. 225th & 227th Co working in forward area. 234th Co in back area.	
	4th		CRE to Trenches with O's C Cos Pioneer Bn to point out work to be done. Capt MEARES adjutant goes on leave. Capt KIRBY 234th Co officiates.	
	5th		CRE to Trenches with O.C. Signal Co reconnoitring dugouts in front line.	
	6th		CRE to DE ZON Camp (between SCHERPENBERG and LA CLYTTE) to inspect site of proposed Div H.Q. Heavy thunderstorm in evening.	[initials]
	7th		CRE to Trenches to select site for A.D.S in ZWARTELEEN also visual station with O.C Signal Co.	
	8th		CRE to Trenches to inspect work on Tracks & Tramway.	
	9th		CRE to Trenches — do — — do —	
	10th		CRE to Trenches to reconnoitre front line dugouts. Suggestions made for allotment of these as Bn H.Q. etc.	
	11th		Nil. Fine. Major J.T. ARGENT returned from leave.	
DE ZON Camp.	12th		Div. H.Q. moved to DE ZON CAMP near LA CLYTTE.	
	13th		CRE to Trenches. Cold. Rain in evening.	
	14th		CRE to ZWARTELEEN with A.A. & Q.M.G. inspecting roads & tracks.	

1875 Wt. W593/826 1,000,000 4/15 J.B.C. & A. A.D.S.S./Forms/C. 2118.

Instructions regarding War Diaries and Intelligence Summaries are contained in F. S. Regs., Part II. and the Staff Manual respectively. Title Pages will be prepared in manuscript.

WAR DIARY
or
~~INTELLIGENCE SUMMARY~~

(Erase heading not required.)

Army Form C. 2118

H. Q. R. E 39th Div — Sept 1917

Place	Date	Hour	Summary of Events and Information	Remarks and references to Appendices
DE ZON Camp BELGIUM.	15th		Adjt returned from leave.	
	16th		Nil.	
	17th		CRE to LARCH WOOD to see 225 & 227 Field Cos.	
	18th		CRE. to ZWARTELEEN. Dull slight drizzle	
	19th		CRE to trenches inspecting new Trench board track. Fine, windy, rain at night	
	20th		39th Div attacked 5.40 a.m. Parties from 227th Field Co accompanied Infantry with mobile charges to blow in dugout doors if required. No doors were found. Parties had only 2 casualties. Remainder of 227th Co made strong points, 234th Co extended a Trench board track beyond original front line. 225th Co in reserve. Fine	Appendix A
	21st		CRE visited Field Cos & Pioneer Bn. Very fine.	
	22		CRE visited trenches	
ZEVECOTEN BELGIUM	23		H.Q. moved to ZEVECOTEN took over from CRE 37 Div	
	24		CRE visited trenches	
	25th		L-Cpl J.T.C. Fogerty killed (227 Fld Coy) 2nd Lt TS Beach 227 Coy wounded (slight)	
	26th		39 Div attacked 5.40 am. Field Coys were employed on construction of forward track to captured position. Casualties missing 4 wounded 5.	Appendix B
ST JANS CAPPEL FRANCE	28		Headquarters moved to St Jans Cappell.	
	29		CRE went on 10 days leave to U.K. Major Hammonds acting CRE.	
	30		of CRE adj, & Coy Commdrs visited site for parade before GOC tomorrow and made necessary arrangements with Coy Commdrs.	

1375 Wt. W593/826 1,000,000 4/15 J.B.C. & A. A.D.S.S./Forms/C. 2118.

W M Hammonds
Major RE
A/CRE 39th Division

SECRET. G.969. Appendix A

O.C., 225th Field Co.R.E.
O.C., 227th -do-
O.C., 234th -do-

At ZERO hour on Attack Day Field Coys. will be assembled as follows:-

1 section 227th Coy. LARCH WOOD Tunnels.

225th Field Coy.)
227th -do- (less 1 Sect) Present rear billets.
234th -do-.)

The sections of 225th and 227th Coys. (less 1 section 227th Coy) now in LARCH WOOD and DUMP tunnels will move to rear billets after work on 18/19th night.

None of these troops will use the road between road junction I.31.d.5.3. and SPOIL BANK between the hours of 10.15 pm and 12.45 am on 18/19th night.

The following work will be carried out on Attack Day as soon as the situation permits.

1 section 227th Coy. is placed at the disposal of G.O.C., 117th Inf.Bde and will supply parties as necessary to blow in doors of dugouts if required.

Further details will be issued. These parties will probably accompany the H.Q. of attacking companies.

227th Field Coy (less 1 section) will construct strong points at about J.26.c.2.0, J.26.c.3.9., J.32.a.1.5., and J.32.a.88. The two latter points are close to concrete dugouts, the two former form part of the line it is intended to consolidate throughout.

227th Field Coy. will detail an officer and the necessary N.C.O's and men to reconnoitre the exact sites for these strong points as early as possible. This officer will wire to O.C. 227th Field Coy. from cable head dugout in ravine about J.25.c.95.40 on proceeding to reconnoitre and will again wire on return to cable head when the situation admits of 227th Coy. proceeding to work.

234th Field Coy. will construct a trench board track forward from the Ravine about J.26.c.9.1. following roughly the line of the 40 contour to the RED LINE.

234th Field Coy. will detail an officer and the necessary N.C.O's and men to tape out the line of this track as early as possible and to inform 234th Field Coy. by wire from cable head when work can be commenced.

227th and 234th Field Coys. will be prepared in any case to move forward so as to be in our present front line by 8.30 pm ready to work during the night.

225th Field Coy. will be in reserve and in the event of 227th and 234th Coys. being able to work on Attack Day will be prepared to relieve them that evening.

It is the intention to form a main line of resistance along the approximate line - J.31.b.40.75 - J.32.a.10.85 - J.26.c.25.20 - J.26.c.15.65 - J.26.a.4.0.

ACKNOWLEDGE.

sd. H.J.Couchman, Lieut-Col R.E.
17.9.17. C.R.E.; 39th Division.

Appendix B

SECRET.

INSTRUCTIONS FOR R.E. AND PIONEERS.

Field Companies and Pioneer Battalion will assemble in their present lines at ZERO hour and be prepared to carry out the following work:-

225th Field Coy. will main TRACK B and carry it forward from its present terminus about J.20.c.6.2. towards TOWER HAMLETS.

234th Field Coy. will maintain TRACK D and carry it forward from its present terminus about J.26.a.7.7. towards J.27.a.1.7.

Tracks will be cleared of obstacles and marked with pickets and not trenchboarded in the first instance.

2 sections of each of the 225th and 234th Field Coys will leave billets at ZERO plus 4 hours and be relieved by remaining 2 sections after 6 hours work.

227th Field Coy. will be in reserve and be prepared to continue trenchboarding of TRACK D during the night.

1 Coy. 13th Gloucester Regt. working in 4 shifts will maintain the trench tramway from LARCH WOOD to R.A.P. at J.25.a.3.8. The first shift will be on this tramline ready to start work at ZERO hour.

13th Gloucester Regt (less 1 Coy) will extend the pack track forward. 1 Coy. will leave billets at ZERO plus 2 hours and be relieved by 2 Coys. after 6 hours work½.

sd. H.J.COUCHMAN, Lt-Col R.E
C.R.E. 39th Division.

24/9/17.

Vol 20

W A R   D I A R Y

F O R

Headquarters, 39th Divl. R.E.

FROM OCTOBER 1st TO OCTOBER 31st, 1917.

Army Form C. 2118

Instructions regarding War Diaries and Intelligence Summaries are contained in F. S. Regs., Part II. and the Staff Manual respectively. Title Pages will be prepared in manuscript.

WAR DIARY
or
~~INTELLIGENCE SUMMARY~~
(Erase heading not required.)

H.Q. R.E. 39th Div   Oct 1917.

Place	Date	Hour	Summary of Events and Information	Remarks and references to Appendices
St JANS CAPPEL	1/10/17		225th & 227th Fd Coys were inspected by the Mj. Gen. FEETHAM. Companies were drawn up in line behind one another with transport. 234th Fd Coy having moved to OULTERSTEENE (yesterday) to work for XIII Corps, was not present at the inspection. 227th Coy was warned to move in afternoon to VOORMEZEELE but order was cancelled about 7 p.m. CRE went round camp work with OC 225th Coy	MMcA
"	2/10/17		227th Coy moved to near VOORMEZEELE at 6am to work on roads in forward area under 9th Corps. 225th Coy moved to POMPIER Camp near La CLYTTE and started work on camps. CRE visited 225 & 234 Coys with Adj also corps RE yard. 2 sections of 234th moved to TERDEGHEM	MMcA
"	3/10/17		CRE visited ~~[illegible]~~ corps workshop in Bailleul with adjutant.	MMcA
"	4/10/17		CRE and adjutant visited Corps ~~[illegible]~~ yard, 227th Coy and 225th Camp.	MMcA
"	5/10/17		~~[illegible]~~ Warning that the 2 sections 234 Coy at TERDEGHEM were to be withdrawn were received from CE on telephone. On authority of GSO1, orders were got out to relieve 227th Coy by 234th Coy and v.v. These were to be cancelled later on hearing from 227th Coy that they were to be relieved by 283 AT Coy.	MMcA
"	6/10/17		Notification of relief of 227th Coy by 283 AT Coy were received from Div about midday. Orders for 227th Coy to move back to REDVERS Camp were accordingly got out. CRE went round camps with AA & QMG 39th Div in morning.	MMcA

Instructions regarding War Diaries and Intelligence Summaries are contained in F. S. Regs., Part II. and the Staff Manual respectively. Title Pages will be prepared in manuscript.

WAR DIARY

~~or~~

~~INTELLIGENCE SUMMARY~~

(*Erase heading not required.*)

Army Form C. 2118

H.Q. R.E. 39th Div   Oct 1917.

Place	Date	Hour	Summary of Events and Information	Remarks and references to Appendices
ST JANS CAPPEL	6 & 7/10/17		CRE & Adjutant went round work on camps in morning and to Oudendom [illegible]	MH
"	8/10/17		CRE visited 34th and 19th Divisions with HA & O.C.G. and looked at camp work. 2 sections of 234th Coy ordered to move from TERDEGHEM to KRABBENHOF farm, to come under OC 225th Coy for work on Camps.	MH
"	9/10/17		CRE and Adjutant went round Camp work on Corse. New orders allotting work on camps between 225th & 227th Coys issued.	MH
"	10/10/17		Lt Col. COUCHMAN wired to say he had 6 days sick leave extension.	MH
"	11/10/17		C.R.E. went round camps on motor bike.	MH
"	12/10/17		Warning order that 39th Div was to relieve 37th Div received. CRE visited CRE 34th Div ~~[illegible]~~ and arranged preliminaries.	MH
"	13/10/17		CRE went round line with CRE 34th Div. Attended conference at D Hd. ~~[illegible]~~. Move of division postponed 24 hours. Issued orders to Fd Coys	MH
"	14/10/17		Got out orders for work cancelled later. Had conference of Fd Coy Cmdrs. at D. Hd.	MH
"	15/10/17		Arranged handing over with 34th Div.	MH

1875 Wt. W593/826 1,000,000 4/15 J.B.C. & A. A.D.S.S./Forms/C. 2118.

Instructions regarding War Diaries and Intelligence Summaries are contained in F. S. Regs., Part II. and the Staff Manual respectively. Title Pages will be prepared in manuscript.

WAR DIARY
or
~~INTELLIGENCE SUMMARY~~
(Erase heading not required.)

Army Form C. 2118

H.Q. R.E. 39th Div — Oct 1917

Place	Date	Hour	Summary of Events and Information	Remarks and references to Appendices
DE ZON CAMP	16/10/17		Moved from St JANS CAPPEL and took over from CRE 37th Div. 225th Coy were bombed at Dominion camp in night and had 57 casualties (including attached inf.). CRE returned from leave in evening	JMP
	17th		227th & 234th Co working in forward area, 225th Co moved to VOORMEZEELE. Orders received that CRE 7th Div will be in charge of forward work from 20th	
	18th		CRE visited CRE 7th Div & went round portion of line. CRE visited CRE 5th Div in evening re. taking over work on forward roads.	
	19th		CRE to C.E. X Corps re forward road work.	
	20th		CRE with O.C. 225th Co along PLUMERS DRIVE to see work to be done under CE X Corps. Fine.	
	21st		CRE to inspect mule & duckboard tracks in morning, to see CRE 7th Div, 225th Co, & Pioneer Bn. in afternoon. Very fine. 225th Co & Pioneers started work on PLUMERS DRIVE	
	22nd		CRE & adjt visited three Field Cos in afternoon. Lieut HAYCRAFT 234th Fd Co arrived to take over duties of adjutant.	
	23rd		CRE to PLUMERS DRIVE in morning to inspect work. Wet	
	24th		Lt a/Capt A.M.S. MEARES. Adjutant left on appt as O.C. 55th Field Co	
	25th		225th Co & Pioneers ceased work on PLUMERS DRIVE. 227th & 234th Cos ceased work in trenches. All units resting. CRE attended conference at Div H.Q. 7th Div relieved 39th Div in TOWER HAMLETS sector. Div H.Q. remain at DE ZON Camp	

1875 Wt. W593/826 1,000,000 4/15 J.B.C. & A. A.D.S.S./Forms/C. 2118.

Army Form C. 2118

WAR DIARY
or
~~INTELLIGENCE SUMMARY~~
(Erase heading not required.)

Instructions regarding War Diaries and Intelligence Summaries are contained in F. S. Regs., Part II. and the Staff Manual respectively. Title Pages will be prepared in manuscript.

H.Q. R.E 39th Div — Oct 1917.

Place	Date	Hour	Summary of Events and Information	Remarks and references to Appendices
DE ZON Camp	26th	.	Nil. ~~[illegible]~~	
	27th		227th & 234th Cos on hutting near KRUITSTAATHOEK under CRE X Corps Troops.	
	28th		Nil	
	29th		39th Div took over TOWER HAMLETS Sector from 7th Div. RE. relief to take place on 30th. CRE to CRE 7th Div to arrange this. ~~227th~~	
	30th		227th & part of 234th Cos moved to CANADA ST & LARCHWOOD tunnels. 225th Fd Co working in back area.	
	31st		CRE to line to see portion of left sector.	
			225th & 227th Field Cos are considerably under strength and as many men are now away on leave the working capacity of the Field Cos is much reduced.	
			[signature] Lt Col RE. CRE 39th Div	

1875 Wt. W593/826 1,000,000 4/15 J.B.C. & A. A.D.S.S./Forms/C. 2118.

CONFIDENTIAL.

Vol 21

W A R D I A R Y

O F

HEADQUARTERS 39TH DIVL. R.E.

FROM 1st to 30th November, 1917.

Instructions regarding War Diaries and Intelligence Summaries are contained in F. S. Regs., Part II. and the Staff Manual respectively. Title Pages will be prepared in manuscript.

WAR DIARY

~~or~~

~~INTELLIGENCE SUMMARY~~

(Erase heading not required.)

H.Q. RE. 39th Div   Nov. 1917

Army Form C. 2118

Place	Date	Hour	Summary of Events and Information	Remarks and references to Appendices
			Sheet 28	
DE ZON Camp	1st		CRE to Right subsector of line with O.C. 234th Co. Also visited O.C. 227th Co.	
	2nd		CRE to left subsector with O.C. 227th Co & 3 Pioneer Officers to choose site of Reserve Line & inspect work. Reported on proposed line & suggested one further back. Proposal approved.	
	3rd		Nil	
	4th		CRE to LARCH WOOD to see O.C. 234th Fd Co re. work.	
	5th		CRE to Left subsector	
	6th		Nil	
	7th		CRE to Right subsector. Capt HAYCRAFT adjt RE proceeds on leave. Capt KIRBY officiates	
	8th		Nil. 225th Co relieved 227th Co in line	
	9th		CRE to left subsector. To BEDFORD House in afternoon.	
	10th 11th 12th		} Nil.	
	13th		CRE to left subsector	
	14th		Nil	
	15th		CRE to Right subsector	
	16th		Div HQ. moved to WESTOUTRE	
WESTOUTRE	17th		227th Co relieved 234th Co in line.	
	18th		CRE to left subsector.	
	19th		Nil	
	20th		CRE to Right subsector	
	21st		Nil	
	22nd		CRE to left subsector. Capt HAYCRAFT rejoined from leave.	

1875 Wt. W593/826 1,000,000 4/15 J.B.C. & A. A.D.S.S./Forms/C. 2118.

Army Form C. 2118

WAR DIARY
or
~~INTELLIGENCE~~ SUMMARY
(Erase heading not required.)

Instructions regarding War Diaries and Intelligence Summaries are contained in F. S. Regs., Part II. and the Staff Manual respectively. Title Pages will be prepared in manuscript.

H. Q. R.E. 39th Div — Nov. 1917

Place	Date	Hour	Summary of Events and Information	Remarks and references to Appendices
WESTOUTRE	23rd		CRE O.O 48 issued	A.
GOLDFISH Chateau	24th		H.Q. RE moved to GOLDFISH chateau. Fd Co. & Pioneer Bn to YPRES & near for work under C.E. VIII Corps.	
	25th		CRE with C.E. VIII Corps inspecting forward roads.	
	26th		CRE & adjt to inspect FREZENBURG – ZONNEBEKE – SEINE road.	
	27th		CRE to conference at office of C.E. VIII Corps re road & Frontline programme	
	28th		CRE & adjt with Field Engineer to select line of new plank road DEVILS CROSSING to SEINE. to 234th Co in afternoon.	
	29th		CRE to see 234th Fd Co re new road work.	
	30th		CRE to inspect work started today on DEVILS CROSSING – SEINE road	
			All 3 Field Cos still considerably under strength.	
			30.11.17	
			[signature] Lt Col RE. CRE. 39 Div.	

Copy No........

SECRET.

C.R.E. 39TH DIVISION OPERATION
ORDER NO. 48.

23/11/17.

1. R.E. and Pioneers of 39th Division will relieve and be relieved by R.E. and Pioneers of 30th Division on 24th and 25th November, 1917, in accordance with the attached table.

2. On relief, these units will work in VIIIth Corps area, and in the absence of other instructions, will take over all work in hand by the units they relieve.
This work is forward roads and tramways.

3. The 2 Coys. of 13th Gloucestershire Regt moving on the 24th Nov. will take over from the 2 Coys. 11th S.Lancs. working on repair of GRAVENSTAFEL - BELLEVUE Road, and will send 4 platoons to work on this road on 25th Nov. Other units will start work on 26th Nov.

4. All units will leave 1 Officer (2 Officers for 13th Glouc. R) and 10 N.C.O's and men in present forward billets to hand over work in hand to relieving units, who will leave similar rear parties. These rear parties will be rationed by relieving units and will rejoin their units on 26th Nov, or earlier if handing over is complete.

5. All units will send small advance parties to take over billets on morning of 24th Nov.

6. All secret maps, lists of dugouts and details of work in hand will be handed over to relieving units.

7. C.R.E's office will close at WESTOUTRE at 10 a.m. Nov. 24th and re-open at GOLDFISH CHATEAU, H.11.central at 11 a.m. on same day.

8. ACKNOWLEDGE.

Lieut-Col R.E.
C.R.E., 39th Division.

Copies issued at p.m. to :-
1. 225th Field Coy.
2. 227th Field Coy.
3. 234th Field Coy.
4. 13th Glouc. R.
5 & 6 H.Q., 39th Division.
7. 39th Signals.
8. 39th Divl. Train.
9. S.S.O.
10. C.R.E., 14th Div.
11. C.R.E., 30th Div.
12. C.E., VIII Corps.
13. C.E., IX Corps.
14. 15. War Diary.
16. File.

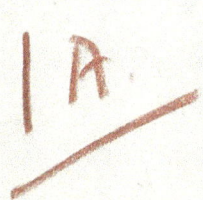

1A

Date.	Unit.	Relieved by	Relieves	Location.		Remarks.
				Billets.	Horse Lines.	
Nov. 24th.	225th Field Coy.	201st Field Coy.	200th Field Coy.	I.2.c.2.7.	H.2.d.95.35.	201st Field Coy. will put ½ Coy. in JASPER Tunnels & ½ Coy in CANADA STREET. 200th Field Coy. will all be in CANADA STREET. Field Coys. 30th Div. have no attached infantry at present.
"	227th Field Coy.	200th Field Coy.	201st Field Coy.	I.1.d.3.8.	H.3.c.0.0.	
"	234th Field Coy.	202nd Field Coy.	202nd Field Coy.	I.7.d.9.9.	H.3.c.1.5.	
"	13th Glouc. Regt. (less 2 Coys).	11th S.Lancs.R. (less 2 Coys).	11th S.Lancs.R. (less 2 Coys).	I.1.d.1.6.	Near VLAMERTINGHE.	
Nov. 25th.	2 Coys. 13th Glouc. Regt.	2 Coys. 11th S.Lancs R.	2 Coys. 11th S.Lancs.R.	-do-	-do-	

5 lorries, 1 for each Field Coy. and 2 for Pioneers Bn. will be at BRASSERIE Cross Roads at 10 a.m. 24th Nov.

2 lorries, for Pioneer Bn. will be at same place and time on 25th Nov.

H.465.

H.Q.39th Division.
C.E.Xth Corps.

Herewith report submitted in accordance with Second Army G.447 dated 26/10/17.

(sd) H.W.COUCHMAN.
Lieut Col.R.E.

9.11.17. C.R.E.39th Division.

SECRET.

Four separate sectors of the YPRES Salient have been prepared for Offensive Operations by this Division. These are:-

(i) HILL TOP for 31st July.
(ii) KLEIN ZILLEBEKE for Sept. 20th. x
(iii) SHREWSBURY FOREST for Sept. 20th.
(iv) TOWER HAMLETS for Sept. 26th and Oct. 26th. /

x 19th Division attack.
/ 7th Division attack.

Dealing with these separately, the work in (i) followed the usual lines of a deliberate preparation and consisted generally of the following :-

(a) Forward Assembly trenches 2500 yards.
(b) Extra communication trenches.
(c) Splinter proofs for 3 Bn. H.Q.
3 R.A.P's and an advanced Collecting Post for wounded. (Tunnelling Coy. also made tunnelled dugouts for Bde & Bn. H.Q.)
(d) Shell proof R.A. Group H.Q.
(e) Extension of trench tramway system, including sidings to gun positions.
(f) Causeway over YPRES-BOESINGHE Canal and 20' plank road 600 yards long. Widening forward road.
(g) Transport track from CANAL forward, including cutting through Canal Bank.
(h) Clearing track for artillery to move forward after Zero.
(i) Splinter proof visual station and O.P's.
(j) Erection of screens to conceal movement above ground.
(k) Digging shallow wells in forward area.
(l) Formation of advanced Divl. and Bde. Dumps of R.E. stores.

The whole of the work planned could not be completed. This was largely due to hostile artillery and gas during the latter half of July which caused considerable casualties, especially to the 3 Field Coys. of another Division who were working under my orders during this period. An immense amount of labour was expended over the assembly trenches.

After the attack on 31st July 1 Field Coy. (relieved at night by another) cleared a track forward of our old front line. By 2 a.m. Aug. 1st a track for mules had been cleared and marked with pickets for 2500 yards; about 800 yards of this was widened for guns. A Field Coy. of the reserve Division completed the track up to our old front line. Owing to the rain, however, the track soon became almost impassable for wagons in spite of improvements made on subsequent days by rough corduroy with salved timber.

The third Field Coy. was detailed to construct 4 strong points, the sites of which had been previously selected on the map. Owing, however, to the failure to capture the final objective, these could not be made, though some work was done on one of them. The Field Coy. was sent out to work about 11 a.m. and communication afterwards was very slow. It seems advisable to face the fact that, except in rare cases, strong points cannot be made before dusk. By that time the situation is usually clear enough for a selection of sites to be made.

A certain amount of digging and wiring was also done on subsequent days by the Field Coys. chiefly round various concrete dugouts.

The Pioneers were exclusively employed on clearing the HILL TOP - ST JULIEN Road forward of our old front line and corduroying it.

For the subsequent attacks which the Division has made, preparations have necessarily been much simpler and the following has usually been the order of urgency :-

1. Trenchboard Tracks.
2. Track for pack transport.
3. Clearing concrete dugouts.
4. Extension of tramways.
5. Communication trenches.

In addition to these main items, various minor work has been done, viz:-

Construction of Advanced Collecting Post.
Splinter proof visual Stations.

After these later attacks, the Field Coys. and Pioneer Battn. have been almost exclusively employed on maintaining and carrying forward trenchboard and mule tracks and very little consolidation has been done by them.

Taking the point referred to in Second Army letter -

i. Plank Roads. The present method of construction with 3 or 4 runners for a 10' width seems the best, but the slabs should be fixed with 6" spikes and not nails. The formation of the road is all important, a good camber should be given and the runners well bedded in, so that slabs rest on the formation and not only on the runners. Double width roads are far preferable but as speed is all important, it is better to make the road single width to start with, provided frequent crossing places, say every 300 yds, are made at the same time. The single track road will be laid with a transverse slope. So little plank road work has been done under me that I cannot estimate the rate of construction. This depends almost entirely on the length of carry which may vary enormously.

ii. Mule tracks have been largely used in this Division. The light mule board made by Xth Corps seems very suitable, provided a good earth formation is made first.

iii. Trench board tracks are an absolute necessity. They should be made double width, though a single track should be pushed through first, and the stout wire netting, not rabbit wire, is a great advantage. This need not cover the whole width of the board and it is better to cover the centre 1' of the boards with wire at the Divisional Yard.

iv. Trench board tracks do not require marking but until the track is made, tape or pickets are necessary. Infantry also require numerous tracks to Coy. and Bn. H.Q. etc., and as it is not possible to trench board all these, some form of marking is required. I do not think that Infantry would use pickets for these forward tracks for they are far heavier than tape, and a large consumption of the latter must be faced.

v. Light Railways are not, I think, of much use for Divisional R.E. work in 'battle' times. My small experience of them is that they cannot guarantee a train load of stores on any particular day, and as large forward dumps of stores are not advisable, they have been little used. A considerable amount of stores were, however, sent up by Light Railway before July 31st.

vi. We have not attempted to organise a forward tramway system for carriage of stores and supplies. Any extensions made have been used for conveyance of wounded.

vii. Corps has generally provided wells at or near Bde. H.Q. but owing to frequent changes of Divisions these have often not been properly looked after, and have been badly fouled.

viii. This entirely depends, of course, on the time available. In the KLEIN ZILLEBEKE sector where there was no attack (I believe) between July 31st and Sept 20th, considerable lengths of revetted C.T's were made and a revetted support line begun. It is far better to start right away with a revetted trench, the bottom 2 or 3 feet at least, and lay trenchboard than to dig long lengths of trench which in this ground, except in rare places, will only stand for a day or two. The construction of shelter is a difficulty which has been much reduced by the many concrete dugouts available, and considerable work has been done to clear and drain these. Practically no wiring has been done.

ix. One or more small parties of R.E. under an Officer were sent on ahead on July 31st and Sept. 20th to reconnoitre sites for strong points and lay out the line of a forward track.

On Sept. 20th these parties were valuable.

On July 31st 3 of the 4 sites previously selected for strong points were not reached by our troops, and the reconnoitring parties did not do very much. If strong points are to be made, they should, where possible, be reconnoitred before dark but I do not think it is worth while attempting this for 5 or 6 hours after Zero.

A small party of R.E. was also sent forward on July 31st to search for wells in the captured lines. Several were found but all were subsequently condemned. This information was, of course, valuable.

x. Parties of a Tunnelling Coy. were sent forward on 2 occasions on attack day to report on condition of dugouts.

I am doubtful of the necessity of this being done so early. If there is reason to suspect the existence of tunnelled dugouts, it is important that they should be inspected by experts without delay, both with a view to their repair and to the detection of possible "booby traps". Concrete shelters, if undamaged, only require clearing and this ought to be done by the infantry. They should, and have been, examined and reported on later by R.E., but I do not think it is necessary to do this at once.

No special arrangements have been made for fixing position gained. This is a real difficulty for contours are usually inaccurate and do not show minor features. The only landmarks are old trenches and edhes of woods, and these are often not visible from a distance. I consider it unfortunate that new editions of trench maps omit the old German trenches behind our lines. More air photos taken of our lines would also be a help.

xi. No remarks.

xii. This is most valuable. We have 1 officer and 100 men attached to each Field Company, and the constant demands for small parties are obviated. Also if the infantry remain for some time with the Field Coy. and can get a certain amount of training, they are worth twice as much as the occasional party.

I have never had Infantry attached to the Pioneer Battn. and I do not think this would work well. The Field Coy. is wasted without labour to do the carrying, and unskilled jobs, the Pioneers on the other hand have a high proportion of unskilled labour.

(Sgd) H.J.COUCHMAN, Lieut.-Col. R.E.,
C.R.E., 39th Division.

9.11.17.

SECRET.

Four separate sectors of the YPRES Salient have been prepared for Offensive Operations by this Division. These are:-

(i) HILL TOP for 31st July.
(ii) KLEIN ZILLEBEKE for Sept. 20th. x
(iii) SHREWSBURY FOREST for Sept. 20th.
(iv) TOWER HAMLETS for Sept. 26th and Oct. 26th. /

x 19th Division attack.
/ 7th Division attack.

Dealing with these separately, the work in (i) followed the usual lines of a deliberate preparation and consisted generally of the following :-

(a) Forward Assembly Trenches 2500 yards.
(b) Extra communication trenches.
(c) Splinter proofs for 3 Bn. H.Q. 3 R.A.P's and an advanced Collecting Post for wounded. (Tunnelling Coy. also made tunnelled dugouts for Bde & Bn. H.Q.).
(d) Shell proof R.A. Group H.Q.).
(e) Extension of trench tramway system, including sidings to gun positions.
(f) Causeway over YPRES-BOESINGHE Canal and 20' plank road 600 yards long. Widening forward road.
(g) Transport track from Canal forward, including cutting through Canal Bank.
(h) Clearing track for Artillery to move forward after Zero.
(i) Splinter proof visual station and O.P's.
(j) Erection of screens to conceal movement above ground.
(k) Digging shallow wells in forward area.
(l) Formation of advanced Divl. and Bde. dumps of R.E. stores.

The whole of the work planned could not be completed. This was largely due to hostile artillery and gas during the latter half of July which caused considerable casualties, especially to the 3 Field Coys. of another Division who were working under my orders during this period. An immense amount of labour was expended over the assembly trenches.

After the attack on 31st July 1 Field Coy. (relieved at night by another) cleared a track forward of our old front line. By 2 a.m. August 1st a track for mules had been cleared and marked with pickets for 2500 yards; about 800 yards of this was widened for guns. A Field Coy. of the reserve Division completed the track up to our old front line. Owing to the rain, however, the track soon became almost impassable for wagons in spite of improvements made on subsequent days by rough corduroy with salved timber.

The third Field Coy. was detailed to construct 4 strong points, the sites of which had been previously selected on the map. Owing, however, to our Infantry being forced back from their final objective consequent on the failure of the Division on our right to capture theirs, these points could not be made, though some work was done on one of them. The Field Coy. was sent out to work about 11 a.m. and communication with it afterwards was very slow. It seems advisable to face the fact that, except in rare cases, strong points cannot be made before dusk. By that time the situation is usually clear enough for a selection of sites to be made, if the original scheme cannot be adhered to.

A certain amount of digging and wiring was also done on subsequent days by the Field Coys. chiefly around various concrete dugouts.

The Pioneers were exclusively employed on clearing the HILL TOP - St JULIEN Road forward of our old front line and corduroying it.

For the subsequent attacks which the Division has made,

SECRET.

Four separate sectors of the YPRES Salient have been prepared for Offensive Operations by this Division. These are:-

(i) HILL TOP for 31st July.
(ii) KLEIN ZILLEBEKE for Sept. 20th. x
(iii) SHREWSBURY FOREST for Sept. 20th.
(iv) TOWER HAMLETS for Sept. 26th and Oct. 26th. /

x 19th Division attack.
/ 7th Division attack.

Dealing with these separately, the work in (i) followed the usual lines of a deliberate preparation and consisted generally of the following :-

(a) Forward Assembly Trenches 2500 yards.
(b) Extra communication trenches.
(c) Splinter proofs for 3 Bn. H.Q. 3 R.A.P's and an advanced Collecting Post for wounded. (Tunnelling Coy. also made tunnelled dugouts for Bde & Bn. H.Q.).
(d) Shell proof R.A. Group H.Q.).
(e) Extension of trench tramway system, including sidings to gun positions.
(f) Causeway over YPRES-BOESINGHE Canal and 20' plank road 600 yards long. Widening forward road.
(g) Transport track from Canal forward, including cutting through Canal Bank.
(h) Clearing track for Artillery to move forward after Zero.
(i) Splinter proof visual station and O.P's.
(j) Erection of screens to conceal movement above ground.
(k) Digging shallow wells in forward area.
(l) Formation of advanced Divl. and Bde. dumps of R.E. stores.

The whole of the work planned could not be completed. This was largely due to hostile artillery and gas during the latter half of July which caused considerable casualties, especially to the 3 Field Coys. of another Division who were working under my orders during this period. An immense amount of labour was expended over the assembly trenches.

After the attack on 31st July 1 Field Coy. (relieved at night by another) cleared a track forward of our old front line. By 2 a.m. August 1st a track for mules had been cleared and marked with pickets for 2500 yards; about 800 yards of this was widened for guns. A Field Coy. of the reserve Division completed the track up to our old front line. Owing to the rain, however, the track soon became almost impassable for wagons in spite of improvements made on subsequent days by rough corduroy with salved timber.

The third Field Coy. was detailed to construct 4 strong points, the sites of which had been previously selected on the map. Owing, however, to our Infantry being forced back from their final objective consequent on the failure of the Division on our right to capture theirs, these points could not be made, though some work was done on one of them. The Field Coy. was sent out to work about 11 a.m. and communication with it afterwards was very slow. It seems advisable to face the fact that, except in rare cases, strong points cannot be made before dusk. By that time the situation is usually clear enough for a selection of sites to be made, if the original scheme cannot be adhered to.

A certain amount of digging and wiring was also done on subsequent days by the Field Coys. chiefly around various concrete dugouts.

The Pioneers were exclusively employed on clearing the HILL TOP - St JULIEN Road forward of our old front line and corduroying it.

For the subsequent attacks which the Division has made,

SECRET.

Four separate sectors of the YPRES Salient have been prepared for Offensive Operations by this Division. These are:-

(i) HILL TOP for 31st July.
(ii) KLEIN ZILLEBEKE for Sept. 20th. x
(iii) SHREWSBURY FOREST for Sept. 20th.
(iv) TOWER HAMLETS for Sept. 26th and Oct. 26th. /

x 19th Division attack.
/ 7th Division attack.

Dealing with these separately, the work in (i) followed the usual lines of a deliberate preparation and consisted generally of the following :-

(a) Forward Assembly Trenches 2500 yards.
(b) Extra communication trenches.
(c) Splinter proofs for 3 Bn. H.Q. 3 R.A.P's and an advanced Collecting Post for wounded. (Tunnelling Coy. also made tunnelled dugouts for Bde & Bn. H.Q.).
(d) Shell proof R.A. Group H.Q.).
(e) Extension of trench tramway system, including sidings to gun positions.
(f) Causeway over YPRES-BOESINGHE Canal and 20' plank road 600 yards long. Widening forward road.
(g) Transport track from Canal forward, including cutting through Canal Bank.
(h) Clearing track for Artillery to move forward after Zero.
(i) Splinter proof visual station and O.P's.
(j) Erection of screens to conceal movement above ground.
(k) Digging shallow wells in forward area.
(l) Formation of advanced Divl. and Bde. dumps of R.E. stores.

The whole of the work planned could not be completed. This was largely due to hostile artillery and gas during the latter half of July which caused considerable casualties, especially to the 3 Field Coys. of another Division who were working under my orders during this period. An immense amount of labour was expended over the assembly trenches.

After the attack on 31st July 1 Field Coy. (relieved at night by another) cleared a track forward of our old front line. By 2 a.m. August 1st a track for mules had been cleared and marked with pickets for 2500 yards; about 800 yards of this was widened for guns. A Field Coy. of the reserve Division completed the track up to our old front line. Owing to the rain, however, the track soon became almost impassable for wagons in spite of improvements made on subsequent days by rough corduroy with salved timber.

The third Field Coy. was detailed to construct 4 strong points, the sites of which had been previously selected on the map. Owing, however, to our Infantry being forced back from their final objective consequent on the failure of the Division on our right to capture theirs, these points could not be made, though some work was done on one of them. The Field Coy. was sent out to work about 11 a.m. and communication with it afterwards was very slow. It seems advisable to face the fact that, except in rare cases, strong points cannot be made before dusk. By that time the situation is usually clear enough for a selection of sites to be made, if the original scheme cannot be adhered to.

A certain amount of digging and wiring was also done on subsequent days by the Field Coys. chiefly around various concrete dugouts.

The Pioneers were exclusively employed on clearing the HILL TOP - St JULIEN Road forward of our old front line and corduroying it.

For the subsequent attacks which the Division has made,

W A R D I A R Y

O F

H.Q., 39TH DIVL. R.E.

FROM 1st December to 31st December 1917.

Army Form C. 2118

Instructions regarding War Diaries and Intelligence Summaries are contained in F. S. Regs., Part II. and the Staff Manual respectively. Title Pages will be prepared in manuscript.

WAR DIARY
or
INTELLIGENCE SUMMARY
(Erase heading not required.)

H.Q. RE 39 Div — Dec 1917

Place	Date	Hour	Summary of Events and Information	Remarks and references to Appendices
GOLDFISH Chateau	Dec 1st		Nil.	
H 11. central Sheet 28	2nd		Nil	
	3rd		CRE. visited SOUTH Road up to SEINE. Very cold. C.E. Second Army visited CRE.	
	4th		Nil.	
	5th		CRE rode inspected SOUTH Road.	
	6th		CRE to C.E. VIII Corps re handing over work to CRE 8th Div. Cold	
	7th		Handed over all work in hand to CRE. 8th Div as from 7 p.m. Warmer. rain at night	
EECKE	8th		H.Q.R.E. moved to EECKE by lorry & road.	
"	9th		Transport marched to MAISON BLANCHE area. Wet	
COLEMBERT	10th		H.Q.R.E. moved to COLEMBERT chateau. Transport to SAMETTE. Fine, cold	
Sheet 13 1/100000	11th		Transport to COLEMBERT. CRE to conference at Div H.Q.	
	13th		CRE visited 227 & 234 Cos with G.O.C. Division.	
	15th		G.O.C. inspected 227 & 234 Fd Cos on parade near BAINGHEM LE COMTE.	
	16th		CRE to Div H.Q. snow in evening.	
	17th		CRE to conference at Div H.Q.	
	20th		Orders received for CRE to report to C.E. II Corps for work on Army Line.	
	21st		CRE to II Corps & Div H.Q. returning to COLEMBERT.	
	23rd		CRE to CANAL BANK YPRES to take charge of wiring in front of Army Line. H.Q.R.E. remain at COLEMBERT	
CANAL BANK YPRES	24th		CRE visited Army Line with C.E. II Corps to lay out lines of wire.	

1875 Wt. W593/826 1,000,000 4/15 J.B.C. & A. A.D.S.S./Forms/C. 2118.

Army Form C. 2118

Instructions regarding War Diaries and Intelligence Summaries are contained in F. S. Regs., Part II. and the Staff Manual respectively. Title Pages will be prepared in manuscript.

WAR DIARY
or
INTELLIGENCE SUMMARY
(Erase heading not required.)

H.Q. RE 39th Div   Dec 1917

Place	Date	Hour	Summary of Events and Information	Remarks and references to Appendices
CANAL BANK YPRES	26th		CRE visited Army Line wire with C.E.	
	27th		CRE went round forward area with CRE 32 Div	
	29		CRE visited Army Line with C.E.	
	30th		Adjt RE arrived CANAL BANK	
	31st		H.Q. R.E. ~~and~~ Transport arrived CANAL BANK. 39th Div took over from 32nd Div at 10 a.m.	

[signature] Lt Col R.E.
CRE 39 Div

1875 Wt. W593/826 1,000,000 4/15 J.B.C. & A. A.D.S.S./Forms/C. 2118.

Copy No.....10

SECRET.

C.R.E., 39th DIVISION OPERATION ORDER
No. 49.

Ref Map 1/100,000 HAZEBROUCK 5A.

7/12/17.

1. H.Q., R.E., 227th and 234th Field Coys.R.E. will move to LUMBRES area, and 225th Field Coy. to BOESCHEPE and COIN PERDU in accordance with attached table.
Details of trains will be notified later.

2. (a). Billets in EECKE area will be allotted by Town Major, EECKE to whom advanced parties will report by 2 p.m. 7th December in accordance with instructions issued.
(b). Billets in LUMBRES area will be allotted by Area Commandant 'C' area at HENNEVEUX. Advanced parties will proceed by train in accordance with instructions issued.
(c). H.Q. R.E. and 234th Field Coy.will be billetted in COMBERT.

3. 225th Field Coy (less 1 section) will be rationed by X Corps School, BOESCHEPE from 9th Dec. inclusive.
1 Section 225th Field Coy will be rationed by X Corps Heavy Artillery from 9th Dec. inclusive.

4. The following distances will be maintained on the march -

Between Field Coys dismounted	100 yards.
Between each group of 6 vehicles	100 yards.

5. C.R.E's office will open at EECKE at 11 a.m. Dec 8th and close there on Dec 10th morning. Location of C.R.E's office in LUMBRES areanwill be notified later.

6. ACKNOWLEDGE.

[signature]
Lieut-Col R.E.
C.R.E., 39th Division.

Copies issued at a.m. to
1. 225th Field Coy.
2. 227th Field Coy.
3. 234th Field Coy.
4.) H.Q., 39th Div.
5)
6. 39th Signals.
7. 116th Inf.Bde.
8. 39th Divl. Train.
9. S.S.O.
10.) War Diary.
11.)
12. File.

Date.	Unit.	To.	Route and Remarks.
Dec. 8th.	225th Coy dismounted (less 1 Section).	BOESCHEPE.	Train to GODEWAERSVELDE, thence march. Report to X Corps School on arrival.
	Transport 225th Coy. (less 1 Section).	BOESCHEPE.	POPERINGHE. Head to enter POPERINGHE at 11 a.m.
	1 Section 225th Coy. (dismounted).	COIN PERDU.	Train and march. Report to X Corps heavy Artillery CLAIR MARAIS on arrival.
	Transport 1 Section 225th Coy.	COIN PERDU.	Any.
	H.Q., R.E., 227th & 234th Field Coys. (Dismounted).	EECKE Area.	Train to GODEWAERSVELDE, thence march.
	Transport 227th Coy.	do.	POPERINGHE. Head to enter POPERINGHE at 11.20 a.m.
	Transport 234th Coy & H.Q. R.E.	do.	POPERINGHE. Head to enter POPERINGHE at 11.45 a.m.
" 9th.	Transport of H.Q. R.E. 227th & 234th Field Coys.	RENESCURE Area.	CASSEL. March under orders of 116th Inf. Bde group.
" 10th.	-do-	LUMBRES Area.	ARQUES and WIZERNES. March under orders of 116th Inf.Bde. group.
" 10th.	H.Q.,R.E., 227th & 234th Field Coys. (dismounted).	LUMBRES Area.	Train from GODEWAERSVELDE to NIELLES.

Copy No. 7

SECRET.

C.R.E., 39TH DIVISION ORDER NO.50.

27/12/17.

1. The H.Q. R.E. and 3 Field Coys 39th Division will relieve H.Q. R.E. and 3 Field Coys of 32nd Division as shown below :-

Field Coy.	Relieve	Location.
H.Q., R.E.	H.Q., R.E.	C.25.c.7.0.
225th Coy.	218th Coy.	H.6.d.7.5.
227th Coy.	206th Coy.	C.25.c.7.4.
234th Coy.	219th Coy.	C.19.d.55.20.

2. Orders for move of H.Q., R.E. will be issued as soon as known.

3. 225th and 227th Field Coys are moving under orders of 2nd Corps.

4. 234th Field Coy. will move in accordance with attached table.

5. (a) Transport of 2 detached sections will join remainder of transport of 234th Field Coy. at SAMETTE on Dec 29th.
(b) 234th Field Coy. will arrange to pick up dismounted portions of 2 detached sections from SAMETTE on Dec 31st.

6. Rations for 234th Field Coy. will be in accordance with the attached table.

7. As regards intervals on the march, attention is drawn to Fourth Army Standing Orders.

8. Lorries will be provided as follows :-

Date.	Unit.	No.	FROM	TO	Remarks.
---	H.Q.R.E.	1	COLEMBERT	CANAL BANK	
Dec 30	234th Co.	1	do.	HARLETTE	2 journeys.
" 31	-do-	2	HARLETTE	Destination	

Actual times that lorries will report will be notified later.

9. ACKNOWLEDGE.

Capt & A/Adj R.E.
for C.R.E., 39th Division.

Copies issued at 11 p.m. to:-
1. 234th Field Coy.
2. C.R.E., 39th Div.
3. 118th Inf. Bde.
4)
5) H.Q., 39th Div.
6. 39th Divl. Train.
7)
8) War Diary
9 File.

TABLE SHOWING MOVEMENTS OF 234TH FIELD COY.

Date.	Unit.	From.	To.	Route.	Remarks.
Dec 28th.	2 detached sections.	HONNEGOVE and NORTBECOURT.	Rest Camp, SAMETTE.	---------	Under orders of II Corps.
Dec 29th.	Transport (less 2 Sections).	COLEMBERT.	Rest Camp, SAMETTE.	Turn off SR 1 Kil W of LUMBRES.	
Dec 30th.	234th Field Coy. (less 2 Sects)	COLEMBERT.	HARLETTE.	LONGEVILLE.	Billets vacated by 13th Glouc. R. on 30th.
Dec 30th.	Transport.	Rest Camp, SAMETTE.	ST. MOMELIN.	ST MARTIN AU LAERT.	Under orders of 118th Bde. Transport.
Dec 31st.	234th Field Coy.	HARLETTE.	C.19.d.55.20.	Entrain WIZERNE Detrain ST.JEAN (IRISH FM)	Dismounted entrain 7 a.m. Cyclists " 10 a.m.
Dec 31st.	Transport.	ST. MOMELIN.	ST.JANS-TER-BIEZEN "A" Area.	WEMAERS CAPPEL, WINNIZEELE WATOU.	Under orders of 118th Bde.
Jan 1st.	Transport.	ST.JANS-TER-BIEZEN.	Destination Forward Area.	POPERINGHE, N. SWITCH RD, VLAMERTINGHE.	do.

Vol 23

W A R   D I A R Y

F O R

HEADQUARTERS 39TH DIV1. R.E.

FROM 1st January TO 31st January 1918.

Instructions regarding War Diaries and Intelligence Summaries are contained in F. S. Regs., Part II. and the Staff Manual respectively. Title Pages will be prepared in manuscript.

WAR DIARY
or
INTELLIGENCE SUMMARY
(Erase heading not required.)

Army Form C. 2118

HQ RE 39 Div — Jan 1918

Place	Date	Hour	Summary of Events and Information	Remarks and references to Appendices
CANAL BANK YPRES	Jan 1st		CRE round forward area with G.O.C. & G.S.O.1.	
	2nd		— do — — do —	
	4th		CRE ~~round~~ with Asst Controller of Mines 4th Army & O.C. 257 Tunnelling Co visited tunnelled dugouts in hand	
	6th		CRE round forward area with G.O.C. & G.S.O.1	
	7th		CRE with O.C. 234 Fd Co to lay out trenches along line of WINCHESTER SWITCH	
	9th		CRE & Adjt round forward area. Thaw in afternoon	
	10th		CRE to WALLEMOLEN with G.O.C. & G.S.O.1	
	11th		CRE to forward area to select alignment of proposed mule track.	
	13th		CRE to WALLEMOLEN with O.C. 227 Fd Co	
	14th		CRE to BLENDECQUES to attend conference of CRE's. Major HAMMONDS D.S.O. M.C. acts as CRE	
	15th		CRE returned from BLENDECQUES in evening. Heavy rain	
	17th		CRE round forward area. Trenches very wet. Heavy snow. YPRES canal running very full.	
	19th		C.R.E. with CRE 35 Div round forward area.	
	20th		Adjt to Tunnelling Camp to see billets for HQ. R.E.	
	21st		3 Field Cos moved by rail (transport by road) to Tunnelling Camp on relief by 35th Div. Handed over to CRE 35 Div.	
	22nd		Moved to TUNNELLING CAMP.	

1375 Wt. W593/826 1,000,000 4/15 J.B.C. & A. A.D.S.S./Forms/C. 2118.

Instructions regarding War Diaries and Intelligence Summaries are contained in F. S. Regs., Part II. and the Staff Manual respectively. Title Pages will be prepared in manuscript.

WAR DIARY
or
INTELLIGENCE SUMMARY
(Erase heading not required.)

Army Form C. 2118

Place	Date	Hour	Summary of Events and Information	Remarks and references to Appendices
TUNNELLING CAMP	23/1/18		CRE visited Fd Coy camps.	
"	24/1/18		Lt Col COUCHMAN went on leave handing over to MAJ. D.H. HAMMONDS. RE HQrs entrained at PROVEN at 16.40. 227th Coy entrained.	
MERICOURT SUR SOMME	25th		~~[illegible]~~ Detrained at MERICOURT L'ABBAYE at 5.30 a.m. Proceeded to MERICOURT-SUR-SOMME by lorry. 234th Coy entrained. 224th Coy arrived at ECLUSIER.	
"	26th		A/CRE and Adj. visited 224th and 234th Coys. 225th Coy entrained. 234th Coy arrived at BRAY	
"	27th		A/CRE and Adj visited CRE's 9th and 21st Divns to arranged details of relief (Whole of 9th Divn and left Bde. of 21st Divn to be taken over) 225th Coy arrived at VAUX-SUR-SOMME.	
"	28th		Issued orders for move of Fld Coys. to forward area.	
"	29th		A/CRE and Adj went by Car to NURLU (HQrs 9th Divn) and went round the works with Lt Col HEARN CRE 9th Divn. 224th & 234th Coys moved to forward area.	
"	30th		Issued order re. allotment of works. 225th Coy moved to forward area.	
"	31st		A/CRE proceeded to 21st Divn HQrs and went round ~~[illegible]~~ ~~[illegible]~~ the line with CRE 21st.	
			DHHammonds Major RE A/CRE 39th Divn	

1875 Wt. W593/826 1,000,000 4/15 J.B.C. & A. A.D.S.S./Forms/C. 2118.

Confidential

War Diary

of

Headquarters 39th Divl RE.

From 1st To 28th Feb. 1918.

Instructions regarding War Diaries and Intelligence Summaries are contained in F. S. Regs., Part II. and the Staff Manual respectively. Title Pages will be prepared in manuscript.

WAR DIARY
or
INTELLIGENCE SUMMARY
(Erase heading not required.)

Army Form C. 2118

Place	Date	Hour	H.Q. RE 39 Div — Summary of Events and Information — Feb 1918.	Remarks and references to Appendices
MERICOURT	1/2/18		A/CRE proceeded to 9th Div by car, visited Fd Coys and spent night with CRE 9th Div.	MM
NURLU	2/2/18		RE HQrs moved by lorry to NURLU and took over from 9th Div at 10 a.m. A/CRE went round work with officers of 9th SEAFORTHS PIONEERS (who are att to 39th Div for work). Work on Reserve line arranged.	MM
"	3/2/18		A/CRE and Adjt went round work with OC 234th Coy and visited OC 63rd Fd Coy (attached 39th Div)	MM
"	4/2/18		A/CRE went round RED LINE work with OC 12th G Cutters and arranged details of work. Conference at DHQ.	MM
"	5/2/18		A/CRE went round work with OC 225 and OC 227 and visited 117th Bde HQrs.	MM
"	6/2/18		Inspected defences of HEUDICOURT.	
"	7/2/18		Went round Corps line with OC 63rd Fd Coy and [illegible] posts	
"	8/2/18		63rd Fd Coy relieved by 64th Fd Coy. Worked out defence scheme for [illegible] and Sorel-le-Grand.	
"	9/2/18		Inspected post on Yellow line with 9th Seaforths.	

1875 Wt. W593/826 1,000,000 4/15 J.B.C. & A. A.D.S.S./Forms/C. 2118.

Instructions regarding War Diaries and Intelligence Summaries are contained in F. S. Regs., Part II. and the Staff Manual respectively. Title Pages will be prepared in manuscript.

WAR DIARY
or
INTELLIGENCE SUMMARY
(Erase heading not required.)

Army Form C. 2118

Place	Date	Hour	Summary of Events and Information	Remarks and references to Appendices
NURLU	10/2/18		Went round red line with OC 13th Glosters and completed details of posts & wire	
"	11/2/18		Visited left Bde sector	
"	12/2/18		—	
"	13/2/18		Went round with ~~9th Seaforths~~ OC 234th Coy and inspected work in left Bde sector.	
"	14/2/18		Visited the GOUZEAUCOURT defences with the Gen. Feltham and G 30.	
"	15/2/18		Sited posts on Yellow support line with 9th Seaforths.	
"	16/2/18		Went round Red line with OC 13th Glosters and sited extension to post R.3. 9th SEAFORTHS rejoined their Division.	
"	17/2/18		Went with OC 227th Coy to reconnoitre bridges on ~~S~~ SOMME between PERONNE & CAPPY	
"	18/2/18		Went round Centre Bde area with OC 225 Fd Coy and discussed the proposed strongpoints QUENTIN REDOUBT & GAUCHE WOOD.	
"	19/2/18		Sited CTs on Yellow System.	
"	20/2/18		Set out CTs between Yellow & Red line systems with OC 13th Glosters. And went round right Bde front with OC 224th Coy. Work on W23 cutting started	

1875 Wt. W593/826 1,000,000 4/15 J.B.C. & A. A.D.S.S./Forms/C. 2118.

Army Form C. 2118

Instructions regarding War Diaries and Intelligence Summaries are contained in F. S. Regs., Part II. and the Staff Manual respectively. Title Pages will be prepared in manuscript.

WAR DIARY
or
INTELLIGENCE SUMMARY
(Erase heading not required.)

HQ RE 39 Div — Feb 1918

Place	Date	Hour	Summary of Events and Information	Remarks and references to Appendices
NURLU	21/2/18		Went round with GOC Div and GSO, and finally decided on siting of CTs between Yellow & Red line and on details of strong points in GAUCHE WOOD and QUENTIN REDOUBT.	
"	22/2/18		Taped out 2 CTs in Yellow line. Visited HQs in Gouzeaucourt and OC 225 Fd Coy. Div conference in evening. Main line of resistance altered from Red line to Yellow line. 13th Glosters consequently to	
"	23/2/18		be moved from Red to Yellow line. Orders for this issued.	
"	23/2/18		Set the 13th Glosters on new work. Issued orders for 8th Bn Leicesters (21 D.) attached to the Div for work on Yellow line.	
"	24/2/18		Went round with GSO, siting dugouts HQs etc in connection with new Yellow line scheme.	
"	25/2/18		Sited strong points in northern portion of Yellow support line and inspected pioneer work. Lt Col COUCHMAN MC RE returned from leave.	
	26th		Went round Yellow line with Maj Hammonds	
	27th		Taped out new switch S. of CHAPEL HILL	
	28"		Inspected new switch dug previous night by Pioneer Bn.	

[signature] Lt Col RE
CRE 39 Div

1875 Wt. W593/826 1,000,000 4/15 J.B.C. & A. A.D.S.S./Forms/C. 2118.

WAR
DIARY

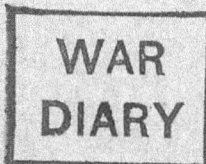

Headquarters,

ROYAL ENGINEERS, 39th Division.

M A R C H

1 9 1 8

Attached:-

Narrative of Operations
21st to 31st March.

W A R D I A R Y

O F

HEADQUARTERS 39TH DIVL. R.E.

FROM 1st March 1918
TO 31st March 1918.

Army Form C. 2118

Instructions regarding War Diaries and Intelligence Summaries are contained in F. S. Regs., Part II. and the Staff Manual respectively. Title Pages will be prepared in manuscript.

WAR DIARY
or
~~INTELLIGENCE SUMMARY~~
(Erase heading not required.)

Place	Date	Hour	Summary of Events and Information — H.Q. RE 39 Div — March 1918	Remarks and references to Appendices
NURLU	1st		Went round Yellow Line with of CRE. 9th Div. Visited 225th Co.	
	2nd		Went round portion of Brown (Corps) Line with of CRE 9th Div. Very cold & snow	
	3rd		Went round Red Line inspected 13 platoons at work there.	
	4th		1 Bn 9th Division started work on Yellow systems with 225 Field Coy. CRE with G.O.C. & G.S.O.1 to RAILTON to site alignment of Corps Line on our right boundary	
	5th		CRE inspected Yellow Line with O.C. 234 Field Coy & visited 225th Field Coy. Work started on 2 concrete pillboxes & 4 tunnelled dugouts. Adjutant taped out CTs in Yellow system.	
	6th		CRE with O.C. 227 Field Coy to fix alignment of Corps (Brown) Support Line	
	7th		CRE with O.C. 227 Field Coy to RAILTON to select new alignment of Corps (Brown) Line at our Right boundary	
	8th		CRE inspected Yellow Line in Right Sector & with O.C. Pioneers selected sites of strong points in Yellow Reserve Line	
	9th		CRE inspected Red & Yellow lines in Left Sector. Orders received in evening to start work on 13 new strong points behind Yellow Line & also in Yellow Reserve Line	
	10th		Work started ~~on~~ as above. CRE with O.C. Pioneers to tape out some of these	
	11th		CRE with GSO1 & CRE 9th Division to select & tape out new strong points along a switch line between Yellow & Brown systems	
HAUT ALLAINES.	12th		Work started on 8 more strong points. H.Q. RE move to HAUT ALLAINES in afternoon. CRE remains to assist CRE 9th Division. 225th Co. to HAUT ALLAINES for the night, 227th Co to GURLU WOOD, 234th Co HQs + 2 secs. to MARICOURT 2 secs to TEMPLEUX LA FOSSE.	

1875 Wt. W593/826 1,000,000 4/15 J.B.C. & A. A.D.S.S./Forms/C. 2118.

Instructions regarding War Diaries and Intelligence Summaries are contained in F. S. Regs., Part II. and the Staff Manual respectively. Title Pages will be prepared in manuscript.

WAR DIARY
or
INTELLIGENCE SUMMARY
(Erase heading not required.)

Army Form C. 2118

Sheet 2.

Place	Date	Hour	H.Q. R.E. 39 Divn. Summary of Events and Information March 1918.	Remarks and references to Appendices
HAUT ALLAINES	14th		Capt. Ross 227 Co. to H.Q. as a/adjt whilst Capt Haycraft on leave to U.K.	
	15th		Capt Haycraft on leave to U.K. Instrns. issued to Fd. Coys. re procedure entraining or embussing whilst Divn. in G.H.Q. reserve and re concentration should Divn. be called upon to counter-attack in Corps Area.	
	16th		227 Co. move from GURLU Wd. to TINCOURT for work on GREEN Line under CRE rear zone E.	
	17th		Adjt. to see 225 Co. at FALVY.	
	18th		Adjt. to see 227 Co. at TINCOURT. C.R.A. 39th Div. killed in action.	
	19th 20th		Nil	
" " "	21st		German offensive began. Detailed narrative attached.	

[signature] Lt Col. R.E.
CRE 39th Divn.

1875 Wt. W593/826 1,000,000 4/15 J.B.C. & A. A.D.S.S./Forms/C. 2118.

Detailed narrative March 21st - 31st.
H.Q., 39th Divl. Engineers.

March 21st.

On 21st March Divl. Engineers were situated as follows:-

C.R.E., with 9th Div at NURLU; H.Q.,R.E. with 39th Div H.Q at HAUT ALLAINES; 225th Field Coy working on GREEN line at FALVY; 227th Field Coy. working on GREEN line at TINCOURT; 234th Field Coy (less 2 sections) at MARICOURT; 234th Field Coy 2 sections at TEMPLEUX LA FOSSE; 13th Gloucesters (Pioneers) at HANCOURT.

At 2 p.m. the Coys and Pioneers were ordered to concentrate in HAUT ALLAINES (225th Coy), GURLU wood (227th and 234th Coys) and TEMPLEUX (13th Gloucesters) by march route. At about 5 p.m. Division issued orders for a new switch line to be dug and wired connecting BROWN line with GREEN line near TINCOURT wood, a length of about 6000 yards. 227th Coy., 2 sections 234th Field Coy and 13th Gloucesters were detailed for this in addition to 117th and 118th Inf Bdes. C.R.E., went with G.S.O. 3 to 21st Div H.Q. LONGAVESNES, the centre of the line, and pointed out on the ground the general alignment of the northern portion to an officer of 117th Inf Bde. This officer then went over the line and guided 117th Bde officers on arrival. G.O.C., 118th Inf Bde and G.S.O. 2 taped out roughly the southern portion of the line. Meanwhile Adj R.E. had arranged for 10 lorry loads of wire, pickets and tools to be sent to 21st Div H.Q. These arrived about 11 p.m. R.E. and Pioneers arrived about 10 p.m. and were employed on northern portion of line, R.E. wiring and Pioneers reinforcing Infantry on digging. C.R.E. showed these units work to be done. By dawn platoon posts had been dug along the whole length and more than half the whole line wired. 225th Coy and 234th Coy (less 2 sections) arrived at their concentration stations about 11 p.m., the rest of the R.E. and Pioneers returning there at dawn.

March 22nd.

C.R.E. returned to NURLU 5 a.m. and rejoined 39th Div at HAUT ALLAINES about noon. At 4.30 p.m. 225th Coy were ordered to mark out and start digging a new line just E of BUSSU. Other 2 Coys and Pioneers remained in GURLU wood and TEMPLEUX. During the evening Pioneer Bn was placed at disposal of Bde as fighting troops and the 2 Coys ordered to be prepared to reinforce infantry if required. Later, orders were issued for these Coys to march at 2 a.m. and to carry on with the new line E of BUSSU. Prior to moving off, Field Coys destroyed many of the huts in GURLU Wood.

March 23rd.

Divl. H.Q. moved to CLERY at 9 am; a few shells were falling near the HAUT ALLAINES Camp before our departure. C.R.E. met C.E., VII Corps at CLERY and was ordered to prepare certain bridges over the SOMME river and canal for demolition. 177th Tunnelling Co. was placed at our disposal and O.C.Coy with Adj R.E, went round all bridges. Schemes for demolition had been got out a month earlier by 227th Coy and these were given to these Officers to work on. No 39th Div Field Coys being available at the moment, we were given explosives etc. from 21st Div Field Coys. who were close by. C.E. had wired Army for a lorry load of explosives but this did not come. 177th Tunnelling Coy. proceeded to prepare bridges for demolition (12 in our sector). O.C. Coy was ordered not to destroy the bridges unless (1) the enemy were seen approaching or (2) C.R.E. issued written orders. Meanwhile 225th Coy had returned to HAUT ALLAINES after work near BUSSU. 227th and 234th Coys. were detained by 116th Inf Bde at BUSSU after work to reinforce line if required.

On arrival at CLERY about 10 am, Division issued orders for all 3 Coys to move at once to OMIECOURT to prepare a line of defence from this place to LA MAISONNETTE. On receipt of this order Field Coy. transport moved off from HAUT ALLAINES. 225th Coy who were the last to leave got blocked on the road by shelling in front of them, and enemy being seen approaching, had to abandon the whole of their wagons except tool carts which had pushed on ahead.

Drivers and teams got through with trifling casualties. 227th and 234th Coys. less transport, were still at BUSSU when the orders reached them and they were at once permitted to withdraw. An officer from each Coy. reported to C.R.E. at CLERY and was shown on the map the work to be done. 225th Coy arriving first were put on to dig posts covering each bridge head, and at LA MAISONNETTE the other 2 Coys. dividing the line between them.

Divl. H.Q. moved from CLERY to FRISE about 4 p.m. At 8 p.m. on instructions from Div, C.R.E. ordered bridges over SOMME to be destroyed. This had however been done about 7 pm. as the enemy were seen approaching and in one case were so close that it is believed that some of them were actually on a bridge at the moment of its destruction. The demolition parties had no casualties. During the night the 3 Field Coys withdrew to near FEUILLERES.

March 24th.

Pioneer Bn placed at C.R.E's disposal 8 a.m. and ordered to work on a line between DOMPIERRE and FRISE. C.R.E. reconnoitred line 10 am and met Pioneer officers on site of work to be done. Line followed an old trench for practically the whole way and work consisted mainly in digging out firesteps. Field Coys. were ordered to move to DOMPIERRE in afternoon and worked on this line in evening. Efforts were made to get 2 lorry loads of wire and pickets to DOMPIERRE from Army but nothing materialised. 3 bridges over SOMME blown up by 177th Tunnelling Co. the previous night not having been destroyed, a party of 225th Coy were sent out to complete demolition. This party under 2/Lt McLACHLAN carried out this job without casualties at dusk although we were holding the western bank only of the river and canal. 1 Section of 234th Coy. worked on clearing tracks for Artillery from HERBECOURT Westwards.

During the day many alarming rumours were in circulation and 234th Field Coy and 1 Coy Pioneers working round DOMPIERRE were ordered in evening by a Brigadier of 66th Div to move up to right of HERBECOURT and work on a line of posts there. C.R.E. visited northern portion of DOMPIERRE - FRISE line in evening. Div H.Q. moved from FRISE to CHUIGNES about midnight.

March 25th.

Field Coys and Pioneers ordered 4 am to occupy the DOMPIERRE - FRISE line by 9 am. C.R.E. visited line about noon and found Coys at work improving trench and putting out wire salved from round about. It may here be noted that this line was never held by our troops. At 3 p.m. Division issued orders for a new line to be made between HERBECOURT and FEUILLERES. Field Coys and Pioneers were ordered to move out to work at 6 p.m. At 5.15 p.m. this was cancelled and these units were ordered to work on a line between HERBECOURT and FRISE. This order did not reach units until they had gone out to work and some time was lost. C.R.E. visited the line at night returning 2 a.m. and found work proceeding well and infantry coming back to occupy the line as ordered. Field Coy. transport moved to BOIS OLYMPE near CAPPY in evening.

March 26th.

Field Coys and Pioneers withdrew to CAPPY on relief by infantry arriving about 5 a.m. A further withdrawal being contemplated Field Coys were ordered to move at 9 a.m. and dig a new line from FRAMERVILLE to PROYART. C.R.E. proceeded at 8.30 a.m. to reconnoitre this line and pointed out work to Field Coy. officers on arrival. Pioneers were placed at disposal of 118th Inf.Bde in morning. C.R.E. met G.S.O.2 on the new line; this consisted of line of posts 100 to 200x East of FRAMERVILLE - PROYART road. A party of men were later seen digging another line some 500 yards further East. These were subsequently found to be the 16th Div. Pioneers and this work had apparently been ordered by Corps, though 39th Division were not informed. C.R.E. ordered Field Coys. to withdraw to CERISY as soon as task was completed and work shown to Infantry officers on arrival and this was done. Meanwhile Division issued orders at 1.35 p.m. for Field Coys. to hold the line dug, until relieved by G.Os.C. Inf.Bdes not later than 9 p.m. when they would withdraw to MORCOURT. This did not reach C.R.E. until 4.20 p.m. at HAMEL by which time Coys. had withdrawn.

Orders were at once sent to them to report to Inf. Bdes, which was done. Previous to withdrawal 225th Field Coy. was engaged with the enemy who had advanced through FRAMERVILLE about 4.30 p.m; this Coy. had also been shelled in the posts they were digging by our own artillery which did not appear to know the line being held. At 11.15 p.m. Division issued orders for Field Coys. to be prepared to cover left flank of 16th Div. (on our left) by occupying ridge above MORCOURT, enemy being reported to have advanced to CHIPILLY north of SOMME. Div. H.Q. moved from CHUIGNES to PROYART at 9 a.m. and to HAMEL at 4 p.m.
Great efforts were made to get tools and wire to the PROYART line but lorries promised did not appear and some wire and pickets that had been got up to CHUIGNES the day before had to be abandoned. An empty lorry finally reached HAMEL at 6 p.m. too late to do anything.

March 27th.

227th Coy. ordered to destroy ammunition dump at LA FLAQUE. Adjt R.E. proceeded to ST FUSCIEN 7 a.m. in car to bring explosives. When however O.C. 227th Coy. arrived near this dump enemy was found in occupation. Field Coys. were ordered in morning to move up to valley behind Bde H.Q. across main AMIENS road, to be prepared to support infantry. In afternoon Field Coys. were placed at disposal of 117th Inf.Bde. From this time therefore no organised work was possible. During afternoon 234th Coy. took part in a counter-attack organised personally by Major-General FEETHAM, G.O.C., 39th Division to restore situation on our left flank caused by retirement of 16th Div.

Divl. H.Q. moved to HAMELET at 3 p.m. and to FOUILLOY at 6 p.m.

March 28th.

39th Division ordered to withdraw to line S. of WIENCOURT - S. of MARCELCAVE. C.R.E. ordered 227th Coy. transport to dump shovels along this line and 234th Coy. to form a dump of shovels at MARCELCAVE Church, which was done. It is doubtful if these were used as line taken up was along railway line just North of these two villages. C.R.E. visited forward area near MARCELCAVE about noon with G.S.O. 3 but did not find Field Coys. who were in process of withdrawal to new line above. Enemy shelling was heavy during this withdrawal but Coys had few, if any, casualties. Major ARGENT M.C., O.C. 227th Coy. wounded in afternoon and 2/Lt LAWRIE of same Coy. injured (sprained knee). Field Coys. especially 225th Coy. who were on exposed right flank, were engaged during afternoon.

Divl. H.Q. moved to DOMART at 10 a.m.

March 29th.

Division ordered all superfluous transport to be sent across the AVRE. Pontoon wagons and half the tool carts sent 7 a.m. to BOVES. C.R.E. to 117th Inf.Bde with O.C., Signals in morning. Met Major HAMMONDS, O.C. 225th Field Coy. there. He reported his Coy. to be in the line between AUBERCOURT and MARCELCAVE.

All Field Coys. were engaged from noon onwards and report having killed many of the enemy.

Divl. H.Q. moved to BOVES 3.30 p.m.

March 30th.

Division issued orders in morning for Field Coys. to be withdrawn to vicinity of BOVES, but E of the AVRE. As Field Coys. were holding the line this withdrawal could not be carried out until Division was relieved the same night. Field Coys. were heavily engaged during the day and had many casualties. Major D.H.HAMMONDS, D.S.O.,M.C. Commanding 225th Field Coy. being killed and 2/Lt J.MCLACHLAN M.C. of same Coy. Wounded. The former was shot immediately after leading a counter-attack with very great gallantry. He was a most valuable officer whose loss is very heavily felt.

March 31st.

Field Coys withdrawn during night on relief of 39th Div. Div H.Q. moved to GUIGNEMICOURT 2 p.m. Casualties of Field Coys. during period March 21st - 30th were as follows :-

	225th.		227th.		234th.	
	Off.	O.R.	Off.	O.R.	Off.	O.R.
Killed	1	2	0	3	0	3
Wounded	2	33	1	38	0	30
Missing	0	3	0	15	0	2

39th Divisional Engineers

C. R. E.

39th DIVISION.

APRIL 1918.

Vol 26

WAR DIARY

OF

H. Q. 39TH DIVL. R.E.

FROM 1-4-18
TO 30-4-18

Instructions regarding War Diaries and Intelligence Summaries are contained in F. S. Regs., Part II. and the Staff Manual respectively. Title Pages will be prepared in manuscript.

WAR DIARY
or
INTELLIGENCE SUMMARY
(Erase heading not required.)

Army Form C. 2118

H.Q. R.E. 39th Div — April 1918

Place	Date	Hour	Summary of Events and Information	Remarks and references to Appendices
GUIGNEMI-COURT (Amiens Sheet)	1st		Div HQ halted. Warning order to move by train & road received but cancelled later. Funeral of late Maj. Gen. FEETHAM in afternoon.	
" "	2nd		Moved 10 a.m to BELLOY-ST LEONARD by road.	
BELLOY-ST-LEONARD (Dieppe Sheet)	3rd		Moved 10 a.m to OISEMONT. CRE with D.A.Q.M.G. round OISEMONT re bathing facilities. Capt HAYCRAFT adjt rejoined from leave having been detained 7 days at BOULOGNE.	
OISEMONT	4th, 5th		Halt	
"	6th		C.R.E. with G.S.O.2 to ST OMER to examine training facilities in RECQUES and EPERLECQUES areas. 39th Div" becomes training nucleus for American troops. Two Field Cos (227 & 234) detached from Division to remain behind.	
"	7th		H.Q R.E moved to GAMACHES. CRE at ST OMER.	
"	8th		" " entrained WEINCOURT for ST OMER 8 p.m. CRE at ST OMER.	
WOLPHUS	9th		CRE rejoined H.Q R.E. at WOLPHUS Chateau in afternoon. CRE with GSO1 & AA & QMG to CASSEL in morning to conference re. Training of Americans.	
"	10th		Halt. CRE round RECQUES area detailing work to be done on short ranges & assault courses.	
"	11th		Moved 10 a.m to EPERLECQUES.	

1375 Wt. W593/826 1,000,000 4/15 J.B.C. & A. A.D.S.S./Forms/C. 2118.

Army Form C. 2118

Instructions regarding War Diaries and Intelligence Summaries are contained in F. S. Regs., Part II. and the Staff Manual respectively. Title Pages will be prepared in manuscript.

WAR DIARY
or
INTELLIGENCE SUMMARY
(Erase heading not required.)

Place	Date	Hour	Summary of Events and Information — H.Q. R.E. 39' Div — April 1918.	Remarks and references to Appendices
EPERLEC-QUES	12th – 16th		Working on short & long ranges & assault courses in RECQUES, EPERLECQUES areas for use of American Troops on arrival	
	17th		302nd Regt American Engineers 77' Div arrived at RUMINGHEM. CRE to see Regt Commander to fix details of attachment of R.E. Officers & N.C.O.s to assist in instruction.	
	18th		2 R.E. Officers & 4 N.C.O's sent to American Engineers.	
	19th – 30th		Work continued & practically completed by end of month. We are extremely fortunate in having an established dump at EPERLECQUES on which to draw. As a rule R.E. stores in back areas are very difficult to obtain.	

[illegible] Lt Col RE
CRE 39 Div.

3.5.18

Instructions regarding War Diaries and Intelligence Summaries are contained in F. S. Regs., Part II. and the Staff Manual respectively. Title pages will be prepared in manuscript.

Confidential

WAR DIARY
or
INTELLIGENCE SUMMARY.
(Erase heading not required.)

Army Form C. 2118.

HQ RE 39 Dvn

Vol 26 7

Place	Date	Hour	Summary of Events and Information — H.Q. RE 39' Div — May 1918.	Remarks and references to Appendices
EPERLECQUES	1st – 31st		Work continued throughout the month on improvements to the RECQUES & EPERLECQUES areas. The whole of 77' American Division arrived by the first week of the month. A new 39' Div H.Q. at WOLPHUS was started on May 24th most of the offices & many of the officers having to be in huts.	
	26'		CRE with D.A.A.G. reconnoitering the new HARDINGHEN area	
	28'		CRE moved to BOULOGNE & commenced detailed reconnaissance of HARDINGHEN area. H.Q. RE remained at EPERLECQUES. Side car issued to CRE by C.E. II Army on loan; without this or a car work would have been impossible.	
	31st		CRE moved to BELLE.	
			Fine weather continued throughout the month.	

[illegible] Lt Col
CRE 39 Div

A5834 Wt. W4973/M687 750,000 8/16 D. D. & L. Ltd. Forms/C.2118/13.

WAR DIARY

OF

H.Q. 39TH DIVL. R.E

FROM 1ST TO 30TH JUNE

Vol 28

Army Form C. 2118.

Instructions regarding War Diaries and Intelligence Summaries are contained in F. S. Regs., Part II. and the Staff Manual respectively. Title pages will be prepared in manuscript.

WAR DIARY
or
INTELLIGENCE SUMMARY.

(Erase heading not required.)

H. Q. R. E. 39th Div — June 1918

Place	Date	Hour	Summary of Events and Information	Remarks and references to Appendices
EPERLECQUES (Map 1/100000 (Hazebrouck 5. A)	1st - 6th		C.R.E. at BELLE until 7th supervising work by 302nd Regt Engineers (77th American Division) on training facilities (short ranges & assault courses) in new WIERRE EFFROY area.	
	7th		Div H. Q. moved to WOLPHUS, R. E H.Q. to LA RECOUSSE. CRE rejoined in evening having handed over work in WIERRE area to 34th Div.	
LA RECOUSSE	8th - 30th		Continued work in RECQUES area. On June 18th 39 Div took over the training of 78th American Div in the LUMBRES area in addition to 30th American Div in RECQUES area. 1 Section 225 Co moved to LONGUEVILLE on 19th to continue work in hand in LUMBRES area. Work has mainly consisted in construction of 2 new long ranges but many minor jobs have been done.	

[signature]

CRE 39 Div

A5834 Wt. W4973/M687 750,000 8/16 D. D. & L. Ltd. Forms/C.2118/13.

CONFIDENTIAL.

W A R D I A R Y

F O R

H. Q., 39TH DIVL. R.E.

FROM 1st JULY
TO 31st JULY, 1918.

Instructions regarding War Diaries and Intelligence Summaries are contained in F. S. Regs., Part II. and the Staff Manual respectively. Title pages will be prepared in manuscript.

WAR DIARY
or
INTELLIGENCE SUMMARY.
(Erase heading not required.)

Army Form C. 2118.

H.Q. RE 39 Div — July 1918

Place	Date	Hour	Summary of Events and Information	Remarks and references to Appendices
LA RE-COUSSE			During the month work has generally been light owing to the 30th and 78th American Divisions having left the area. 225 Field Co have completed various jobs notably ~~[illegible]~~ a 400ˣ range ~~near~~ AUDRESHEM & bath houses at BOURSIN & BLEQUIN. During the last fortnight of the month 3 sections of this Field Co have been working on a new 500ˣ range at COLEMBERT & have practically finished it. On July 31st CRE & Adjt proceeded to CALAIS to inspect sites for a proposed Officers Training Depot. Weather has generally been fine but a good deal of rain fell in 3rd & 4th weeks.	
			[signature] Lt Col RE CRE 39 Div 1-8-18	

A5834 Wt. W4973/M687 750,000 8/16 D. D. & L. Ltd. Forms/C.2118/13.

WAR DIARY

OF

H.Q 39th DIVL RE

FROM 1st - 31st AUG 1918

Vol 30

Instructions regarding War Diaries and Intelligence Summaries are contained in F. S. Regs., Part II. and the Staff Manual respectively. Title pages will be prepared in manuscript.

Army Form C. 2118.

WAR DIARY
or
INTELLIGENCE SUMMARY.
(Erase heading not required.)

Place	Date	Hour	Summary of Events and Information — H.Q. R.E. 39 Div — Aug 1918	Remarks and references to Appendices
LA RECOUSSE	1st – 14th		225 Fd Co completed work on COLEMBERT range and were concentrated at GUEMY on 8th. 2 machine gun ranges built alongside existing ranges of GUEMY + AUDREHEM	
	15th		Div H.Q + H.Q 225 Fd Co moved to near DIEPPE. Sections of 225 Fd Co are divided among ROUEN, HAVRE, ETAPLES + CALAIS to work on new Officers Training Depôts. H.Q. R.E. remain behind at disposal of C.E. VII Corps and are to assist CRE No 2 Sector 2nd Army Defences under whom 227 + 234 Fd Co 39 Div are working.	
	19th		CRE proceeds on leave.	
	20th		Site of new H.Q. chosen, tents drawn + erected at N 30 d 70 Sheet 27 close to CRE No 2 Sector	
	21st		H.Q. RE moved to above location	
	22nd		Adj reported to CRE No 2 Sector + took on duties of A/Camp Commnt	
	24th		Adj visited 227 + 234 Fd Cos	
	25th – 31st		Routine work of administering detachment under CRE No 2 Sector, about 60 strong.	

T W R Haycraft Capt RE
Adj. for CRE 39th Div.

39

WO 31

CONFIDENTIAL.

W A R D I A R Y

F O R

H.Q., 39TH DIVISIONAL R.E.

FROM 1st to 30th Sept. 1918.

7

Instructions regarding War Diaries and Intelligence Summaries are contained in F. S. Regs., Part II. and the Staff Manual respectively. Title pages will be prepared in manuscript.

WAR DIARY
or
INTELLIGENCE SUMMARY.
(Erase heading not required.)

Army Form C. 2118.

H.Q. RE 39th Div — Sept 1918.

Place	Date	Hour	Summary of Events and Information	Remarks and references to Appendices
Sheet 27 N.30.d.7.0	1st – 10th		Adjutant continued ~~duties~~ duties of Camp Commandant to CRE No. 2 Sector.	
	11th		227th & 234th Fd Co transferred to XV Corps for work on remaking old aerodrome BAILLEUL. H.Q. RE ordered to move to BAILLEUL area.	
	12th		Order for move cancelled for present. Administration of 227 & 234th Co taken over by CRE 39th Div.	
	20th		CRE returned from leave (extended by medical certificate)	
	23rd		CRE to inspect work at BAILLEUL aerodrome.	
	24th		CRE & Adjt to select site for camp.	
	26th		CRE to inspect work at BAILLEUL	
	28th		— do — Personnel of HQ RE moved to new camp	
	29th		CRE & Adjt moved to new camp. CRE visited 227th Co	
PHINCBOOM Sheet 27 X.8.	30th		Very wet.	

[signature]
Lt Col RE.
CRE 39th Div

A5834 Wt. W4973/M687 750,000 8/16 D. D. & L. Ltd. Forms/C.2118/13.

4 VR 32 39

39th Div. R.E.

War Diary for H.Q. 39th Div R.E.

(1-10-18 — 31-10-18)

Army Form C. 2118.

Instructions regarding War Diaries and Intelligence Summaries are contained in F. S. Regs., Part II. and the Staff Manual respectively. Title pages will be prepared in manuscript.

WAR DIARY
or
INTELLIGENCE SUMMARY.
(Erase heading not required.)

Place	Date	Hour	Summary of Events and Information — H.Q. RE 39th Div — Oct 1918.	Remarks and references to Appendices
PHINCBOOM Sheet 27 X.8. central	Oct 1st - 3rd		Work continued on BAILLEUL Town aerodrome	
	4th		234th Co moved to PONT DE NIEPPE to construct bridge over R. LYS. XV Corps supervising the work	
	5th		Capt HAYCRAFT Adjt proceeds on leave	
	6th		227th Co join 234th Co. CRE continues to be responsible for work on aerodrome. A succession of units are now employed on this work for periods varying from ½ day to 14 days.	
	21st		Capt HAYCRAFT rejoins from leave	
	23rd		" " left on appt as O.C. 83rd Field Co.	
	24th		Orders received that no more work is required on aerodrome which is now practically complete.	
	25th		CRE to XV Corps H.Q. Orders received 7pm for H.Q. RE & Field Cos to move to ARQUES. CRE to arrange about train for personnel. Time did not permit this & orders were issued for Field Cos to move on 27th. Wired C.E XV Corps for lorries for H.Q. R.E. Lieut N.A. REW joined H.Q. RE from 207th Field Co.	
	26th		Waiting for lorries or reply from C.E	
	27th		—do— —do— . C.E wired 10pm that no lorries available	

A5834 Wt. W4973/M687 750,000 8/16 D. D. & L. Ltd. Forms/C.2118/13.

Instructions regarding War Diaries and Intelligence Summaries are contained in F. S. Regs., Part II. and the Staff Manual respectively. Title pages will be prepared in manuscript.

WAR DIARY
or
INTELLIGENCE SUMMARY.
(Erase heading not required.)

Army Form C. 2118.

Place	Date	Hour	Summary of Events and Information — H.Q.R.E. 39 Div — Oct 1918.	Remarks and references to Appendices
PHINC -BOOM Sheet 27 X.8	28th		CRE moved to ARQUES & wired C.E. Army for lorries to bring tackle & stores for dismantling bridge at ARQUES on which work 227 & 234 Field Cos are to be employed.	
ARQUES	29th		H.Q.R.E. moved to ARQUES. Lt Col COUCHMAN appointed CRE 47th Div. No reply from C.E. re lorries for bridging tackle.	
	30th		Work on dismantling bridge at a standstill owing to non arrival of tackle. First consignment of this arrived this evening.	
	31st		Work on bridge proceeding well but not yet at full speed owing to non arrival of essential stores.	

Couchman Lt Col RE.
CRE. 39 Div.
31.10.18

A5834 Wt. W4973/M687 750,000 8/16 D. D. & L. Ltd. Forms/C.2118/13.

3

D. A. G.,
G.H.Q., 3rd Echelon.

Herewith War Diaries for the month of November for the undermentioned units.

H.Q., 39th Divl. R.E. ✓
234th Field Coy., R.E. ✓

Noel A Kerr. Capt., R.E.
Adjt., 39th Divisional R.E.

1.12.18.

C O N F I D E N T I A L.

W A R   D I A R Y.

Headquarters, 39th Divisional Royal Engineers

NOVEMBER, 1918.

Volume XXXIII

Instructions regarding War Diaries and Intelligence Summaries are contained in F. S. Regs., Part II. and the Staff Manual respectively. Title pages will be prepared in manuscript.

WAR DIARY
or
INTELLIGENCE SUMMARY.
(Erase heading not required.)

Army Form C. 2118.

Place	Date	Hour	Summary of Events and Information — H Q R E 39th DIV. — NOVEMBER 1918.	Remarks and references to Appendices
			C R E visited work on bridge at ARQUES	
ARQUES	1		Lt Col H J Couchman D.S.O. M.C. CRE 39th Div left to take up appointment as C R E 47th DIV.	
			Major G S Marston M.C. R E (O.C. 234 Field Company) took over duties as Acting C.R.E.	
	2		A/CRE and A/Adj went to ROUBAIX in 255 Tun Co's Box Car to see C.E. 2nd Army re lorries to fetch material from Bridging Store at BAILLEUL to bridge at ARQUES. A/CRE saw C.E. 2 lorries & 2 trailers promised for 7 A.M. the following morning. Called round on the way back & fixed these up with R.E. officer in charge of lorries etc. Owing to frequent breaks down of car did not arrive back until 1 A.M. 3.11.18.	
			Orderly Room Sgt (Sgt Matthews) went on leave.	
	3		Nothing to note.	
	4		Nothing to Note	
	5		Nothing to Note	
	6		C.E. 2nd Army came over to see ARQUES bridge moved.	
	7		2/Lieut VOELCKER R.E joined ~~234 Field Company~~ H Q R.E. 39 DIV from ROUEN.	
			~~234~~ 227 Field Company entrained at ARQUES for VII CORPS area (BOVES)	
	8		Nothing to note	
	9		Nothing to note	
	10		Orders received for 234 Field Company to move by train to VICHTE (near COURTRAI)	

A5834 Wt. W4973/M687 750,000 8/16 D. D. & L. Ltd. Forms/C.2118/13.

Army Form C. 2118.

Instructions regarding War Diaries and Intelligence Summaries are contained in F. S. Regs., Part II. and the Staff Manual respectively. Title pages will be prepared in manuscript.

WAR DIARY
or
INTELLIGENCE SUMMARY.
(Erase heading not required.)

Place	Date	Hour	Summary of Events and Information	Remarks and references to Appendices
ARQUES.	Nov 11	7-19	234 Field Company + CRE's HQ entrained at ARQUES for VICHTE.	
		19.30	Arrived at VICHTE - orders received to move on the 12th to ESCANAFFLES. Armistice signed	
VICHTE	Nov 12	9-0	234 Field Company + CRE's HQ moved by road to ESCANAFFLES to work on bridge.	
ESCANAFFLES	" 13		Nothing to note	
✓	" 14		234 Field Coy started work on INGLIS BRIDGE over the ESCAUT RIVER at ESCANAFFLES.	
✓	15		234 ✓ worked on Bridge	
✓	16		✓ ✓ ✓ ✓	
✓	17		✓ ✓ ✓ ✓	
✓	18		✓ ✓ ✓ ✓	
✓	19		Sergt Matthews returned from leave in U.K.	
✓	20		Nothing to note	
✓	21		39 Div RE HQ + 234 Field Coy again come under XV Corps	
✓	22		A/CRE attended CE's conference (XV Corps) at ROUBAIX re educational scheme. Work on Inglis bridge at ESCANAFFLES completed.	
✓	23		234 Field Company working on improvements to Billets etc.	
✓	24		CRE X Corps Troops called to see A/CRE, but latter was out	
✓	25		234 Field Company working on repairing village of ESCANAFFLES	
✓	26		Do Do	
✓	27		Do Do	
✓	28		Do Do	

Instructions regarding War Diaries and Intelligence Summaries are contained in F. S. Regs., Part II. and the Staff Manual respectively. Title pages will be prepared in manuscript.

WAR DIARY
or
INTELLIGENCE SUMMARY.
(Erase heading not required.)

Army Form C. 2118.

Place	Date	Hour	Summary of Events and Information	Remarks and references to Appendices
ESCANAFFLES	29		234 Field Company working on repairing Village of ESCANAFFLES	
	30		Do Do	
			Staff Officer Education officer from XVth Corps called re Educational & Recreational proposals - officer from 234 Field Company went over to MENIN to arrange for billets for these H Q & attachments from 234 Field Company.	
	1-12-18		G. [signature] Major C.R.E. 39TH DIVISION	

A5834 Wt. W4973/M687 750,000 8/16 D. D. & L. Ltd. Forms/C.2118/13.

W A R   D I A R Y.

HEADQUARTERS, 39th DIVISIONAL ROYAL ENGINEERS.

DECEMBER, 1918.

Volume XXXIV.

Instructions regarding War Diaries and Intelligence Summaries are contained in F. S. Regs., Part II. and the Staff Manual respectively. Title pages will be prepared in manuscript.

WAR DIARY
or
INTELLIGENCE SUMMARY.
(Erase heading not required.)

Army Form C. 2118.

Place	Date	Hour	Summary of Events and Information DECEMBER 1918	Remarks and references to Appendices
ESCANAFFLES	1/12/18		H.Q. 39th DIV RE, with 234th Field Coy RE have been preparing workshops for instructional purposes under the Educational scheme at Escanaffles. Carpenters shops complete. Fitters shop with lathe & drilling machine in sugar factory only requires an engine, which has been located but not yet put in working order.	
"	2/12/18.		A/CRE took over work on heavy bridging in MENIN. H.Q. 39 DIV. RE & small detachment of 234 Field Coy RE moved to MENIN.	
MENIN	3/12/18.		The Bridges to be constructed are 2-60 ft. Class "A" & one 120 ft. Hopkins bridge all on the Menin Halluin Road. RE Coys under CRE for work on bridges are 214 AT Coy RE 236 AT. REG. & 46 Labour Coy.	
"	4/12/18		Nothing of interest to report.	
"	5/12/18			
"	6/12/18		A/CRE attended XV Corps Conference, after which visited CRE 36 DIV. to arrange for a field coy RE to report for work on bridges in Menin.	
"	7/12/18			
"	8/12/18.			
"	9/12/18		Orders received for A/Capt & adj R.N. REW, RE from L of C through 39th DIV. to proceed forthwith to 93 Field Coy RE & relinquish acting rank of Capt.	
"	10/12/18		Nothing of interest to report.	

Instructions regarding War Diaries and Intelligence Summaries are contained in F. S. Regs., Part II. and the Staff Manual respectively. Title pages will be prepared in manuscript.

WAR DIARY
or
INTELLIGENCE SUMMARY.
(Erase heading not required.)

Army Form C. 2118.

Place	Date	Hour	Summary of Events and Information	Remarks and references to Appendices
MENIN	11/12/18		A/CRE visits Ecanoffles & Power Station SWEVINCHAM. The latter plans for arranging with the electrical coy assistance of enemy in repairing transmission line & machinery for light & power which would be useful to troops in XV Corps area.	
"	12.		Nothing of interest to report. (Capt MORLAND MC. proceeds to XV Corps Troops CRE HQ for duty)	
"	13.		Nothing of interest to report	
"	14			
"	15		Orders received to proceed to Izeghenck on 17th Dec.	
"	16		Nothing of note to report	
"	17		HQ. 39th Div RE & 234 Fd. Coy. proceed to Izeghenck to build demobilization Camp under 19th Corps. – A/CRE remains at Menin to finish construction of bridges.	
Izeghenck	18		Work on demobilization camp started. – Capt Morland returned from XV Corps & attached to HQ.	
"	19th		Nothing of note to report	
"	20th		Bridges at Menin completed; A/CRE returned to H.Q – A/CRE interviews CRE XIX Corps Troops.	
"	21st		A/CRE proceeds on leave.	

A5834 Wt. W4973/M687 750,000 8/16 D. D. & L. Ltd. Forms/C.2118/13.

Instructions regarding War Diaries and Intelligence Summaries are contained in F. S. Regs., Part II. and the Staff Manual respectively. Title pages will be prepared in manuscript.

WAR DIARY
or
INTELLIGENCE SUMMARY.
(*Erase heading not required.*)

Army Form C. 2118.

Place	Date	Hour	Summary of Events and Information	Remarks and references to Appendices
[illegible]	22/12/18		Order received from 39th Div. stating that OR of 39th Div HQRG are to proceed to the base for use as reinforcements	
"	23		a/Adjutant interviews CE XIX Corps re order received from 39th Div. a/Adj. writes to 39th Div pointing out that their order cannot be carried out until further instructions are received as to transport etc. – Capt Morland [proceeds to 86th Bde RGA to be attached	
"	24		Nothing to report.	
	25		Nothing of note to report	
	26			
	27			
	28			
	29			
	30			
	31			

R [illegible] Cdg. 39th Div R[illegible]

C.R.E.Southern Training Area.No.T.A./10/20

D.A.A.G.,
G.H.Q.,3rd Echelon.

Reference attached correspondence, herewith War Diary referred to. This diary being the only one passed to this office, was treated as being for information.

R.G. Whiteman

Captain & Adjt., R.E.,
for C.R.E.Southern Training Area.

29/10/18.

D.A.G.
3rd Echelon.G.H.Q.

Reference your 140/452 dated 7/10/18.

1. War Diaries for Headquarters R.E. and 234th Field Company R.E. were forwarded to C.R.E. Vll Corps Troops about 1st. Sept.18. These units are now detached from this Division.

2. War Diary for General Staff 39th Divn. will be forwarded as early as possible.

3. The 39th Divisional Trench Mortar Batteries were disbanded in May last. (Please see this office 39/113/A dated 27/8/18 and your 140/452 dated 31/8/18)

A.G.'s OFFICE AT THE BASE
12 OCT 1918

HEADQUARTERS.
A.A. & Q.M.G.,
39TH DIVISION.
No. 39/113/A

E. Taylor Major
for Major-General,
October 10th 1918. Commanding 39th Division.

C.R.E.

VIIth Corps Troops.

Reference reverse, ~~Min~~ Para. 1, will you please say how the War Diaries of the H.Q.R.E. 39th Division and 234th Field Coy R.E. for the month of August were disposed of.

A.G.'s BRANCH,
G.H.Q. 3rd ECHELON,
WAR DIARIES &
"SECRET" RECORDS
No. 140/452
Date

G.H.Qrs.,
3rd Echelon,
24/10/18.

[signature]
Major,
D.A.A.G. for
D.A.G.

CRE
VII CORPS TROOPS.
No. 1/40
Date

C.E. VIIth. Corps.

CHIEF ENGINEER
No. 5084/22
Date
VII CORPS

Forwarded for your information please.

[illegible] 11Lt + a/adj. RE.
for. Lieut. Colonel. R.E.
C.R.E. VIIth. Corps Troops.

2nd. September, 1918.

CRE VII Corps Troops
noted - returned
[illegible]
S.O.R.E. VII Corps
2/9/18

www.ingramcontent.com/pod-product-compliance
Lightning Source LLC
Chambersburg PA
CBHW080859230426
43663CB00013B/2576